Viburnums

Viburnums

Flowering Shrubs for Every Season

MICHAEL A. DIRR

Illustrations by
Bonnie L. Dirr

TIMBER PRESS

Frontispiece (colored pencil drawing of *Viburnum plicatum* f. *tomentosum*) and other illustrations by Bonnie L. Dirr. All photographs are by Michael A. Dirr.

Published in 2007 by
Timber Press, Inc.
The Haseltine Building
133 S.W. Second Avenue, Suite 450
Portland, Oregon 97204-3527, U.S.A.
www.timberpress.com

For contact information regarding editorial, marketing, sales, and distribution in the United Kingdom, see www.timberpress.co.uk.

Designed by Susan Applegate
Printed in China

Library of Congress Cataloging-in-Publication Data

Dirr, Michael.
    Viburnums: flowering shrubs for every season/
Michael A. Dirr; illustrations by Bonnie L. Dirr.
        p.   cm.
    Includes bibliographical references and index.
    ISBN-13: 978-0-88192-853-2
    1. Viburnum. I. Title.

QK495.C199D57 2007
635.9′3392—dc22   2007002627

A catalog record for this book is also available from the British Library.

Contents

Viburnum plicatum f. *tomentosum*, fruits

Acknowledgments

THROUGHOUT MY CAREER, I planned to write a book on viburnums but mused whether time would expire on the Dirr garden clock. Pleased to report that the biological machinery is still ticking. Never for a millisecond did I tire of the process while assembling this book. Book writing can prove excruciatingly painful; this effort, only exhilarating.

Who to acknowledge for making it to this juncture of life's journey? Actually easy . . . for Dad, Mom, Bonnie, Dirr children, great academic mentors L. C. Chadwick and K. W. Reisch (The Ohio State University) and A. V. Barker (University of Massachusetts)—all were part of making me spiritually and academically whole and persistent. The pioneering breeding research by Donald R. Egolf, geneticist, U.S. National Arboretum, provided road maps for those who followed.

Opportunities for study, travel, and self-improvement were provided by the University of Illinois, the University of Georgia (UGA), the Arnold Arboretum of Harvard University, the great Sir Harold Hillier Gardens and Arboretum, Hampshire, England, and every garden in between that housed viburnums . . . Never would have gained the insight and information without your sharing. Thanks for the memories.

Timber Press, a company that smiles at my idiosyncrasies and allows the author freedom of thought and voice. Books are better from Timber because the author executes the subject matter, while the company edits, designs, markets, and supports the new tomes.

To Margie Boccieri, who passionately and professionally engineered typing, proofing, organization, all with an eye to excellence . . . great appreciation. I look forward to our next collaboration since the *Viburnum* book was so seamless.

To my mentors, colleagues, viburnum lovers, and students, who painted with a viburnum brush and fashioned an educational mosaic, I offer sincere thanks. To all these named, and those I missed—never would have happened without you.

And again to Bonnie . . . 37 years and still laughing, enjoying every day, providing beautiful paintings that render viburnums . . . *art in the garden.*

Viburnum nudum 'Pink Beauty', flowers

Introduction

WHY A SINGULAR MINI-TOME dedicated to *Viburnum*? Timber Press and I discussed detailed, dedicated, readable, and garden-oriented treatments of specific tree and shrub groups. *Acer, Cornus, Hydrangea, Lagerstroemia, Viburnum*, and others were considered. The text and quality photos would engage amateur and professional gardeners. The books would be read, again and again, and carried to garden centers and nurseries, providing guidance and inspiration.

For too many years, I planned to pen a horticultural monograph on *Viburnum*, researched, detailed, and perhaps too intense for everyday gardeners. Neal Maillet, then Executive Editor at Timber Press, and I discussed *this* book in terms of presenting the best of the best for gardeners. As the outline crystallized, I became more excited about shaping and molding the text. My horticultural education at The Ohio State University infused me with great enthusiasm and love for the genus. Memory (somewhat cloudy) recalls approximately 22 viburnums that were taught in my woody plants courses. To achieve an A, students had no choice but to learn viburnums. Anyone who has read *Manual of Woody Landscape Plants* (Dirr 1998a) senses my unbridled passion for the genus.

In preparation for writing this book, I referenced my 1999 sabbatical (England) notes on viburnum. Amazingly, 163 *Viburnum* taxa were documented. This included photographs, field notes, locations, dates of flowering, and impressions. *Viburnum ×bodnantense* and cultivars were listed 39 times, meaning notes and/or photos were recorded each of these times. I travel with camera and notebook and used these records, and more recent ones, for flowering dates, fragrances, and nuances as minuscule as hairs on bud scales. Timber Press was gracious, including 424 photographs. Bonnie has spiced and enhanced the book with illustrations of selected viburnums. She would labor for days and then show the work to me. My consistent refrain . . . Wow!

There will always be room for improvement, and the paucity of botanical and horticultural information on the genus sometimes made cross-checking authenticity difficult. I utilized paragraph format rather than the template characteristics common to my *Manual of Woody Landscape Plants*. Typically habit, foliage, flower, fruit, culture, and uses are presented. The photographs were chosen to represent the species and cultivars at their garden best. Chapters on nomenclature, breeding, culture, diseases and pests, and propagation undergird the species and cultivar presentations of chapter 2 without redundancy. A list of gardens with notable *Viburnum* collections appears at the end of chapter 4.

For the majority of species and cultivars, I have observed, touched, sniffed, collected, photographed, and made copious notes. Dates of flowering are presented to afford readers/gardeners a chance to interpolate and estimate flowering and fruiting times for their own locales. Atlanta and Athens, Georgia, are approximately four weeks ahead of Urbana-Champaign, Illinois, and Boston; probably six to seven weeks ahead of Minneapolis. Remember that flowering dates are dictated by weather conditions, not the calendar. Spring, as defined at a particular longitude and latitude, may be seven days early one year, seven days late the next—a swing of two weeks.

Sizes have been included based on actual landscape specimens; each is a gauge to where a specific viburnum can travel. Don't be discouraged by a 15- by 15-foot *V. sargentii* 'Susquehanna'. Either prune at an early age to maintain size and shape or choose another. Such a size represents an approximately 20-year-old plant, residing in an arboretum or botanical garden, never approached by pruning equipment. For some viburnums, their USDA hardiness zones are at best estimates, often cobbled from the literature. They serve as a ballpark guide, so if the adventuresome gardening spirit moves, give a particular species or cultivar an opportunity.

This small book represents the synthesis of my lifelong passion for and pursuit of viburnums. Viburnums are not flashy, gaudy, knock-your-socks-off plants like hydrangeas. They comport themselves with understated dignity, the sum of all their seasons greater than their parts. A viburnum exists for virtually every garden, and I hope the reader believes as much after perusing the book. I look forward to constructive comments about viburnum performance in the readers' gardens.

Viburnum rafinesquianum, flowers

Viburnum nudum 'Pink Beauty', fruits

CHAPTER 1

Brief History, Nomenclature, and Taxonomy

MOST GARDENERS TAKE MINIMAL INTEREST in the taxonomic gerrymandering associated with higher plants. The use of DNA (deoxyribonucleic acid) to elucidate taxonomic affinities is changing established patterns that were based on floral and fruit (i.e., reproductive) characteristics. DNA goes to the heart of the organism, where the naked eye and microscope cannot penetrate. We have used DNA technology to determine whether hydrangea seedlings are, in fact, hybrids. The DNA gives a clear pattern of the maternal, paternal, and hybrid progeny. Where looks deceive, DNA does not.

I suspect there will be studies within *Viburnum* that determine whether the variations associated with the polymorphic *V. dentatum* complex are genetically meaningful or minor deviations. I remember attempting to differentiate by vegetative characteristics (hairs, primarily) the various *V. dentatum* types as an undergraduate at The Ohio State University. The future of these nebulous species will be decided by their DNA.

Viburnum L. was designated as such by Linnaeus in *Species Plantarum* (1753). A reproduction of the early classified species shows the name for *Viburnum lantana* L. as *Viburnum foliis cordatis serratis venosis subtus tomentosis*. Be thankful for the Latin binomial system devised by Linnaeus, which gives every plant species a generic name (in this case, *Viburnum*) and a specific epithet (like *dentatum*), resulting in a universally accepted scientific name for the species that is utilized worldwide. The abbreviation after the scientific name (in this case L., for Linnaeus) is the authority who first and/or correctly named the plant. So the humble arrowwood viburnum becomes *Viburnum dentatum* L.

Occasionally, varieties (or subspecies) are applied to variants of the species which occur in certain geographic regions or because of inheritable traits. For example, *V. dentatum* var. *scabrellum* occurs along the Gulf Coast to east Texas. The leaves are smaller, its calyx and corolla are densely hairy, and it flowers three to four weeks later. At one time, this variety was classified as a separate species, *V. ashei*. To be sure, it is eyeball-different from everyday *V. dentatum*. Allow the botanists to ultimately give it the "correct" name. Regardless, the garden attributes will remain the same.

The genus *Viburnum* is now classified within the family Adoxaceae, of the order Dipsacales, of the class Magnoliopsida, of the division Magnoliophyta. Formerly viburnums were included, with *Abelia*, *Diervilla*, *Dipelta*, *Lonicera*, *Weigela*, and others, in the honeysuckle family, Caprifoliaceae; the movement of *Viburnum* to the Adoxaceae from the Caprifoliaceae was a recent change, and many references still cite Caprifoliaceae as the home base.

A logical question to proffer: "What biological ingredients (leaf, flower, fruit, seed, stem, pubescence) constitute a viburnum?" In other words, can the average gardener or horticulturist assess the viburnosity of an unknown woody shrub? No! and No! Those two No's apply to the reader and the author. I have been fooled too often, although I am learning.

Viburnums umbrella many morphological characteristics. According to the list that follows, assembled late on a May night with no reference source but the wandering mind as a guide, they may be . . .

HABIT:	INFLORESCENCES:	FLOWERS:
trees	cymose	white (most)
shrubs	paniculate	pink
evergreen		all fertile
semi-evergreen	BUDS:	fertile and sterile
deciduous	imbricate	all sterile and showy
large (60 feet)	valvate	fragrant
small (3 feet)	connate	foul
	glabrous	no discernible odor
LEAVES:	pubescent	
large	red	FRUITS:
small	green	yellow
entire	brown	orange
serrate	naked	red
dentate		black
lobed		purple
glabrous (no hairs)		blue
tomentose (woolly pubescence)		

. . . or combinations and permutations of the above.

Where is this leading? Actually, to anarchy, because there are no common characteristics that can be applied across all species of *Viburnum* except that ...

1. the fruit is a drupe, generally ellipsoidal, flattened, ovoid to rounded, with a fleshy coat, hard bony endocarp, and a single seed within; and,

2. the leaves are always arranged opposite; a few species, occasionally, have three leaves at a node.

The flowers? Mostly white (sometimes pink) with or without the sterile, showy, ray florets, calyx small, 5-lobed, corolla 5-lobed, campanulate, platter-like or tubular (*V. cylindricum*), 5 stamens; short pistil, 3-lobed stigma, short style, inferior 3-celled ovary, only one ovule developing into a seed, the others abortive, each flower perfect (all parts), except for marginal ray florets, which are showy and sterile. These ray flowers, which are reminiscent of the lacecap inflorescences of *Hydrangea macrophylla*, occur in *V. opulus*, *V. plicatum* f. *tomentosum*, *V. sargentii*, *V. trilobum*, *V. macrocephalum* f. *keteleeri*, and others.

For best fruit set, another seedling or clone of the same or closely related species should be in proximity. Viburnums trend toward self-sterility, meaning pollen from the same flower will not successfully pollinate and fertilize the ovules (forerunners of seeds) of that flower. I have noticed this in *V. dilatatum*, less so in *V. dentatum*, where isolated specimens set reasonable fruit.

The exact number of *Viburnum* species is debatable. References tend to copy from each other, and none of us has observed and confronted all the wild species. Lloyd Kenyon (2001) noted approximately 250 species in cold-temperate to semi-tropical climates: approximately 20 species from North America, 60 from Central and South America, four from Europe, 30 from North Africa, and better than half from Asia. I did note that C. V. Morton (1933) classified 30 *Viburnum* species from Mexico and Central America, where only five were previously identified. Hara (1983) recognized 158 species in ten sections, Rehder (1951) recognized 120 species, Bean (1981) well over 100, and Krüssmann (1985) about 200. The species conundrum is further exacerbated by Michael J. Donoghue, who researched *Viburnum* for his graduate work at Harvard and continues his studies to the present; two recent papers provide the current status of taxonomic relationships within the genus (Donoghue et al. 2004; Winkworth and Donoghue 2005). Interestingly, the number of species is cited as "approximately 175" in the 2004 paper, "circa 160" in the 2005. I question the disappearance of approximately 15 species in one year.

If the reader is consumed with speciation within *Viburnum*, I recommend Web visits to the Harvard University Herbaria (www.huh.harvard.edu). This site lists holdings, collection sites, and even photos. Other useful sites include the following:

- The Arnold Arboretum of Harvard University (www.arboretum. harvard.edu)
- Chicago Botanic Garden (www.chicagobotanic.org)
- Minnesota Landscape Arboretum (www.arboretum.umn.edu)
- Missouri Botanical Garden (www.mobot.org)
- The Ohio State University–Plant Facts (http://plantfacts.osu.edu)
- Royal Botanic Gardens, Kew (www.rbgkew.org.uk)
- USDA Germplasm Resources Information Network (www.ars-grin.gov)
- U.S. National Arboretum (www.usna.usda.gov)
- University of British Columbia Botanical Garden (www. ubcbotanicalgarden.org)
- University of Washington Botanic Gardens Washington Park Arboretum (http://depts.washington.edu/wpa)

Viburnum species are splintered into sections that are meaningful for plant breeders and botanists. These sections are structured largely on the sculpturing of the stone (endocarp wall). A successful cross (hybridization) is more likely consummated between two species within a specific section. For example, according to Krüssmann (1985), within section Lantana reside *V. bitchiuense, V. buddleifolium, V. burejaeticum, V. ×burkwoodii, V. ×carlcephalum, V. carlesii, V. cotinifolium, V. ×juddii, V. lantana, V. macrocephalum, V. mongolicum, V.* 'Pragense', *V. ×rhytidocarpum, V. ×rhytidophylloides, V. rhytidophyllum, V. schensianum, V. urceolatum, V. utile,* and *V. veitchii*. Refer to the species and cultivar text in chapter 2, and you will note how many hybrids that grace our gardens are derived from species within this group.

The molecular work by Winkworth and Donoghue (2005) proposed 12 sections; they and their respective species (those that were included in the study) are shown below. Certainly Donoghue's perspective on *Viburnum* taxonomy has evolved over his 25-year research career. Future changes are possible as more species are molecularly analyzed.

- Lobata—*V. acerifolium, V. kansuense*
- Succodontotinus—*V. dilatatum, V. japonicum, V. lobophyllum, V. melanocarpum*
- Megalotinus—*V. cylindricum*
- Tinus—*V. cinnamomifolium, V. davidii, V. tinus*

- Oreinodontotinus—*V. dentatum, V. hartwegii, V. jucundum, V. stenocalyx, V. triphyllum*
- Mollodontotinus—*V. ellipticum, V. molle, V. rafinesquianum*
- Opulus—*V. edule, V. sargentii, V. trilobum*
- Lantana—*V. carlesii, V. lantana, V. utile*
- Lentago—*V. elatum, V. lentago, V. nudum, V. prunifolium, V. rufidulum*
- Pseudotinus—*V. cordifolium, V. furcatum, V. lantanoides*
- Solenotinus—*V. erubescens, V. farreri, V. odoratissimum, V. sieboldii, V. suspensum*
- Tomentosa—*V. plicatum*

I have several thoughts concerning the horticultural significance of the sections just named. In Lobata, *V. kansuense* (Asian, red-fruited) is closely allied with *V. acerifolium* (eastern North America, purple-black fruited). I would hope to see hybrids of these two species. In Mollodontotinus, *V. rafinesquianum* (eastern North America) is molecularly aligned with *V. ellipticum* from the West Coast of the United States; however, *V. rafinesquianum* and *V. dentatum* (in section Oreindontotinus), at times almost indistinguishable by leaf characteristics, grow together in similar understory habitat around Chapel Hill, North Carolina. The latter consistently flowers three weeks later than the former.

Nothing is absolute in biology, and these sections will no doubt be subject to further refinement as molecular work advances.

CHAPTER 2

Viburnum Species and Cultivars

Viburnum acerifolium L.

MAPLELEAF VIBURNUM

Seldom recognized as a viburnum because of the maple-shaped leaves, this wide ranging, colonizing, suckering, native species dwells on the forest floor, often in the suffocating shade of noble trees. Definitively, it will never ascend to the garden acceptance and use of *V. carlesii* and *V. dentatum*, but it does have a niche in naturalized landscapes. The fall color is exceptional—in shades of fluorescent pink and rose-red to grape-juice purple-red—and effective for an extended period in October–November. I have experienced *V. acerifolium* in the wild from Maine to Indiana to Georgia, always as a spreading-colonizing shrub, 2 to 3 (occasionally 4 to 6) feet high, usually inhabiting slopes and hillsides. In mid October 2003, Bonnie and I chanced upon a thicket of vibrating fall color near Wiscasset, Maine. We were lumbering down a slope to find an open view of the marsh for photographic purposes. I believe this viburnum actually followed us from Georgia to Maine.

The 2- to 5-inch-long and -wide leaves, blue-green to dark green, are often 3-lobed with prominent jagged serrations and impressed veins. I have also observed plants with unlobed leaves. Leaves have black dots on the lower surface. Flowers, off-white, nonoffensive odor (offensive on a Florida provenance), in 1- to 3-inch-wide, flat-topped cymes, open in early May (Chapel Hill, North Carolina; 25 April 2006 in Athens, Georgia). On occasion, pink-budded flower forms occur. Unfortunately, as the flowers mature, the pink fades to white.

Viburnum acerifolium, habit, foliage, flowers, fall color, and fruits

Fruits, almost camouflaged among the foliage, are black, ellipsoidal, ⅓-inch-long drupes. I seldom see them persisting into fall and suspect that they are taken early by the birds.

Any woodland, organic, humusy, well-drained soil is suitable for cultivating *V. acerifolium*. Truly remarkable that in my travels, I cannot remember a plant in a cultivated, man-intervened, garden setting. Cultivars are occasionally listed but are doubtfully sufficiently unique from the species to warrant purchasing. Prospers quite contentedly, in the wild, from New Brunswick to Florida, west to Minnesota and Texas. Zones 3 to 7(8). Introduced 1736.

Viburnum atrocyaneum C. B. Clarke

Observed in only a few gardens by the author and rather refined compared to its big-leaf brethren. Evergreen leaves, ovate to ovate-elliptic, serrate, acute at apex, cuneate to rounded at base, 2 to 3 inches long, 1¼ to 1¾ inches wide, with 5 to 7 vein pairs, emerge bronze to purplish, eventually dark green, and finally bronze-purple-green in winter. Petiole is ⅓-inch-long, maroon, glabrous, with the color extending to the midvein below. Completely glabrous, which is seldom true for viburnums; whorled leaf arrangement (3 at a node) occasionally occurs. The May–June flowers (29 May 2006, Hillier Arboretum) are greenish white and are followed by ellipsoidal, ⅕-inch-long, steel-blue fruits. Develops into a small, 3- to 4-foot-high and -wide shrub, although I observed a 15-foot-high and -wide specimen at Hillier in 1999. This plant was multi-stemmed, vase-shaped, with rounded crown. Lancaster (1989) reported a 20-foot-high plant in China. Appears to tolerate sun and partial shade. Small plants reside at

Viburnum atrocyaneum, foliage and flowers

the JC Raulston Arboretum and in the superb garden of Charles Keith in Chapel Hill, North Carolina. Zones 7 and 8. Native to the Himalayas. Cultivated plants are derived from Kingdon-Ward's 1931 collection.

Viburnum awabuki K. Koch

Heavenly taxonomic nightmare! In recent years, this taxon has been assigned variety (subspecies) and cultivar status under *V. odoratissimum*, and maintained as a legitimate species. Leaves, when crushed, do not have the foul odor of *V. odoratissimum*. It has also been listed as *V. macrophyllum* and *V. japonicum* (a legitimate species). The uniqueness of this taxon, compared to its so-called brethren, deserves a legitimate designation. I have observed gigantic old plants in Augusta, Georgia, and in Raleigh and Chapel Hill, North Carolina, exceeding 20 feet in height and exhibiting no mature growth characteristics comparable to *V. odoratissimum* and *V. japonicum*. The narrow, elliptic, 3- to 7-inch-long, ½- to 2-inch-wide leaves, as thick as orange peel, mirror-reflective upper surface, toothed on the margins, are beautiful throughout the sea-

Viburnum awabuki

Viburnum awabuki, foliage, flowers, and fruits

Viburnum awabuki 'Variegata'

sons. In fact, the foliage is the principal reason to utilize the plant. It makes a great screen or group planting and can be pruned into a respectable hedge. The leaves are so large and thickish that the cut edges may look the worse for wear after pruning.

Bonnie and I had a plant of 'Chindo' given to us by J. C. Raulston of North Carolina State University. This, in reality, does not appear vegetatively different from the species, except Raulston mentioned observing "large pendulous masses (6 to 10 inches in diameter) of bright red fruits hanging in the 15-foot-tall plant like ornaments on a Christmas tree." 'Chindo' and the species are initially shy flowering and fruiting. I observed the white, fragrant flowers in late May on a large, 20-foot-high specimen at the JC Raulston Arboretum in Raleigh. I suspect that fruit set is minimal because the species is largely self-sterile and requires another seedling or clone to effect cross-pollination. The plant at the JC Raulston Arboretum produced a fair display of ⅓-inch-long, red, oval fruits in August 2005.

The species is reliably cold hardy in Zone 7; however, the foliage may be discolored or injured when temperatures drop below 0°F. In the early 1980s, temperatures dropped to between −5°F and −10°F in Griffin, Georgia, and large plants were killed to the ground but did resprout. The species requires well-drained soil and is remarkably drought tolerant once established. I have observed it prospering in sandy and clay-based soils in sun and shade. In fact, extremely dense-foliaged specimens develop in the shade of pine trees in Georgia.

For grouping or screening, or as a bold-textured specimen plant, *V. awabuki* is a topflight choice. Remember, pruning is a requisite to keep it in bounds. Matures 15 to 25 feet high, 10 to 15 feet wide. Ancient trees in Japan are recorded as growing 66 feet high. Zones 7 to 9(10). Native to Korea, Japan, eastern China, and Taiwan. Grows in evergreen forests on hills and in valleys in warm coastal areas at altitudes of 30 to 2,500 feet. See Lancaster 2000.

CULTIVARS & VARIETIES

'Variegata' is spectacular with milk-white marginal variegation. Unfortunately, the chimera is unstable. This means that all green, all white, and white-margined leaves can occur. For the collector who has time to remove the stray reversion shoots.

Viburnum betulifolium Batal.
BIRCHLEAF VIBURNUM

I had only read about this species and dreamed of the magnificent red fruit displays that are typically described. Then in Trewithen Gardens, Cornwall, on a chilly February day, I chanced upon several 15-foot-high plants—the fruits still persistent. Since that initial encounter, sightings have increased, and I ponder why the species is not more common in American commerce.

Typically, a large shrub with arching branches. The 2- to 4-inch-long, 1½- to 3-inch-wide, dark green leaves resemble those of a birch: apex acuminate, base rounded, sharply serrate, with 7 to 9 vein pairs, veins prominent with tufts of hairs in axils below, and petiole about ¾ inch long. On the leaf underside are a pair of pitted glands, one on either side of the midrib near the base. The white flowers occur in 2- to 4-inch-wide, 7-rayed cymes in May–June in England; they were in full flower 6 May 2006 at the Sarah P. Duke Gardens, Durham, North Carolina. My notes state, "Fragrance not bad" on the Sarah P. Duke plant. The bright red fruits are spectacular, each ¼ inch long, ovoid in shape, and long persistent. For maximum fruit expression, plant several seedlings for cross-pollination. A well-drained, slightly acid soil is best. Provide full sun to partial shade. Excellent plant for the back of the border or as a loose screen or grouping. In England I witnessed plants 10 feet high and 15 feet wide at Hillier, 15 feet high and wide at RHS Wisley, 15 feet high and wide at Hinton Ampner, and 10 feet high and wide ('Marchant') at RHS Hyde Hall. Lancaster (1989) noted a 13- by 13-foot specimen in China. Zones 6 and 7(8). Native to China, Taiwan.

CULTIVARS & VARIETIES

'Hohuanshan' was described by Crûg Farm as a small, deciduous, well-branched shrub to 13 feet high in the wild. New leaves emerge deep bronze and are followed by white flowers and bright red fruits. Their collection was from Tayuling, Taiwan, at approximately 10,000 feet.

'Marchant' has smaller leaves than the species and pinkish fruits.

'Trewithen' is a heavy-fruiting selection. I believe that this was derived from the plants I saw at Trewithen Gardens.

Viburnum betulifolium, habit, foliage, flowers, and fruits

Viburnum bitchiuense Mak.
BITCHIU VIBURNUM

This species is closely allied to *V. carlesii* and absolute identification is not easy. The habit is looser, with more slender stems, smaller leaves, and smaller, pure-white flowers. Leaves, dull, dark blue-green, 1 to 3 inches long, 1 to 2 inches wide, may turn dull reddish purple in fall; however, I have observed plants with sheeny, blue-green leaves. Leaves emerge by late March at the JC Raulston Arboretum, Raleigh, North Carolina. The flowers, in 2- to 3-inch-wide, hemispherical cymes, open in late March–early April (Athens, Georgia). The emerging buds are pink, opening white, and sweetly fragrant. Fruits are approximately ¼ inch long, ripening red to black. The species is taxonomically difficult to put one's arms around. Plants labeled as such may be *V. carlesii*. In our Georgia trials, a wild-collected *V. bitchiuense* by Dan Hinkley flowered profusely as a small plant, with inflorescences to 4 inches in diameter. The leaves are dull gray-green and larger than typical *V. bitchiuense*. In my observations, *V. bitchiuense*, to the envy of *V. carlesii*, appears more heat tolerant. The fact that *V.* ×*juddii* (*V. carlesii* × *V. bitchiuense*) performs better in Zones 7 and 8 of the South than *V. carlesii* supports these contentions. Not fussy about soils as long as they are well drained. Site in full sun to partial shade. Will grow 8 to 10 feet high and wide. Zones 5 to 7. Native to Japan and Korea. Introduced 1911.

Viburnum ×*bodnantense* Stearn
BODNANT VIBURNUM

My affection for this group of hybrids between *V. farreri* and *V. grandiflorum*, named after Bodnant Garden in Wales where they originated, ebbs and flows with the seasons. From fall to spring, fragrant flowers are often present. The floral effect is not overwhelming, but the fragrance and unique timing more than compensate. I grew *V. farreri* in our Urbana, Illinois, garden, where it prospered; *V.* ×*bodnantense* in Georgia, where it perished. This was my fault for I sited it in full sun and a dryish location. 'Dawn', in other southern gardens, properly sited, has performed with dignity. The foliage is akin to *V. farreri*, 2 to 4 inches long, 1 to 2 inches wide, bronze when emerging, later medium green, narrowly oval, tapering at the ends and regularly toothed except at the base. Described in European literature as having good autumn color, this has not occurred under my watch in the United States. The fragrant flowers appear from the naked branches in cymes that are 1 to 2 inches wide by approximately 1 inch high. The buds are pink (varying degrees) and open to lighter colors (pink to almost

*Viburnum
bitchiuense,*
habit, foliage,
flowers, and
fruits

Viburnum
×bodnantense
'Dawn', habit,
flowers, and fruits

Viburnum
×bodnantense
'Charles Lamont',
flowers

Viburnum ×bodnantense 'Deben', flowers and foliage

white). The red fruits mature in summer (June in England) and in my experience are limitedly produced. They eventually turn black at maturity, but I have yet to witness this latter color stage. The habit is cumbersome and stiff, upright in youth, eventually somewhat rounded. Certainly more appealing when fully foliaged than naked-stemmed. Will grow from 8 to 10(15) feet high and wide, or wider. Behemoth-like specimens are common in English gardens. Quite adaptable, sun and shade, with reasonable moisture. Grows from Chicago, Illinois, to Atlanta, Georgia. Zones 5 to 7, 8 and 9 on West Coast.

CULTIVARS & VARIETIES

The three cultivars—'Charles Lamont', 'Dawn', and 'Deben'—have separate origins. The original crosses were made by Charles Lamont in 1933 at the Royal Botanic Garden, Edinburgh, using *V. grandiflorum* as the maternal parent. Initially, none were considered worthy of naming.

Flowers open over an extended period, so if injured by cold, another spurt follows. There is a surreal, mystical aura to the flowers, and as I traipsed around the Hillier Arboretum in February and March in the dank and cold, I had the "feeling" that I was being watched. Can plants see?

Certainly worthwhile plants for the winter garden. Their oafishness can be masked by groundcover shrubs and perennials like *Sarcococca, Danae, Helleborus,* and *Skimmia.*

'Charles Lamont'. A seedling with brighter pink flowers (than 'Dawn') and a more free-flowering nature. Leaves are the largest of the three cultivars (the *V. grandiflorum* trait). An upright-spreading, stiff, coarse plant, 15 feet high and 10 feet wide, grew at Hillier in 1999. A 15- to 18-foot-high specimen grew at RHS Wisley on 25 May 2006.

'Dawn' was derived from *V. farreri* × *V. grandiflorum* (1934) by Charles Puddle, head gardener at Bodnant Garden, Wales. The flowers are pink with dark purple-pink anthers. This is the most common form in cultivation in the United States. Witnessed a 12- by 8-foot plant with great foliage at Hillier on 2 July 1999.

'Deben' appeared as a chance seedling at Notcutts Ltd., England. The buds are pink, opening apple-blossom pink, and fading to white. Flower clusters are larger than those of 'Dawn'. May be a cross with *V. farreri* 'Candidissimum' as one parent. The flowers show cold injury (browning) more so than 'Dawn' and 'Charles Lamont'. There was an upright-spreading form, 12 feet high by 10 feet wide, at Hillier in 1999.

Viburnum bracteatum Rehd.
BRACTED VIBURNUM

Even for the advanced gardener, this is a difficult species to properly identify. Consider it a souped-up version (72 chromosomes, an octaploid) of *V. dentatum* with glossier, thicker-textured leaves. Otherwise I see little difference between the two species, and, within the complex *V. dentatum*, individual plants that resemble *V. bracteatum* do appear. I have grown a selection, 'Emerald Luster', for ten years in the UGA trials that is 10 feet by 8 feet in outline: a respectable haystack. This lone specimen is tightly branched and, in foliage, lustrous dark green. Over the years, I have observed a number of plants labeled as *V. bracteatum*, but I am never absolutely convinced. The basis for the epithet is the presence of distinct bracts that subtend the inflorescence. Leaves, 2 to 5 inches long, 1½ to 3 inches wide, almost rounded at times, with 5 to 6 vein pairs, ending in coarse dentate teeth, turn yellow to bronze in fall. Leaves are pubescent on impressed veins below; petiole is about ½ inch long and pubescent. Leaves display *remarkable* heat tolerance and hold up better than those of most named *V. dentatum* cultivars in Athens. Flowers, white and malodorous, open in early to mid May (Athens), in 2- to 3(5)-inch-wide, flat-topped cymes. On 'Emerald Luster' the flowers are borne in profusion, producing a striking contrast to the glossy dark green foliage. Tolerates sun and shade (will be more open in shade) in well-drained soils. Excellent drought tolerance as evidenced by ten years in Georgia trials without flinching. Makes a great screen, shrub border, or naturalizing and wildlife shrub. Unique in that the purple-blue-black fruits (at least of 'Emerald Luster') occur in profusion without cross-pollination, meaning a single plant is self-fruitful. Easy to root from cuttings and to grow in containers. The species grows to 10 feet high and wide. A 15-foot-tall plant of the species resides in the Hillier Arboretum. Zones 6 to 8. Native to the southeastern United States.

*Viburnum
bracteatum*
'Emerald Luster',
habit, foliage,
flowers, and fruits

Viburnum buddleifolium C. H. Wright

WOOLLY VIBURNUM

Common neither in literature nor in gardens, *V. buddleifolium* serves as a lure for the collector. The fuzzy, bunny-ear leaves, resembling those of *Buddleia*, are the benchmark for identification. Leaves in outline resemble *V. rhytidophyllum*, 4 to 6(8) inches long, 1 to 2 inches wide, shallowly toothed with 8 to 10 vein pairs, and a woolly pubescent petiole that is approximately ½ inch long. Leaves softly pubescent above, gray-felted below. Leaves tend toward semi-evergreenness with at least those below the terminal bud persisting in Zone 7. The stems and buds are covered by fine pubescence.

Pink buds give rise to white flowers in April (10 April 2004 in Chapel Hill, North Carolina), in 2- to 4-inch-wide, 7-rayed cymes. I kept smelling the flowers, expecting the off-odor, but was unable to detect anything, sweet or foul. I checked the field notes from my study leave at Hillier in 1999 and read the abbreviated passage, "No floral fragrance, April 13." The flowers are reminiscent of *V. lantana* but occur before the new leaves develop: the entire effect rather rickety. This is by no means a dainty plant, and habit is distinctly upright, to 10 feet high and greater. Usually taller than wide. Noted a dense, 10- by 6-foot plant with clean foliage at Hillier, 1 July 1999; 10- to 12-foot-high plant in Chapel Hill, North Carolina. Fruit, oval, red to black, average ½ inch long. A parent of *V. ×rhytidocarpum*. Deer will browse. Zones 6 and 7. Native to central China. Introduced in 1900 by E. H. Wilson.

Viburnum buddleifolium, foliage and flowers

Viburnum burejaeticum Regel & Herder
MANCHURIAN VIBURNUM

Viburnum burejaeticum has a *V. lantana* aura with its stinky flowers and the fact it served as the parent (with *V. ×rhytidophylloides* 'Alleghany') of 'Emerald Triumph'. This is a large upright shrub, typically over 10 feet high; I recorded heights of 10, 12, 15, and 18 feet at different venues. The literature states the species grows as wide as high, but I have yet to see this. The Hillier plant was 15 feet by 12 feet, full, dense, with abundant developing fruits on 31 May 2006. The leaves are shinier and more narrow than *V. lantana*, 2 to 4 inches long, 1 to 2 inches wide, almost setosely serrate, pubescent (slightly) on both surfaces, prominently on veins below. Apex is acute, base rounded, and margins have uniform sharp-pointed serrations. The pubescent petiole ranges from ⅛ to ⅓ inch long. The white flowers, malodorous, in 5-rayed, approximately 2-inch-wide, flat-topped cymes, open in early April (Chapel Hill, North Carolina, and Hillier Arboretum) as the leaves are developing. They do not overwhelm! Fruits, up to ⅜ inch long, ellipsoidal in outline, red maturing black, ripen in late summer (August) to fall. Although not common in commerce, it appears adaptable as it grows in many collections in sun or partial shade and in heavy soils. Like *V. lantana*, it will grow in drier, calcareous soils. At best a shrub border plant. *Viburnum burejaeticum* is native to northern China, Korea, and eastern Russia. Described from the Bureja Mountains, hence the epithet. Zones 3 to 7. Introduced about 1900.

Viburnum burejaeticum

*Viburnum
burejaeticum*,
foliage, flowers,
and fruits

Viburnum
'Emerald
Triumph'

CULTIVARS & VARIETIES

'Emerald Triumph' was bred by Harold Pellett, University of Minnesota, for its superior, lustrous dark blue-green foliage, red to black fruits, maroon fall color, and more compact habit. I have tracked the excellent performance of this hybrid from the Lyle E. Littlefield Ornamental Gardens at the University of Maine, Orono, to the JC Raulston Arboretum in Raleigh, North Carolina. In the author's opinion, it is superior to everyday *V. burejaeticum*, *V. lantana*, or *V. ×rhytidophylloides*. 'Emerald Triumph' is more compact than *V. burejaeti-cum*, probably 6 to 8 feet high and wide. Leathery lustrous dark green foliage. White flowers in 2- to 3-inch-wide cymes and green-red-black, ⅜- to ⅝-inch-long, ovoid fruits that mature earlier than *V. lantana*. Red coloration lasts for three to four weeks. An excellent viburnum for northern Zones 4 to 6(7). This form was about 50 percent leafed out on 23 March 2004 and in full flower 6

Viburnum 'Emerald Triumph', foliage, flowers, fruits, and fall color

April 2004 at the JC Raulston Arboretum. Somewhat resistant to the viburnum beetle. Introduced in 1994 (see Rose and Pellett 1994).

Viburnum ×*burkwoodii* Burkw. & Skipw. ex Anon.
BURKWOOD VIBURNUM

Burkwood viburnum is an all-time favorite of the author's because of the beautiful foliage, spicy-sweet flower fragrance, hardiness, and cultural adaptability. The parentage, *V. utile* × *V. carlesii*, and subsequent backcrosses and other genetic combinations have spawned a dazzling array of worthy garden cultivars. In the process, some fragrance may have been sacrificed for improved habit, foliage, and cultural traits. For this book, most hybrids with traces of *V. utile* are included under *V.* × *burkwoodii*. The original clone resulted from *V. utile* × *V. carlesii*, raised by Burkwood and Skipwith in Kingston-on-Thames in 1924. I cannot detail the original characteristics with certainty, since plants labeled *V.* ×*burkwoodii* are not always the same. In general, *V.* ×*burkwoodii* reaches 8 to 10 feet high and wide. The lustrous black-green leaves, grayish and tomentose below, range from 1½ to 4 inches long, ¾ to 1¾ inches wide, serrated, with a ¼- to ½-inch pubescent petiole. Leaves may be fully deciduous to evergreen. My theory is if winter lows do not drop below 20°F, a significant portion of the foliage remains. For example, two accessions of 'Park Farm Hybrid' in our Georgia trials drop most of their leaves; I travel to Hillier (England) in March, and one of the same accessions is completely evergreen. In fall, older leaves sporadically color wine-red. The smallish, approximately 2- to 3-inch-wide, hemispherical, 5-rayed cymes, are pink in bud and finally white. The cooler the temperature, the more persistent the floral effect. Typically lasts seven to ten days, sometimes as long as two weeks, in late March into early April (Athens, Georgia). Fragrance is sumptuous—like that of *Daphne odora*, and one of the great spices of the spring. Fruit, seldom abundant, is approximately ⅓ inch long, ellipsoidal-flattened in shape, red to black, maturing in July and August. Adaptable to full sun, prominent shade, well-drained soil, and drought once established. Like most of the fragrant, spring-flowering taxa, prune after flowering. Utilize in groupings, shrub borders, and near trafficked areas. Zones (4)5 to 8.

CULTIVARS & VARIETIES
American Spice™ ('Duvone'), a new introduction by Bailey Nurseries, St. Paul, Minnesota, is a relatively compact form; the original selection was 4 feet tall by 4¼ feet wide in 14 years. Foliage becomes lustrous medium to dark green in early summer, and leaves persist late into fall, eventually developing shades of deep red and purple with yellow and orange overtones. Leaves are 2 to 3½

Viburnum ×burkwoodii, habit, foliage, flowers, fruits, and fall color

inches long, 1¼ to 2¾ inches wide, petiole ⅙ to ⅓ inch long. Flowers are reddish in bud and pure white when open, with a spicy fragrance. Inflorescences 1½ to 2 inches wide. Fruits are ⅓ to ½ inch long, oblong-ellipsoidal drupes, red to black at maturity. Plant was discovered in a block of 'Sarcoxie' at Duvall Nursery, South Lyon, Michigan. Differs from 'Sarcoxie' in its compactness, earlier developing flowers and foliage (two to three days), and increased fragrance. Survived ten consecutive days of −20°F without snow cover in winter of 1993–94.

'Anne Russell', the result of a backcross of *V. ×burkwoodii* × *V. carlesii* made in 1951, was selected and named after his wife by John Russell at L. R. Russell Ltd., Richmond Nurseries, Windlesham, England. The habit is more rounded and densely twiggy than typical *V. ×burkwoodii*. The pink-budded, fragrant, 3-inch-wide flowers occur in abundance. I have observed plants with red flower buds in England. At PMA Plant Specialties, Somerset, the red buds were as prominent as Christmas ornaments on a compact specimen. Leaves are primarily deciduous, owing to 75 percent *V. carlesii*, more rounded and more akin to *V. carlesii*, and not as shiny as 'Park Farm Hybrid'. A plant at Wakehurst Place, England, was 5 feet high and wide with leaves like *V. carlesii*: rounded, serrated, and entirely deciduous, 20 April 1999. Plants to 12 feet high have crossed my path, causing me to suspect that some 'Anne Russell', so tagged, may not be true to form. Will flower in late March–early April in Athens. In January 2006, we acquired 'Anne Russell' from Piedmont Carolina Nursery for our Chapel Hill garden; it performs and looks like the real thing. A plant at Hillier in 1999 was dense, 5 feet high and wide, with some leaf spot.

'Carlotta' is derived from the same backcross as 'Anne Russell' and introduced by W. B. Clarke, San Jose, California. Considered an improved *V. carlesii* with larger broad-ovate leaves. I have been unable to track this in cultivation.

'Chenaultii' was listed as *V. ×chenaultii* and, on occasion, shows in the literature as such. Leaves are lustrous dark green, slightly smaller, and more refined than *V. ×burkwoodii*. White flowers average 2 to 3 inches in diameter, slightly pink in bud opening white, and fragrant. The branches are fine-textured, and the overall habit quite refined. Will grow 10 feet high. Plants that large grew at Callaway Gardens, Pine Mountain, Georgia; in England, 7 to 8 feet was the tallest I witnessed. Raised in France.

'Compact Beauty' is listed by the Dawes Arboretum, Newark, Ohio. No additional information available.

'Conoy' is a terrific hybrid, and Bonnie and I have lovingly appreciated its stellar performance in our Athens garden. Habit is compact, 5 to 6 feet high, 6 to 8 feet wide. The foliage is exquisite—a polished dark green, slightly wavy-surfaced, cupping in the cold of winter, 1½ to 2½ inches long. Pink buds open to white, essentially nonfragrant flowers in early April (Athens) and are followed

Viburnum ×burkwoodii 'Anne Russell', habit and flowers (below left)

Viburnum ×burkwoodii 'Chenaultii', foliage (above right) and flowers

by ⅓-inch-long glossy ovoid drupes in late summer that change from red to black. This magnificent garden plant was bred by Don Egolf, U.S. National Arboretum, using *V. utile* × *V. ×burkwoodii* 'Park Farm Hybrid', and introduced in 1988 (for a full description, see Egolf 1988). Cross made in 1968, selected in 1976, named and released in 1988. Continues to grow in stature and prominence among commercial nurserymen and gardeners. Displays superb drought tolerance once established.

'Fulbrook' has the same parentage (supposedly) as 'Anne Russell' with large, sweet-scented, pink-budded flowers that open white. Each flower is ⅜ inch wide, the cymes 3 inches across. Matures 8 feet high by 10 feet wide. Leaves are like *V. carlesii* with more luster, strongly serrated, 3 to 4 inches long and 2 to 3 inches wide. The few plants I observed do not measure up to 'Mohawk' and 'Park Farm Hybrid'. I thought the foliage on the plant at Hillier was inferior to that of *V. carlesii*. Raised by Florence Paget, distributed by Douglas Garden, Fulbrook House, Elstead, Surrey, England. The Hillier plant was 5 feet high and wide in 1999. The more I observe this and 'Anne Russell', the more confused I become. I suspect a mix-up. Typical plants of 'Anne Russell' are always better than the best specimens of 'Fulbrook'.

'Mohawk' is the result of the genius of Egolf, who backcrossed *V. ×burkwoodii* × *V. carlesii* in 1953, selected this taxon in 1960, and released it in 1966. Embryo culture (see chapter 3) was used to expedite seedling growth. Shining dark red buds open to white petals with red-blotched reverse. The fragrance is heavenly. Inflorescences average 3 to 3½(4) inches across and are prime in early to mid April (Athens); full flower 6 April 2004 at the JC Raulston Arboretum, Raleigh, North Carolina. Flowers are abundant. Leaves are glossy dark green, turning orange-red to red-purple in mid November (Athens) and abscissing clean by late November. The habit is rounded to broad-rounded, typically 7 to 8 feet

Viburnum ×burkwoodii 'Conoy', habit and foliage (opposite top left)

Viburnum
×*burkwoodii*
'Fulbrook', habit
(left) and foliage
(above)

Viburnum
×*burkwoodii*
'Mohawk'

*Viburnum
×burkwoodii*
'Mohawk', foliage,
flowers, and fall
color

*Viburnum
×burkwoodii* 'Park
Farm Hybrid',
foliage and flowers
(below)

high, although I have seen plants over 10 feet high. My experiences and observations elevate 'Mohawk' to the Top 5 aristocrats among fragrant viburnums.

'Park Farm Hybrid', in the genuine incarnation, is a choice garden plant. Unfortunately, it is confused in U.S. commerce. I researched its identity throughout gardens and nurseries, never positive that I had the real McCoy in my sights. At Hillier Arboretum, it showed its true brilliance. Raised in 1924 by Burkwood and Skipwith, a sister seedling of *V. ×burkwoodii*, it has larger leaves that are evergreen (completely so at Hillier), lustrous dark green, 3 to 4 inches long, entire or slightly serrated. The leaves are narrow-ovate-elliptic, not as round as the other *V. ×burkwoodii* types and consistently longer; the widest measured by the author was 1⅜ inches by 3⅛ inches long. The deep pink buds open to fragrant white flowers in 3- to 5-inch-wide inflorescences. Often listed as more compact than typical *V. ×burkwoodii* and wider than high. My notes state 8 to 10 feet high and wide (Hillier), 10 feet high and 8 feet wide (RHS Wisley), 10 feet high and 15 feet wide (Hillier). All abundantly endowed with flowers, which persisted for two weeks. In full flower 19 April 1999 at Hillier. I was fortunate to root cuttings of the outstanding Hillier form and now have the plant in our Georgia trials. It is being used in hybridization work with *V. utile* and *V. macrocephalum* f. *keteleeri*. The first generation seedlings of 'Park Farm Hybrid' × f. *keteleeri* were deciduous to evergreen, small to large leaved, glossy to dull surfaced; most of the semi-snowball flowers were fragrant (March–April 2007).

'Sarcoxie' is the result of a backcross of *V. ×burkwoodii* × *V. carlesii* by Dale Wild of Sarcoxie Nursery, Missouri. Described as upright in youth, more rounded with maturity, fragrant flowers 2 to 3 inches across. I have never observed this cultivar.

A world of biological opportunity awaits the breeder who utilizes *V. ×burkwoodii* and its parents in an improvement program. I have open-pollinated seedlings of 'Mohawk' that show remarkable variation in leaf size, summer and winter color, and retention. Three-year-old plants flowered in April 2006, many with the deep red buds that open white and spicy fragrance of 'Mohawk'. I have two selections that are promising; one produces phenomenal quantities of 4-inch-wide flowers.

Viburnum calvum Rehd.

Possibly of greatest significance as a breeding parent with *V. davidii* that resulted in *V. ×globosum* 'Jermyns Globe'. An evergreen shrub, 6 to 8 feet high and wide, with 1½- to 3-inch-long, 1- to 1½-inch-wide, dull dark gray-green, glabrous leaves, pale below, with a petiole that is ¼ inch long. Leaf shape is ovate to rhombic-elliptic, apex acute, base cuneate, entire or with reasonably prominent serrations, and 5 to 8 pairs of deeply impressed veins. Leaves are significantly smaller than *V. ×globosum* and *V. davidii*. A reasonable identification characteristic is the wavy, undulating surface of its leaf. This trait shows in *V. ×globosum*. The nonfragrant, off-white flowers are produced in 2- to 3-inch-wide cymes in May followed by ¼-inch-long, ovoid-globose, lustrous blue-black fruits. I have not experienced this species in the United States, but a single plant grew in the former White Gate border at Hillier. A behemoth, the plant was 15 feet high and 18 feet wide as observed 31 May 2006. A collector's plant. Zones 7 and 8. Native to western China. Introduced by E. H. Wilson in 1904.

Viburnum calvum, habit, foliage, and flowers

Viburnum ×*carlcephalum* Burkw. & Skipw.
CARLCEPHALUM VIBURNUM, FRAGRANT VIBURNUM

A tad unkempt compared to other scented viburnums, but *V.* ×*carlcephalum* is useful in the border for its slightly later, fragrant flowers. Habit is bold, with an ultimate height of 10 to 15 feet. Leaves are coarser, larger, 2 to 4 inches long and 1½ to 3 inches wide, serrated, pubescent, sheeny dark green. Pink-budded, maturing white, snowball cymes, 4 to 5(6) inches wide, are somewhat lumpy in outline. Flowers have the fragrance of *V. carlesii*, *V.* ×*burkwoodii* 'Mohawk', and *V.* ×*burkwoodii* 'Park Farm Hybrid'. This is the latest of the fragrant snowball types, opening about a week later on almost naked stems (9 April 1983, Callaway, Georgia; 19 April 1999, Petworth, England; 24 April 2004, Spring Grove, Cincinnati, Ohio). Witnessed the flattened, egg-shaped fruits, transitioning red to black, in great abundance at the University of North Carolina–Charlotte Botanical Gardens, 10 October 2006. Parentage is *V. carlesii* × *V. macrocephalum* f. *keteleeri*; originated in 1932 at the Burkwood and Skipwith Nursery. Zones 5 to 7(8), although an 11-foot-high plant was reported at the Morton Arboretum, Lisle, Illinois, Zone 4(5).

CULTIVARS & VARIETIES

'Cayuga' is an Egolf introduction that resulted from a backcross of *V. carlesii* × *V.* ×*carlcephalum* in 1953. A superior seedling was selected in 1960 and named in 1966. In general, the plant in all its parts is smaller than *V.* ×*carlcephalum*, although this is somewhat misleading, as I have observed 10-foot-high plants. Leaves are darker green with a bit more polish than the species. I measured leaves 5 inches long, 2¾ inches wide, toothed, pubescent on both surfaces, with a ¼-inch-long, pubescent petiole. Wonderful orange-red fall color

Viburnum ×*carlcephalum*

Viburnum
×*carlcephalum*,
flowers, fruits,
and fall color

Viburnum
×*carlcephalum*
'Cayuga'

Viburnum
×*carlcephalum*
'Cayuga', foliage
and flowers

has occurred in Athens. Flowers, 4 to 5 inches across, are pink in bud, opening white, and fragrant. In full flower 29 April 2005, Swarthmore College, Pennsylvania; 15 April 2004, Hickory, North Carolina. In youth, the habit is distinctly upright, spreading with time, and becoming somewhat leggy. Hardiness is similar to the species, perhaps slightly greater. Plant was 8½ feet high and 11 feet wide at 20 years.

'Chesapeake', as is true for 'Eskimo', appears to belong with *V.* × *burkwoodii* because of the foliage characteristics. Egolf crossed 'Cayuga' with *V. utile* in 1962 and introduced 'Chesapeake' in 1981 (see Egolf 1981a). 'Chesapeake' has lustrous dark green wavy leaves and 2-inch-wide, pink-budded flowers that open white, with minimal (no) or ever-so-slight fragrance. Flowers open after *V.* ×*carlcephalum* in early to mid April (Athens). Fruits are dull red to black and seldom abundant. Size is larger than the 6 feet high and 10 feet wide in 16 years that was originally cited. Plants reach 10 feet high and wide or greater. I witnessed an 8- by 8-foot plant at Savill Gardens, England, on 14 April 1999; a 10- to 12-foot-high and slightly wider plant on the Georgia campus, 20 May 2006. Branches are brittle and difficult to tie up during the balling and burlapping process. The flowers pale by comparison with its sister seedling 'Eskimo', and it is not as cold hardy, probably surviving to –15°F.

'Eskimo' is appropriately named for the white snowball flowers that dot the plant in early to mid April (Athens). Pale cream buds, etched with pink, open pure white, each inflorescence 3 to 4 inches in diameter and nonfragrant. The lustrous dark green leaves are flat surfaced, a reliable trait that permits separation from 'Chesapeake'. The leaves are more evergreen than 'Chesapeake'. Habit

*Viburnum
×carlcephalum
'Chesapeake',
habit and foliage

*Viburnum
×carlcephalum
'Eskimo'*

Viburnum
×*carlcephalum*
'Eskimo', foliage
and flowers (above)

Viburnum
×*carlcephalum*
'Maat's Select' (left)

is upright in youth, oval-rounded with maturity, approaching 8 to 10 feet in height. This is the real deal in flower and makes a great show in the shrub border. 'Cayuga' was crossed with *V. utile* in 1962; a selection from this cross was selfed in 1967. A seedling was selected for evaluation in 1975 and introduced as 'Eskimo' in 1981. See Egolf 1981b.

'Variegatum' is listed, but I have only witnessed 'Maat's Select', an unstable gold-cream-green leaf form named for Dick van der Maat, Boskoop, Netherlands.

Viburnum carlesii,
habit, foliage,
flowers, fruits, and
fall color

Viburnum carlesii Hemsl.
KOREANSPICE VIBURNUM, MAYFLOWER VIBURNUM

Viburnum carlesii is considered the quintessential fragrant-flowered species and still the most popular in garden commerce, particularly in Zones 4 to 6. Typically rounded in outline, dense in foliage, 4 to 8 feet high and wide, with an occasional specimen over 10 feet high. I noted a 12-foot-high specimen at Spring Grove in Cincinnati, Ohio. Leaves are dull dark green, 1 to 4 inches long, ¾ to 2½ inches wide, petiole ¼ to ½ inch, turning wine-red to muted purple in autumn. The pink- to red-budded flowers open white in 2- to 3-inch-wide, hemispherical cymes in late March–April (Athens). In North Carolina, opening 15 March 2006 at the Sarah P. Duke Gardens, Durham, and in full flower 6 April 2005 at the JC Raulston Arboretum, Raleigh. Typically flowers before *V. ×carlcephalum*. Fragrance is among the great perks of spring. Particularly in the Midwest, and to some extent in the East, this viburnum is resolutely adapted and performs as described in the catalogs. The ⅓-inch-long, flattened egg-shaped, red to black fruits mature in August–September. Well adapted to extremes of soil (except wet), sun, and significant shade. Great shrub border plant, mixed in herbaceous borders, in groupings, or as a single specimen. Fragrance actually reaches out and engulfs passersby. Zones (4)5 to 7(8). Native to Korea, Tsushima Island, Japan. Rare, growing on hills, often in calcareous soils. Introduced in 1902 to the Royal Botanic Gardens, Kew.

SLIEVE DONARD CULTIVARS
At the Hillier Arboretum, the Slieve Donard Nursery, County Down, Ireland, introductions 'Aurora', 'Charis', and 'Diana' were carefully studied. These selections resulted from the work of Leslie Slinger, who imported seed from Japan and introduced the three cultivars in 1958.

'Aurora' is an excellent selection that first attracted my attention during my 1991 sabbatical at the Arnold Arboretum. The Arnold plant was 6 to 8 feet high and wide. Rich deep pink-red buds open to pinkish white, spicily fragrant flowers. Inflorescences are larger—to 5 inches—and more substantial than those of the species. It is starting to appear in U.S. nurseries. A 6- by 7-foot plant at Hillier, somewhat scraggly in outline, had some leaf spotting, although leaves were green at emergence.

'Charis' is a vigorous form that is probably larger than 'Aurora' at maturity. Red-budded flowers open to pink and at maturity are white. Highly fragrant. Not impressive at Hillier: loose, open, bedraggled, 6 feet high and wide in 1999, with rounded, toothed leaves and smaller flowers than 'Aurora'.

'Diana' is a vigorous clone of relatively compact habit that is red in bud, opening the same and finally turning pink, and fragrant. Purple-tinged young foliage and young stems and petioles are reddish purple. This is arguably the finest of the Slieve Donard introductions. I witnessed a dense, 6- by 8-foot specimen at Hillier in 1999 with excellent foliage and no leaf spot.

OTHER CULTIVARS & VARIETIES

'Arlene' was listed by the Dawes Arboretum, Newark, Ohio.

'Compactum' is a superb dwarf selection that matures 3 to 4 feet high and wide with dark green leaves and flowers about the same size as the species. Displays greater resistance to bacterial leaf spot. Introduced by Hoogendoorn Nurseries, Newport, Rhode Island, in 1953.

'Marlou' was introduced by Ward van Teylingen, Boskoop, Netherlands.

Spiced Bouquet™ ('J. N. Select') produces dark rose-pink buds that open to soft pink flowers. It has a compact habit, growing to 5 feet high and 6 feet wide

Viburnum carlesii 'Aurora' (above)

Viburnum carlesii 'Diana' (above right)

Viburnum carlesii 'Compactum' (right)

in ten years with good foliage density. Leaves have a pronounced glossy sheen. Selected by Michael Yanney in the late 1980s. Introduced by Johnson's Nursery, Menomonee Falls, Wisconsin.

'Variegata' is listed by Kenyon (2001) as a slow-growing variegated form. I have not observed it.

Viburnum cassinoides L.

WITHEROD VIBURNUM, SWAMP VIBURNUM, APPALACHIAN TEA VIBURNUM, SWAMP BLACKHAW, FALSE PARAGUAY TEA, WILD RAISIN

I had no idea *V. cassinoides* umbrella-ed so many common names until reading the assortment just given in Kenyon (2001). A ubiquitous native suckering shrub that I have tracked from Cadillac Mountain, Maine, to Rabun and Brasstown Balds, Georgia, it produces exquisite pink, rose, robin's-egg blue to blue-black fruits, often with all colors in the same infructescence. Habit is upright-spreading, forming a rounded outline. Size is in the 10- by 10-foot range. In the wild, I have seen many 12- to 15-foot-high plants. The new shoots emerge bronze or tinted chocolate-purple. Leaves are early-emerging and extremely frost resistant. Leaves mature to dull dark green, with yellow, orange, red, and purple tints surfacing to differing degrees in autumn. Leaves, 1½ to 3½(4¼) inches long, ¾ to 2¼ inches wide, are toothed to varying degrees, a trait that separates *V. cassinoides* from *V. nudum* in all the specimens I have studied. The leaves are absolutely not as lustrous as *V. nudum*. Opportunities exist for the selection of superior types with compact habits, red fall colors, and copious fruit production. The white, yellow-stamened (prominent) flowers are held in 2- to 5-inch-wide, flat-topped cymes in late May–early June (Athens, Georgia). The floral effect is often quite potent, especially on plants growing in full sun. Grows from granite mountaintops to the edges of streams in moist, acid soil, in full

Viburnum cassinoides

Viburnum cassinoides, new growth, flowers, fruits, and fall color

sun and shade. Plants in our Georgia trials have performed admirably in full sun and with only the blessing of nature's moisture. Excellent plant for naturalizing, massing, or in the shrub border. Zones 3 to 8. Native to Newfoundland to Manitoba and Minnesota south to Georgia. Introduced 1761.

CULTIVARS & VARIETIES

Buccaneer™ and Defender™ are listed, but I was unable to locate descriptions. 'Deep Pink' is described by Connecticut nurseryman Mike Johnson, Summerhill Nursery, as a deep pink-fruited form that he discovered in Maine.

Hillier Form is a yet untitled clone that botanist Allen J. Coombes was considering naming. Young leaves emerge in early April (Athens) a rich, shiny, deep chocolate-purple. The large dark blue-green leaves turn deep mahogany-purple in fall. Typical white flowers and beautiful robin's-egg blue fruits. This is a large form, easily reaching 10 feet high and 12 feet wide and beyond.

*Viburnum
cassinoides
'Nanum'*

'Nanum' is a dwarfish mound of crinkled, crisped, convex leaves that emerge bronze, deepening to green. Leaves are larger than the species, up to 5 inches by 3 inches. It is a slow-growing and small plant that in our tests does little to impress. Flowering has not been reported. The largest plants in the author's purview grow at the Hillier Arboretum and are 2½ feet high by 3 to 4 feet wide.

'Summer Hill' is listed as a hybrid with shiny green leaves that may stay green in warm climates. Matures 5 to 6 feet high. Offered by the former Roslyn Nursery.

Viburnum chingii P. S. Hu

Not well known, but in forms I have seen and grown, a smallish rounded shrub with leaves approximately 2 to 3½ inches by 1 to 1½ inches wide, dull green, oval, ovate, sharply toothed, and leathery, with short, glossy red petioles. In fall, leaves may turn wine-purple. Size is reported to 15 feet, but the plant has grown extremely slowly in our trials and limps along in the heat of Zone 7. Habit is typically loose, open, and lax. Flowers appear in May in 1- to 2-inch-long and -wide terminal cymes (panicles), pink in bud, fading to white. The lone Georgia plant flowered on 29 March 2003 in our trials. I tried to pick up a scent and, after crawling on the ground with my nose (big) in the inflorescence, decided there was nothing—good or bad. However, the literature mentions fragrance as a floral characteristic. Each flower is about ⅓ inch long and wide, the petals reflexed backward, resulting in an urn-shaped corolla with reflexed lobes. Fruit

Viburnum chingii,
flowers and fruits
(above)

*Viburnum
cinnamomifolium,*
habit, foliage and
flowers

is a ⅓-inch-long, red-to-black drupe, coloring in June. Probably a plant for the insatiable collector. Considered similar to *V. erubescens* (certainly different in leaf characteristics, however) and first described in 1966. Zones 6 and 7. Native to China.

Viburnum cinnamomifolium Rehd.

I liken this to *V. davidii* on steroids—with similar, prominent, impressed, 3-veined, lustrous dark green leaves, 2 to 6(7) inches long, 1 to 2½ inches wide, entire or almost so, and leathery. The thickish petiole, ½ to 1 inch long, is painted green-red to red. This is a large shrub to 10 feet, upright, a near haystack in outline in most forms I observed, with rather coarse reddish brown branches. The flowers, dull white, no odor, appear in May–June (1 May 1999 at RHS Hyde Hall) in 5- to 6-inch-wide, 7-rayed cymes. In full flower 2 April 2003 in Aiken, South Carolina. Fruits, which I have yet to see, are egg-shaped, ¼-inch-long, glossy turquoise-blue to blue-black drupes. Performs more reliably in the South than *V. davidii*. Well-drained, acid soil and partial shade, sheltered from wind and winter sun, suit it best. A classy textural addition to the shade garden. Possibly requires two seedlings or clones to effect cross-pollination and fruit set. Even in Europe, I have not seen fruiting plants. Eleven feet high, 9 feet wide at Hillier in 1999; 7 feet in height at the Atlanta Botanical Garden, 22 December 2005. Zones 6 and 7, 9 and 10 on West Coast. Native to western Sichuan, China. Introduced in 1904 by E. H. Wilson, who discovered the species on Mount Omei.

Viburnum corylifolium Hook. f. & Thoms.

Observed only once by the author, this species is similar to *V. dilatatum*, except the leaves are more rounded (not absolute), 1 to 3 inches long, similar in width, with 6 to 9 vein pairs and prominent serrations. The plant at Kew Gar-

Viburnum corylifolium

dens was 7 feet high with leaves that I noted looked like *Corylus* or *Corylopsis*. White flowers in May–June are followed by egg-shaped, ⅓-inch-long, bright red, long-persistent fruits. May grow 6 to 10 feet high and wide. Stems covered by long, reddish brown hairs. Zones 6 and 7. Native to eastern Himalayas, western China. Introduced in 1907.

Viburnum cotinifolium D. Don

The first time I witnessed this species, I thought I was looking at a roundleaf, semi-evergreen form of *V. lantana*. Differs from *V. lantana* in cymes, 5-rayed, corolla tinged pink, distinctly funnel-shaped, and corolla tube longer than the lobes. All plants I experienced in England were rounded in outline, stiffly branched, with generally a few leaves persisting through winter. The medium to dark green leaves are broad-ovate to rounded, 2 to 5 inches long, 2 to 4 inches wide, with 6 to 8 prominent veins. Leaves are flat gray-green above, whitish,

Viburnum cotinifolium, habit, foliage, and flowers

hairy below, apex abrupt, base subcordate, margins finely serrate from apex to base. Petiole is about ¼ inch long and pubescent. Hillier and Coombes (2002) mentioned that leaves sometimes turn crimson in autumn. The red-budded, nonfragrant flowers open to white from late April (30 April 1999 at Hillier) into May, in 2- to 3-inch-wide, 5-rayed cymes. Fruits, egg-shaped, ⅓ inch long, color red, finally black. Apparently adaptable to a range of pH and soil types. Reaches 10 to 12 feet high, 12 to 15 feet wide in the wild; plants in cultivation are smaller. A plant at Hillier was 10 feet high and wide with abundant fruit and slight viburnum beetle damage on 31 May 2006. A plant at the JC Raulston Arboretum was injured by cold in the winter of 2003–04. Mildew on foliage at Knightshayes, 1 August 2001. Zones 6 and 7. Occurs naturally from Afghanistan to the Himalayas. Introduced about 1830.

CULTIVARS & VARIETIES

Several are described by Kenyon (2001), including var. *lacei* T. R. Dudley and var. *wallichii* T. R. Dudley. I have not seen them in cultivation. Apparently considerable variation exists over the extended natural range.

Viburnum cylindricum Buch.-Ham. ex D. Don
TUBEFLOWER VIBURNUM

Viburnum cylindricum is a bold evergreen species, large in stature, 10 to 15 feet high, with greater potential. The range of sizes I noted were 6 to 8 feet high and 10 feet wide, 10 feet high and 15 feet wide, 15 feet high and 12 feet wide, and 18 feet high and wide. Leaves quite variable, 4 to 6 vein pairs, entire, serrate or with a few serrations toward the apex, dull dark green, pale below, 3 to 8 inches long, 2 to 4 inches wide; the petiole ¾ to 1½ inches long and green to pink. Leaves on seedlings are distinctly toothed; mature plants have largely entire leaves. No odor to crushed leaves. The upper surface is covered with wax, which turns gray

Viburnum cylindricum

when scratched or marked. Good leaf to inscribe one's name. White, scented, cylindrical-shaped flowers with protruding purple stamens opened in late June at Hillier Arboretum. Inflorescences are 7-rayed cymes, 3 to 6 inches across. Fruits are egg-shaped, ⅙- to ¼-inch-long, black drupes. I have yet to observe fruit set on cultivated plants. Unique plant for foliage, with large droopy leaves. Another in the genre of collector plants. A small plant at the JC Raulston Arboretum, Raleigh, North Carolina, survived 10°F in the winter of 2003–04. Zones 7 and 8, 9 and 10 on West Coast. Wide distribution in Southeast Asia, Malaysia, Himalayas, and China. Introduced in 1881 from India, 1892 from China.

CULTIVARS & VARIETIES

A variegated leaf form grows at the Hillier Arboretum. Leaf is green with lighter lime-green center. Not readily evident except on close inspection. Plant was 15 feet high and 12 feet wide in 1999. It has not been named.

Varieties *capitellata* Wright & Arn. and *longiflorum* Kern are listed by Kenyon (2001).

Viburnum cylindricum, seedling foliage and flowers

Viburnum cylindricum, variegated leaf form

Viburnum davidii Franch.

DAVID VIBURNUM

All who see . . . desire . . . for their gardens and their clients' gardens. Enthusiasm must be restrained, for the species itself is temperamental in the eastern–southeastern United States. Forms a compact mound, 3 to 5 feet high, of lustrous dark green leaves with 3 deeply impressed veins. The 2- to 6-inch-long, 1- to 2½-inch-wide leaves are toothed toward the apex, acute, slightly rounded, and glabrous; petiole, ¼ to 1 inch long, is red. In winter, foliage color is largely as in summer, occasionally with slight tints. The pink-budded, eventually dull white, nonfragrant flowers occur in dense, 2- to 3-inch-wide, 7-rayed cymes in April–May. In full flower 11 April 2003 at the UGA Botanical Garden, Athens, Georgia. The bright blue, ¼-inch-long, narrow-oval, blue fruits ripen in fall and persist into winter. No guarantees for fruiting abundance, as plants may be functionally "male" or "female"; plants are self-sterile and require cross-pollination. The heat, humidity, and wet soils of the Southeast mitigate good success. Definitely a plant for cooler climates, ideally the coast of California into the Pacific Northwest. The magnificent specimens in European gardens attest to the importance of cool, moist climates. Used in rock gardens, borders, groupings, and even masses. Truly one-of-a-kind viburnum that knows no equals. Moist, acid, well-drained soil in shade (Southeast). Noticed leaf spot on older leaves at Wakehurst Place, 27 May 2006. Zones (7)8 and 9. Native to China. Introduced in 1904 by E. H. Wilson.

CULTIVARS & VARIETIES

'Angustifolium' is a narrower leaf form with the same traits as the species but a more refined appearance. In habit, as I first witnessed the plant (1999), it was compact and spreading. The same plant is 5 to 6 feet high and looser and more open as viewed in March 2006. I have read mention that it may be a hy-

Viburnum davidii

Viburnum davidii, flowers, fruits, and foliage

Viburnum davidii 'Angustifolium'

brid between *V. calvum* and *V. davidii*, although I see no *V. calvum* in the gene pool. It is faster growing and flowers slightly later than *V. davidii*. May be closer to *V. cinnamomifolium*. Origin unknown. Certainly would be worth testing for adaptability in the United States since the leaf texture is similar to *V. davidii* and *V. cinnamomifolium*.

Viburnum dentatum L.
ARROWWOOD VIBURNUM

This is one of the most durable viburnums for general landscape use. From St. Paul, Minnesota, to Tallahassee, Florida, from Lincoln, Nebraska, to the eastern seaboard, it is impervious to extremes of climate and soils. Wet, dry, acid, high pH, salt—it withstands all. Considered by this author a polymorphic species with significant plasticity in habit, leaf, pubescence, but consistent for the 6 to 10 pairs of impressed veins ending in prominent serrations, the white, unpleasant-to-the-nose flowers, and the blue to blue-black fruits. A multi-stemmed, colonizing, dense, rounded shrub with spreading, arching branches, it forms a large dome. Plants appear almost bulletproof except for deer-browsing and, in recent years, the viburnum beetle. Leaves, flat to lustrous medium to dark green, 2 to 4½ inches long, 1 to 4 inches wide, typically pubescent—at least on veins below, with a ½- to 1-inch petiole, turn yellow to red in fall. Autumn color is seldom flagrant (i.e., brilliant red like *Euonymus alatus*) and is significantly variable from plant to plant; several of the cultivars selected for excellent fall color perform inadequately in Athens. Most of the cultivar selections are derived from northern seed provenances. Enterprising plantsmen need to assess the variation in the South for superior introductions. The white flowers in 7-rayed, 2- to 4(5)-inch-wide cymes on 1½- to 2½-inch-long peduncles, open in May–June (early May in Athens) and are effective for ten to 14 days. The fruits follow in summer–early fall and are often foraged by the birds. Each

Viburnum dentatum

Viburnum dentatum, foliage and immature fruits, flowers, fruits, and fall color

fruit is oval-rounded, ¼ to ⅓ inch long, blue to blue-black. Amazingly adaptable and for that reason a great choice for difficult sites. Use for hedges, groupings, mass plantings, screens, and foundation plantings. Unbelievable variations in size . . . 6 to 15 feet high and wide. There was a 12- by 12-foot plant at Hillier in 1999. Compact forms are needed. Zones (2)3 to 8. Native to New Brunswick to Minnesota and south to Georgia. Introduced in 1736.

CULTIVARS & VARIETIES

Many varieties are listed, but I doubt their validity: no one could separate them without labels.

Autumn Jazz® ('Ralph Senior') has a graceful, vase-shaped habit, 8 to 10 feet high, 10 to 12 feet wide, glossy green summer foliage, white flowers, and blue-black fruits. Fall color is yellow-orange-red-burgundy, and I observed it turning yellow-orange-red at the Chicago Botanic Garden on 28 October 1998. It has minimal fall color in Zone 7. A good-quality, 10- by 10-foot specimen grew at the Minnesota Landscape Arboretum on 20 July 2005. Introduced in 1992 through Chicagoland Grows and selected by Synnesvedt Nursery, Round Lake, Illinois.

Black Forest™ ('KLMnine') is on Roy Klehm's Beaver Creek Nursery production/trial list.

Blue Blaze™ ('Blubzam') has a low spreading habit and moderate growth rate, and matures 5 feet high by 7 feet wide. Two- to 4-inch-wide, cream-white cymes occur in May–June followed by blue fruits. Attractive, 3-inch-long, gunmetal-green leaves have deep wine-colored lower surfaces. This is a Lake County Nursery introduction, part of the Lake Erie Series™.

Blue Muffin™ ('Christom') has glossy dark green leaves, intense blue fruits and grows 5 to 7 feet high, 2 to 4 feet wide. This form was listed as 4 to 5 feet high and wide in ten years but has grown 7 feet high in five years in Athens, Georgia. Selected by Tom Watson, Christom Farms Nursery, Cambridge, Wisconsin. Sold under the Proven Winners® banner.

Viburnum dentatum Autumn Jazz® ('Ralph Senior'), fall color

Viburnum dentatum
Blue Muffin™
('Christom') (above)

*Viburnum
dentatum* Cardinal™
('KLMthree'), fall
color (above right)

Viburnum dentatum
Chicago Lustre®
('Synnesvedt'), fruits
and fall color (right)

*Viburnum
dentatum* var.
deamii (right)

Cardinal™ ('KLMthree') has light green leaves, brilliant red fall color, white flowers, ¼-inch-long, blue fruits on an upright 10- to 12-foot-high and -wide habit. In five years, no fall color in UGA trials. Hardy to Zone 4. Introduced by Roy Klehm, Beaver Creek Nursery, Illinois.

Chicago Lustre® ('Synnesvedt') has glossy dark green foliage, white flowers, and blue-black fruits. Reddish purple in fall but not really striking; no appreciable fall color in Zone 7 (our *V. bracteatum* 'Emerald Luster' is superior). A 1990 Chicagoland Grows introduction, Synnesvedt selection, that grows to be a rounded shrub 10 feet high and wide. I witnessed a 10- by 8-foot plant at the Minnesota Landscape Arboretum on 21 July 2005.

Cream Puffs™ ('Crpuzam') is a large, broad-rounded shrub maturing 10 feet by 12 feet with abundant white flowers, bright blue fruits, and red fall foliage. A Lake County Nursery introduction, Lake Erie Series™.

Crimson Tide™ ('KLMsix') has clean summer foliage, blazing red fall color, exceptional vigor, and an upright habit similar to Autumn Jazz®. Grows 10 to 12 feet high and wide. Zone 4. Introduced by Roy Klehm, Beaver Creek Nursery.

Variety *deamii* (Rehd.) Fernald, with larger leaves and flowers, shows up in collections. Eugene W. Coffman, Ridge Road Nursery, Bellevue, Iowa, lists it as one of the best forms of *V. dentatum*. It is a good representative for the Midwest of the terrific variation within *V. dentatum*. There was a loose, spreading shrub at Hillier, 10 feet high and wide, on 1 July 1999. Leaves are larger than *V. dentatum* with upper and lower surfaces extremely pubescent. Flowers are larger than *V. dentatum* with no odor.

Dwarf Form is a selection that grew 5 feet high while others in seedling population were 8 feet high. Finer-textured branches and leaf size than species. Abundant cream-white flowers, reddish purple fall color, and blue-black fruit that is held above the foliage. Selected at Reeseville Ridge Nursery, Reeseville, Wisconsin. Also listed as 'Compactum', which is invalid.

Fireworks™ ('Firzam') has a compact habit, 6 to 7 feet by 4 to 5 feet, that is somewhat columnar in outline. Thick, glossy green leaves turn ruby-red in autumn. Produces cream-white flowers and blue-black fruits. A Lake County Nursery introduction, Lake Erie Series™.

'Golden Arrow' develops yellow leaves that may photobleach (turn white) and lose their color as they mature in Zone 7 and south. Leaves are smaller than typical *V. dentatum*. Shrub as viewed on 9 April 2006 at the JC Raulston Arboretum was not appealing. Discovered by Jon Roethling. I believe that this is the same as Yellow Leaf Selection.

Grow Low™ ('GrowLo') is listed by Beaver Creek Nursery.

Indian Summer™ ('KLMeight') has clean summer foliage and a blend of orange and red in the fall. It is an upright, rounded, vigorous form that grows

Viburnum
dentatum
'Golden
Arrow'

Viburnum
dentatum
Northern
Burgundy®
('Morton')

Viburnum
dentatum
Papoose™
('Papzam')

8 to 12 feet high and wide. Zone 4. Introduced by Roy Klehm, Beaver Creek Nursery.

Little Joe™ ('KLMseventeen'). True compact form. Original plant was 4 feet high and wide after ten years. Finer-textured branches and smaller leaves than the species. Typical flowers and fruits. Purple-green fall color. Introduced by Roy Klehm, Beaver Creek Nursery.

'Moonglow' ('Moonglo', 'Moon Glow') has a rounded habit at maturity, low-spreading when young. Matures 8 feet high and wide. Inflorescences are cream-white, dome-shaped, rather than flat like the species. The stamens, as they mature, turn reddish, giving the appearance of cinnamon sprinkled on top of the flowers. Fruits are blue, larger than typical for the species, ripening in August–September. Leaves are rounded, lustrous dark green, with wavy margins and few serrations. Introduced by Moon Nurseries, Chesapeake City, Maryland.

Northern Burgundy® ('Morton') has dark green summer foliage that turns burgundy in fall. Grows 10 to 12 feet high, more upright than Autumn Jazz®. Same flowers and fruits as species, again nothing to get excited about in Zone 7. Chicagoland Grows promotion, Synnesvedt introduction in 1992. A 10- to 12-foot-high, quality specimen grew at the Minnesota Landscape Arboretum on 20 July 2005; it had duller and smaller foliage than Chicago Lustre®.

'October Glory' turns brilliant red in October and maintains the red color into November in Zone 5. Produces dense, flat, white clusters (cymes) of flowers in June that are effective for three weeks. Cold hardy and can withstand −20°F without damage. Introduced by William Flemer III, Princeton Nursery, Princeton, New Jersey.

'Osceola' was selected by Rick Webb in the Florida parishes of Louisiana. Found growing at the edge of a pocasin (pine/holly forest) on clay hills. Slightly smaller foliage with late yellow-purple fall color. Good flower and fruit production. Original plant was 9 feet by 10 feet at seven years. The central reason for introduction was to have a true southern provenance that would perform well. I can attest to the disappointing *V. dentatum* cultivar performance in our UGA trials. Of the current five, none have any (much less reliable) fall color. All flower and fruit quite well, probably because of proximity of other pollinators.

Papoose™ ('Papzam') has new pink-tinged leaves that have some gloss in summer and turn gold-red in fall, white flowers, and blue fruits on a compact, 5-foot-high shrub. It is tighter and more densely branched than average *V. dentatum*. Introduced by Lake County Nursery, Lake Erie Series™.

Pathfinder™ ('Patzam') has glossy black-green leaves that are smaller and more deeply serrated than the species, white flowers, and metallic blue-black fruits. Grows 5 to 6 feet by 3 to 4 feet with a slender, upright habit. A Lake County Nursery introduction, Lake Erie Series™.

Viburnum dentatum 'Perle Bleu', fruits (above)

Viburnum dentatum Red Feather® ('J. N. Select'), fall color (above right)

Viburnum dentatum var. *scabrellum* (right)

'Perle Bleu' is described as producing heavy crops of blue fruits. It has medium green leaves and was in full, stinky flower on 4 May 2006 at the JC Raulston Arboretum. Grows 8 to 10 feet high, otherwise like the species.

Variety *pubescens* Ait. is hairy in all its parts, hence its common name, downy viburnum. It is recognized for densely downy pubescent stems and leaf undersides with leaves of thicker texture.

Raspberry Tart™ ('Rastzam') is a true compact rounded form, 4 to 5 feet high and wide, with shiny green leaves that change to raspberry-red in fall. White flowers are followed by blue-black fruits. Another Lake County Nursery introduction, Lake Erie Series™.

Red Feather® ('J. N. Select') has leaves that emerge red-purple, mature lustrous dark green, and then turn a consistent deep red burgundy in fall. Grew 6 feet by 5 feet in nine years. Mature size listed as 8 to 10 feet high and wide. Selected by Michael Yanny in 1989 from open-pollinated seedlings. Introduced by Johnson's Nursery, Menomonee Falls, Wisconsin.

Red Regal™ ('KLMseven') has reddish orange fall color and is upright to 8 to 12 feet high and wide. Zone 4 hardiness. A Roy Klehm, Beaver Creek Nursery introduction.

Variety *scabrellum* Chapm. is, I believe, the same as *V. ashei* Bush and is consistently the last viburnum to flower in the UGA trials. Foliage is smaller, lustrous, heat tolerant, and turns yellow in fall. White flowers with no noticeable odor arrive in late May–early June (12 June 2006, Athens, Georgia) followed by blue fruits. Growth habit appears restrained. Probably maturing in the 5- to 8-foot range. There was a 7- by 10-foot dense, sprawling form with lustrous dark green leaves and scabrous stems at Hillier on 1 July 1999. Appears self-fruiting, as no other viburnums were in flower. The plant labeled var. *scabrellum* has the same characteristics as the UGA *V. ashei*. Found naturally in east Texas, Louisiana, eastward to Florida. In full flower 18 June 2004 at the JC Raulston Arboretum; 17 June 2003 at the University of Georgia.

Tree Form, listed by Louisiana Nurseries, has a small tree-like habit and large white flowers, followed by showy blue-black fruits.

Vanilla Cupcakes™ ('Vacuzam') offers large olive-green leaves and golden fall foliage on an upright-rounded plant that matures 5 to 6 feet high and wide. Large vanilla-white flowers are followed by bright blue fruits. A Lake County Nursery introduction and the heaviest fruiting of the Lake Erie Series™.

Viburnum dilatatum Thunb.
LINDEN VIBURNUM

Wow! Spectacular! Especially when laden with the glossy red fruits. I would be hard-pressed to cite the best planting but the one that comes to mind was at Longwood Gardens—a mass planting dressed in red satin. For a single specimen, I give the nod to a dense, broad-mounded, compact form in the Arnold Arboretum. Habit is variable—upright, arching, straggly, to dense and rounded. Typically 8 to 10 feet high and as wide, although smaller cultivars like 'Catskill' bring size to the 5-foot level. Foliage is maddening for identification, for on the same branch ovate to obovate leaves commingle. Usually dark green, often lustrous, even leathery, the 2- to 5-inch-long and almost as wide leaves, with 5 to 8 vein pairs, turn inconsistent red in fall. Leaves are pubescent above, prominently so below. Petiole is about ½ inch long with prominent pubescence. In

Viburnum dilatatum, habit, flowers, and fall color

Viburnum dilatatum, "the marriage of red and white"

Viburnum dilatatum, laden with fruits

fact, stems, peduncle, and pedicels are covered with hair. The flowers, oh-so-stinky, white, in 3- to 5-inch-wide, mostly 5-rayed cymes, open in May–June. In full flower late April–early May in Athens. Flower numbers are high, and a plant at its best is attractive—from a distance. The heart and soul of the species are embodied in the fruits—red, shiny, ⅓ inch long, ovoid, ripening in September–October, persisting into winter. I have caught (with the camera) the marriage of red and white (snow). A visual feast. Apparently, the fruits are largely unpalatable to the birds. Adaptable but best in acid, moist, well-drained soils. Not as pristine in the heat of the lower South (Zone 8). In Orono, Maine, the species, 'Catskill', and 'Erie' were seriously injured by cold. But in Zones 5 to 7 a choice plant for the shrub border. Utilize two clones or seedlings to promote cross-pollination and abundant fruit set. Native to Korea, China, and Japan. One of the most common shrubs in sunny thickets on hills and low mountains in Japan. Introduced in 1846 by Robert Fortune.

CULTIVARS & VARIETIES

Many, with the best resulting from Egolf's breeding work and several other worthy introductions from plantsmen who kept their eyes open.

'Asian Beauty' has shiny dark green foliage, russet-red fall color, and excellent cherry-red fruit production and color retention. Fruits persist with good color into winter, eventually darkening. 'Asian Beauty' has an upright habit with significant vigor, reaching 10 feet or greater with age. One of the best fruit pro-

Viburnum dilatatum 'Asian Beauty', habit and fruits (below)

Viburnum dilatatum 'Catskill', habit and fruits (above right)

ducers, it is becoming more common in commerce. A Don Shadow introduction, Winchester, Tennessee.

'C. A. Hildebrant's' was observed only once by the author and immediately identified as a selection of *V. dilatatum*. A recent sighting in a nursery catalog lists it as a *V. wrightii* selection. Supposedly grows only 4 feet and has great quantities of bright red fruits. The plants I witnessed were relatively compact, but I have doubts about the 4-foot size at maturity. Probably larger. The leaves are extremely lustrous dark green and perhaps more leathery than the run-of-the mill seedling. Also, the stems and leaf undersides as well as the petioles are covered with dense pubescence. This characteristic is common to *V. dilatatum*, whereas *V. wrightii* is essentially glabrous. A Conard-Pyle introduction.

Cardinal Candy™ ('Henneke') (PP 12,870) has glossy foliage and good vigor. There were stinky white flowers fully open on 10 May 2006 at the JC Raulston Arboretum, Raleigh, North Carolina. Glossy red fruits are persistent, remaining into spring. Fruiting appears heavy without a pollinator. Listed as 5 to 6 feet high; I suspect larger based on the vigor of container plants at the Center for Applied Nursery Research, Dearing, Georgia. Zones (4)5 to 7. A Proven Winners® introduction selected by Rodney Henneke from a batch of seed-grown plants after −30°F killed all except for Cardinal Candy™.

'Catskill' is a dwarf *V. dilatatum* seedling selection made by Egolf in 1958 from plants raised from seed obtained from Japan. 'Catskill' was selected for its compact growth habit, smaller and rounder leaves, and good autumn coloration. The compact, wide-spreading growth habit has been constant. The smaller, dull, dark green leaves, which are more nearly rounded than on most *V. dilatatum* plants, assume good yellow, orange, and red fall coloration. The creamy white inflorescences are produced in May (late April 1994, Athens). The dark red fruit clusters, which are dispersed over the plant, ripen in mid August and provide a display until mid winter. There was an extremely dense 3½ feet high and wide plant at Hillier in 1999. The original plant, at 13 years old, was 5 feet high and 8 feet wide. This selection did not do well in the Illinois field tests; however, it has performed well in Tennessee. A planting in the UGA Botanical Garden is now 6 feet high, densely broad-rounded, and has produced red fruits, although never as abundantly as its neighbor 'Erie'. See Egolf 1966b.

'Erie' forms a rounded-mounded shrub, 6 feet high and 10 feet wide in 14 years. Dark green leaves assume good yellow, orange, and red fall color. Produces white flowers in 4- to 6-inch-wide, flat-topped cymes and prolific red fruits, which after frost become coral and persist as coral to pink. Highly resistant to diseases and insects. Excellent performer in Cincinnati and Athens. In my experience, grows more upright than description just given; in Athens, it is now 10 feet by 8 feet. Excellent fruit set in Zone 7 if a cross-pollinator is avail-

Viburnum dilatatum 'Erie', habit, fruits, and fall color (right, below, below right)

Viburnum dilatatum 'Iroquois', fruits (bottom left)

Viburnum dilatatum 'Michael Dodge', fruits (bottom right)

able. Resulted from open-pollinated seed collected in Japan. Released in 1970. Styer Award recipient in 1992. See Egolf 1971.

'Fugitive' is a name that was attached to a semi-evergreen plant of *V. dilatatum* at Hawksridge Nursery, Hickory, North Carolina, on 19 March 2004. A suspected hybrid (*V. japonicum* × *V. dilatatum*) with white flowers and no fruits.

Forma *hispidum* Nakai has hispid stems.

'Iroquois' resulted from a cross of two *V. dilatatum* selections made in 1953. The cultivar was selected for large, thick-textured, dark green leaves; abundant inflorescences of creamy white flowers; large, glossy, dark scarlet fruits; and dense, globose growth habit. The heavy-textured foliage is ornamental in all seasons, glossy green in summer, and orange-red to maroon in autumn. In mid May the inflorescences transform the plant into a mound of creamy white. The glossy red fruits are larger than those on *V. dilatatum* plants. The flat, wide-spreading fruit clusters contrast well with the dark green leaves. The fruits, which ripen in late August, persist after the leaves have fallen, and often the dried fruits are in abundance in mid winter if not eaten by birds earlier. The original specimen was 9 feet high and 12½ feet wide. Excellent form based on my observations; have seen fruit so heavy it weighs the branches down. This is still one of the best forms and when well fruited is the envy of all the fruiting shrubs. See Egolf 1966b.

Littleleaf Form is a name I attached to a dark green, small-leaf taxon (about one-third to one-half the size of species' leaf) that Rick Crowder, Hawksridge Nursery, Hickory, North Carolina, showed me. I asked Rick about specifics, and he had no background information. Good-looking plant if it flowers and fruits like the species.

'Michael Dodge' is an introduction with all the fine qualities of the species except the large fruits are a beautiful bright yellow that is much more attractive than those of 'Xanthocarpum'. Fall color is reddish. Named after the White Flower Farm horticulturist, discovered by Hal Bruce at Winterthur, in Delaware. Supposedly matures smaller than most *V. dilatatum* types at 5 feet by 6 feet. This plant has a unique history as recounted in a 24 January 2001 letter from its namesake. In 1969, at Winterthur, Michael crossed 'Xanthocarpum' with *V. dilatatum*, and harvested, cleaned, and sowed fruits that same fall. They germinated in great abundance in the spring of 1970, but Michael then accepted a position at White Flower Farm. Hal Bruce lined out seedlings at Winterthur, and told Michael there were several attractive selections. Conard-Pyle, West Grove, Pennsylvania, was given propagation rights. I witnessed it in glorious fruit at Swarthmore College in fall 2001. Truly the best of the yellow-fruiting *V. dilatatum* types and performing admirably in our UGA trials.

*Viburnum
dilatatum* 'Mt.
Airy' (above)

*Viburnum
dilatatum* 'Ogon'
(above right)

Viburnum 'Oneida'
(right), deer
damage below
middle

*Viburnum
dilatatum*
'Xanthocarpum',
fruits

'Mt. Airy' I discovered as a stray, misnamed seedling with lustrous leath-ery dark green foliage and abundant large bright red fruits while surveying the *Viburnum* collection at Mt. Airy Arboretum, Cincinnati, Ohio. Interestingly, about 30 feet away were plants of 'Erie' that were not close in fruit size and abundance; obviously ample opportunities existed for cross-pollination, so if good fruit were to occur, it should have. The new clone was 6 to 7 feet high and wide (10 feet high in 2004) with pleasing upright rounded outline. Cuttings were rooted, and the plant has found a small niche in commerce. Appears to be nothing more than a bird-planted seedling but has all the characteristics of true *V. dilatatum.* Early leafing by early April. Flowered mid April 1995 in the Dirr garden. Don Shadow tells me this cultivar is more cold hardy than most.

'Ogon' is a rare yellow-foliage form that was given to me by Ted Stephens, Nurseries Caroliniana, North Augusta, South Carolina. Unfortunately, in Ath-ens, Georgia (Zone 7), it photobleaches (turns white) in full sun. In shade, it loses the color over time. Beautiful when first emerging, less so later.

'Oneida' resulted from a cross of *V. dilatatum* × *V. lobophyllum* made in 1953. This deciduous shrub was selected for its abundance of nonoffensive flowers in May (late April, Athens, Georgia; late May, Mt. Airy Arboretum, Cincinnati, Ohio) and sporadic flowers throughout the summer; its thin-textured foliage that turns pale yellow and orange-red in autumn; and its upright growth habit with wide-spreading branches. Because of the two or three sporadic flowering periods, abundant fruits are produced that ripen in August and persist on the plant until mid winter. The original plant has grown to a height of 10 feet and a width of 9½ feet. It has not proven as impressive as 'Erie' and 'Iroquois' but is still a good choice. My more recent field notes are more positive, including comments about a 10-foot-high plant with excellent red fruits on 27 September at Brooklyn Botanic Garden and a Swarthmore plant with fruits as good as any typical *V. dilatatum.* Also, the leaves and stems are more glabrous than typical *V. dilatatum* due to *V. lobophyllum* parent. See Egolf 1966b.

Forma *pilosum* Nakai has pilose pubescence that sticks straight out from stems and leaves. I have only observed this form once. Arguable whether it de-serves taxonomic rank.

'Vernon Morris' has cream-white to pale yellow-colored fruits on a large up-right shrub. Introduced in 1993. I have yet to see the plant; however, I met the namesake, a Pottstown, Pennsylvania, doctor.

'Xanthocarpum' (f. *xanthocarpum* Rehd.) has yellow to almost amber-yellow fruits, which are not produced in great abundance and do not make the show of the better red-fruited types. As I have seen the fruits, scarcely yellow in the classical sense, more yellow-orange. A rounded, dense, 6- by 8-foot form was recorded at Hillier on 1 July 1999. A plant grew in the great *Viburnum* collection at the Arnold Arboretum.

Viburnum edule (Michx.) Raf.
MOOSEBERRY, SQUASHBERRY

A straggling shrub that grows 6 to 7 feet high and wide with 2- to 3-inch-long and -wide leaves, 3 to 5 vein pairs, and 3 short lobes at the apex. A dense, aesthetically appealing specimen, 15 feet high and wide, grew at Hillier in 1999. Leaves look like *V. opulus*, with similar glands and stipules, but are heavily pubescent beneath based on the Hillier plant. One reference noted leaves are glabrous beneath. Petiole is 1 inch long with prominent raised glands; I counted 6 on a single petiole. The white flowers in 5-rayed, 1-inch-wide cymes appear in May–June. The egg-shaped, ⅓-inch-long, edible but tart red fruits mature in fall. Fruits can be used to make jelly. One reference said to pick fruits before ripe. Requires moist, shady situation. Allied to *V. opulus* but differs in absence of sterile flowers at the periphery of the inflorescence. Zones 2 to 5, 8 on the West Coast. Native to the Pacific Northwest into Canada and Alaska. Introduced 1880. I question the authenticity of the Hillier plant.

Viburnum edule,
immature fruits

Viburnum ellipticum Hook.

Bonnie and I chased this West Coast native around the Portland, Oregon, area in 2005 and were unable to locate the species in the wild. In the Portland public gardens, it was also *in absentia*, meaning the ornamental characteristics were lacking to support garden use. Typically it is a 5- to 8-foot-tall shrub with greenish yellow, slightly pubescent shoots when emerging. The 1- to 3-inch-long, thickish, leathery, elliptic-oblong leaves are coarsely serrate above the middle. The leaf base is 3-veined, subcordate, with pubescence on the veins beneath. Flowers, white, are borne on long-stalked pubescent, approximately 2-inch-wide terminal cymes. The fruit is an ellipsoidal, ½-inch-long black drupe. It occurs as an understory plant in the wild. Not well suited to the Midwest and eastern United States. Leaf shape and serration pattern are unique among viburnums I observed. Zones 6 to 9. Native to western North America. Introduced 1908.

Viburnum erosum Thunb.
BEECH VIBURNUM

In my limited experience (one specimen at Kew, one at Hillier, one at the Sarah P. Duke Gardens), the species is similar to *V. dilatatum*, just not as hardy. Typically, an upright straggly shrub, 5 to 7 feet high, 3 to 5 feet wide, found naturally in Japan, China, and Korea. A plant at Hillier was 6 feet high and wide in 1999. Leaves are dark green, 1½ to 3½ inches long, 1 to 2 inches wide, with a short (less than ⅕-inch-long) tomentose petiole. Fall color is dull orange-red. White, malodorous flowers in April (15 April 2006, Sarah P. Duke Gardens, Durham, North Carolina) in 2- to 3-inch-wide cymes are followed by ¼-inch-long, globose-ovoid, red fruits. Two varieties are listed: var. *taquetii* Rehd. and var. *vegetum* Nakai. A forma *xanthocarpum* with yellow fruits is also reported. Zones

Viburnum erosum

*Viburnum
erosum*,
foliage,
flowers, and
fall color

6 to 8. Common on sunny hills in warm-temperate Japan. Introduced in 1844 by Robert Fortune.

Viburnum erubescens Wall.

My primary familiarity with this species is attached to Sissinghurst, England, where a large 18- by 12-foot specimen resides in the Rose Garden. This form appears to be var. *gracilipes* Rehd., with larger leaves and flower panicles than the typical species. The glossy green, glabrous (above) leaves average 2 to 4 inches long by 1 to 2 inches wide, with a reddish central lower vein, 7 to 9 pubescent vein pairs, and a 1-inch-long, reddish, glabrous petiole. Leaves emit a fetid odor when bruised. The fragrant flowers, typically white stained pink when emerging, open in May–June. I noted the shrub at Sissinghurst coming into flower on

2 May 1999. In full flower late May–early June in 1984 and 1986 at Sissinghurst. The panicles, loose, pendent, range from 3 to 4 inches wide to 2 inches long. The ¼-inch-wide, ellipsoidal fruits transition from green to red to black. The var. *gracilipes* is a graceful shrub worthy of trial. An upright, loose, open, 10- by 8-foot shrub grew at Hillier in 1999. This is more common in cultivation than the species. Zones 6 and 7. Introduced by Wilson in 1910. Varieties *carnosulum* W. W. Smith and *limitaneum* W. W. Smith are listed, but I have not observed them. Native to Sri Lanka, India, Himalayas, northern Burma, and China.

Viburnum erubescens, habit and foliage (below left and bottom left)

Viburnum erubescens var. *gracilipes*, habit and flowers (below and bottom right)

Viburnum farreri Stern
FRAGRANT VIBURNUM

Viburnum farreri is named after Reginald Farrer, who collected in China, Burma, and the Alps. The old name for this species, *V. fragrans*, is occasionally used and is certainly more appropriate because of the fragrant pink flowers that open in March–April. This species, with a rickety, vase-shaped habit and temperamental flowering response (fall to spring) was ensconced in our Illinois garden. The sweet fragrance is worth the frustration of trying to successfully grow and flower the plant. Late spring freezes often wreaked havoc. Pinkish red flower buds open pink-white before the leaves in 1- to 2-inch-long and -wide panicles. I documented full flower in early to mid April in 1977 at Purdue University. Never overwhelming but worthy of consideration by the viburnum lover. The foliage, 1½ to 4 inches long, 1 to 2¾ inches wide, emerges early, bronzy-green, matures to dark green, occasionally reddish purple in fall. Leaves have 5 to 6 pairs of deeply impressed veins, which produce a pleated pattern. Leaves essentially glabrous above, slight hairiness on raised veins below or in the axils. Petiole, ½ to 1 inch long, glabrous, and red. When crushed (bruised), leaves emit an odor akin to green peppers. This carries through to the cultivars also. Fruits are rare; I suspect the flowers (at least the ovaries) are often injured by cold, and/or no closely related viburnums are flowering to effect pollination. The glossy red, oval fruits, ¼ to ⅓ inch long, mature black. I have only photographed the fruits twice: once at RHS Hyde Hall in England, the other at Mt. Airy Arboretum in Cincinnati. Yet to witness the black coloration on maturing fruits. Fruit are purported to be edible. Not particular about soil as long as well drained. Cooler climates improve performance. Provide adequate moisture. Good choice for shrub border, where legginess can be masked. Grows 8 to 12 feet high and wide. Zones (4)5 to 7(8). Native to China. Introduced 1910.

CULTIVARS & VARIETIES

'Bowles' ('Bowles' Variety'), listed by the University of British Columbia Botanical Garden, is described as superior to the species. Considered lost to cultivation by Kenyon (2001).

'Candidissimum' ('Album') produces pure white fragrant flowers that are more easily singed by cold. Fruits are described as light yellow but I have yet to see. The leaves show no reddish pigmentation in spring or fall. Their summer color is a soft yellow-green. Typically not as vigorous or large as the species although a 10-foot-high specimen grew at RHS Hyde Hall. A 6- by 4-foot upright plant is at Hillier.

Viburnum farreri,
habit, foliage,
flowers, and fruits

Viburnum farreri
'Candidissimum'
(above)

Viburnum farreri
'Farrer's Pink'
(above right)

Viburnum farreri
'Nanum' (right)

'Farrer's Pink' has pink flowers. There was a 10-foot-tall plant at RHS Hyde Hall and a 6- by 3-foot young plant at Hillier in 1999.

'Fioretta' is described as a stocky, compact form with pink flowers from November to March; reported to grow 5 feet high in ten years (Houtman 1998).

'Mount Joni' is listed as an early-flowering form that repeats in spring.

'Nanum' can either delight or shock, depending on condition. Small, to 5 feet, usually less, rounded becoming lumpy with age, it produces small panicles of pink flowers in spring. A dense, compact plant, 3½ feet high and wide, grew at Hillier in 1999. Foliage is similar to the species but smaller. Leaves 1½ to 2½ inches long, ¾ to 1¼ inch wide, petiole ½ to ¾ inch long, shorter intervals between nodes, ½ to 1 inch apart. Overall shrub appears bronze-green. If groomed properly, a respectable garden addition.

Viburnum foetidum Wall.

Seldom encountered in American gardens, this evergreen, semi-evergreen to deciduous, broad-rounded, dense shrub reaches 10 to 15 feet high and wide. A specimen at Hillier Arboretum has reached this stature, but most references understate the size. The dark green, 1- to 3-inch-long, 1- to 1½-inch-wide leaves, glabrous above, pubescent below, with a reddish, ⅓-inch-long, pubescent petiole, are variable in shape. Herbarium specimen from Hillier had rhombic-ovoid leaves, entire to the middle, then with about 5 deep dentate serrations toward the apex. About 3 to 5 vein pairs and a set of stipular leaves at nodes. Leaves, when bruised, are stinky. The flowers, malodorous, white with violet anthers, occur in terminal, 2- to 3-inch-wide cymes; each flower is ¼ inch wide. I noticed flowers emerging on the Hillier plant on 26 April 1999; fully open and stinky 30 June 1999. In full flower 3 June 2004 at the JC Raulston Arboretum, Raleigh, North Carolina. The species is adaptable to varied soils, full sun to partial shade. Fruit, scarlet-red, is broad-oval and about ¼ inch long. I have not observed fruit set on North Carolina, Georgia, or Hillier plants. Have observed an irregular white-variegated leaf form that was collected in Japan by Ted Stephens. Zones 7 and 8, 9 on West Coast. Native to the Himalayas, Burma, China, and Taiwan. Introduced in 1901 by E. H. Wilson.

Viburnum foetidum

CULTIVARS & VARIETIES

Varieties *ceanthoides* (C. H. Wright) Hand.-Mazz., with small leaves, and *integrifolium* Kanchira and Hatushima, with up to 3½-inch-long, 1-inch-wide leaves, are cited by Kenyon (2001).

Variety *rectangulatum* (Graebn.) Rehd., as seen here at Hawksridge Nursery, Hickory, North Carolina, has smaller, obovate leaves. The specimen in our Georgia collection has almost 3-lobed leaves, reminiscent of water oak (*Quercus nigra*) in outline; the plant has not been vigorous and has suffered winter damage in Athens.

Viburnum foetidum, foliage (above)

Viburnum foetidum var. *rectangulatum*, flowers (above right) and foliage (right)

Viburnum furcatum Bl. ex Hook. f. & Thoms.
FORKED VIBURNUM

This Japanese and Taiwanese species and the closely related North American *V. lantanoides* are unique by virtue of their white lacecap flowers, red to black fruits, and large, 4- to 8-inch-long and -wide leaves. Leaves are downy at emergence, eventually dark green, pubescent below, changing to muted bronze, red, and purple in fall. Petiole is about ½ inch long and woolly pubescent. *Viburnum furcatum* develops an upright, stiffly branched outline, 10 to 15 feet high, somewhat sparse in foliage, but displaying 3- to 6-inch-wide, fragrant, white flowers in 5-rayed cymes in late April–early May (Arnold Arboretum, Boston). The shiny, white, ray flowers are up to 1 inch wide; the inner fertile flowers, ¼ inch wide. Flowers appear before and as the bronzy leaves emerge. Fruits are initially red, purple-black with maturity, ⅓ inch long, and broad oval. I have yet to experience fruit set, which I suspect is related to lack of a suitable pollina-

Viburnum furcatum, habit, foliage, and flowers

tor (the species is apparently self-infertile). Culturally, moist, well-drained, acid soil and cooler climates suit it best. Great specimen at the Arnold Arboretum, which I first witnessed in flower in 1979. Certainly a choice plant and a collector's dream. Does not develop the trailing, arching, layered branches of the related *V. lantanoides*. A pink-flowered form, 'Pink Parasol', was discovered in the wild in Japan's Honshu province. Species grows in the cool-temperature, subalpine forests of Japan. Lancaster (1998) mentioned that the species can reach tree-like proportions of up to 23 feet in its native Japanese and Taiwanese habitats. Zones (5)6 and 7, higher elevations in the Southeast. Introduced in 1892.

RELATED SPECIES

Viburnum sympodiale Graebn. is allied to *V. furcatum* but differs by virtue of stipules on the petiole and the smaller, ovate, more finely toothed leaves. Horticulturist Paul Jones, Sarah P. Duke Gardens, showed me an unidentified plant that keyed perfectly to *V. sympodiale*. Leaf shape, venation, serration, and pubescence resemble both *V. furcatum* and *V. lantanoides*. The linear, strap-shaped stipules were clearly distinguishable. Collected by E. H. Wilson in 1890 in central China.

Viburnum ×*globosum* Coombes

A hybrid between *V. davidii* and *V. calvum* raised in 1964 at the Hillier Nursery, this evergreen species forms a dense, rounded shrub, 15 feet high and wide. This size is based on an old specimen growing in the Hillier Arboretum in 1999. I estimate everyday landscape size in the 5- to 10-foot-high and -wide range. The dark green leaves, undulating and wavy, range from 2 to 6 inches long, 1 to 2½ inches wide, and hold the color through winter. Leaves display the 3-veined character of *V. davidii*, and are serrated and essentially glabrous. The pink-budded, dull white, nonfragrant flowers open in 2- to 3-inch densely packed cymes in late April–May, England (full flower on 20 April 2004 at the JC Raulston Arboretum). I observed blue, ¼-inch-long, narrow-oval fruits on the Hillier plant on 22 February 1999, which means that they are quite persistent. The plant prospers in acid and higher pH soils and appears to have increased longevity compared to its female parent, *V. davidii*, at least in the Southeast. Also, *V.* ×*globosum* exhibits good shade tolerance and is sun adaptable. For landscape purposes, easy to maintain as a smaller shrub. Do not fear the 15-feet-high mentioned above. Probably best in Zones 6 and 7 in the East, into 9 and 10 on West Coast. See Coombes 1980 for original description. 'Jermyns Globe' is the best selection from this cross, being more dense and rounded. I observed a 3-foot-high plant at RHS Hyde Hall, England, which did not inspire. A 12- by 12-foot,

Viburnum
×*globosum*
'Jermyns Globe',
habit, foliage,
flowers, and fruits

globose, extremely dense specimen grew at Hillier in 1999. Leaves are narrower with a central midvein, irregularly toothed, essentially glabrous, 1½ to 4 inches long, to 1¼ inch wide; petiole ¼ to ½ inch long and glabrous.

Viburnum grandiflorum Wall.

Seldom with a presence in North American gardens, yet a rather prosperous 6- to 8-foot-high specimen of *V. grandiflorum* grows contentedly in the JC Raulston Arboretum, Raleigh, North Carolina. The foliage is pristine early in the growing season, but heat and drought will render the leaves necrotic (brown). Giant shrubs, multi-stemmed, naked in their lower extremities, grow with abandon in English gardens. Plants 10 to 15 feet high are common, although most references list size as 6 to 10 feet. The spread is less, in the range of 5 to 8 feet. The ovate leaves, with 6 to 10 vein pairs, 3 to 4 inches long, 1½ to 2 inches wide, are dull matt green, turning maroon in fall; the red petiole is about 1 inch long. Have observed leaves with shiny, waxy surface. Leaves emerge early in Zone 7—often by late March. I have yet to see good fall color. The leaves (also stems) are consistently pubescent beneath, a trait that separates the species from *V. farreri*. These two species mated to produce *V. ×bodnantense*, the cultivars with differing degrees of pubescence on the lower surfaces. Leaves, when crushed, emit a sordid, foul green-pepper odor. Flowers, fragrant, typically appear in winter, January–March, on naked stems in 2- to 3-inch-wide, densely packed cymes, carmine-red in bud, pink upon opening. Flowers are apt to be singed by cold, as they are not as frost tolerant as those of *V. farreri*. Flowered on 12 March 2004 in Chapel Hill, North Carolina. An entire shrub in flower does not overwhelm but is a welcome respite from the doldrums of winter. The approximately ½-inch-long, oval fruits, red maturing black-purple, ripen in May–June. Witnessed fruits on a plant at Wakehurst Place, 27 May 2006, just turning red and elliptical-cylindrical in shape. Not fussy about soil as long as well-drained and also adaptable from full sun to partial shade. Best in a border or winter garden. Zones 6 and 7 in the East, 8 and 9 on West Coast. Native from Himalayas to western China. Introduced in 1914.

CULTIVARS & VARIETIES

Forma *foetens* (Decne.) N. P. Taylor & Zappi was listed as *V. foetens* Decne. The white flowers are not as fragrant as those of the species, and my notes indicate that the leaves are distinctly larger, stinky, not as pubescent (almost glabrous), and lighter green with 5 to 6 prominent vein pairs and a petiole ¾ to 1 inch long and glabrous. Taylor and Zappi consider f. *foetens* a more glabrous variant of *V. grandiflorum*, with distribution restricted to the western Hima-

*Viburnum
grandiflorum,*
habit, foliage,
flowers, and fruits

layas. Flowers also are more susceptible to frost (cold browning) damage. The plant ranges from 6 to 8(10) feet in height. I observed a 12- by 10-foot specimen at RHS Wisley, 25 May 2006, and a 7- by 6-foot loose, open, not very appealing plant at Hillier on 30 June 1999. A 12-foot-high plant was also observed.

Forma *foetens* 'Desmond Clarke', 10 feet high by 12 feet wide with large glabrous leaves, was recorded on 14 June 1999 by the author at Kew Gardens. Flowers are pink. Desmond Clarke revised W. J. Bean's great work, *Trees and Shrubs Hardy in the British Isles*, and edited the *Supplement*. See Taylor and Zappi 1997.

'Snow White' should be just that in flower, but plants at RHS Wisley (12 feet by 15 feet) and Hillier produced pink-budded, opening white, minimally fragrant flowers on 18 and 22 February 1999, respectively. This is an upright, vaseshaped, open plant, 10 feet by 8 feet, with clean foliage (Hillier, 2 July 1999). Leaf, 3½ to 4½ inches long, 9 to 10 impressed vein pairs below, prominently pubescent with tufts of hairs in axils of major veins. Red petiole is ½ to 1 inch long. Raised from seed collected in Nepal by Col. Donald Lowndes in 1950.

Viburnum grandiflorum f. *foetens*, foliage and flowers (above)

Viburnum grandiflorum 'Snow White' (right)

Viburnum harryanum Rehd.

This is the poster viburnum for confounding one's plant material friends relative to identity. I can count on one hand the number of sightings, but once encountered, never forgotten. A wispy, irregular, frumpy evergreen shrub, listed as 6 to 8 feet high; the 18- by 10-foot specimen I saw at Hillier Arboretum in 1999 supersedes the published range. The most unique trait is the unusually shaped leaves, which remind me of Mickey Mouse ears. Leaves are flat dark green, virtually entire except at apex, ½ to 1¼ inch long and slightly narrower to as wide, with a ¹⁄₁₆-inch-long, hairy, red petiole. Undersides of leaf are hairy with a reticulate vein pattern. The nonfragrant, white, smallish ⅛-inch-wide flowers appear in 7-rayed, 1- to 1½-inch-wide terminal cymes (umbels) in May–June. I noted flowers just emerging on 14 April 1999 at Savill Gardens; just opening 29 May 2006 at Hinton Ampner; just finishing 4 June 1999 at Hillier. Fruits are described as bluish black, ⅙-inch-long, ovoid-pointed drupes. I have yet to experience fruits on cultivated plants. I have had no experience growing the species

Viburnum harryanum, habit, foliage, and flowers

in the United States but suspect it would prove adaptable on the West Coast. Hawksridge Nursery, Hickory, North Carolina, has maintained a respectable plant in a 3-gallon container by overwintering it in an unheated polyhouse. Hardiness is not known for the United States: Zones 7 to 9? Native to western China. Discovered by E. H. Wilson in 1904.

Viburnum henryi Hemsl.

A beautiful, architectural evergreen shrub with spreading, arching branches and narrow, 2- to 5-inch-long, 1- to 1½-inch-wide, lustrous dark green leaves, lax and arching, the latter a trustworthy characteristic for separation from *V. ×hillieri* 'Winton'. Leaves are so narrow as to suggest *Salix* (willow) foliage. The leaves are serrated above the middle. Petiole about ½ inch long with a few hairs. Leaves, when bruised, do not have an unpleasant odor like 'Winton' (mild) or *V. erubescens* (potent). Flowers occur in 2- to 4-inch-high and -wide, stiffly pyramidal green panicles, opening off-white in June–July. A plant was just coming

Viburnum henryi, habit, foliage, and flowers

into flower at RHS Wisley on 9 June 1999; in full flower at Hillier, 28 June 1999. I could not detect any fragrance. The oval, ⅓-inch-long, red fruits mature black. I have not observed the species in the United States. It is a parent of *V. ×hillieri* 'Winton'. *Viburnum henryi* grows 7 to 10 feet high and wide. I witnessed a 14-foot-high and -wide plant with loose, open, layered branches at Hillier on 31 May 2006. Possibly Zones 7 and 8 in the Southeast, 8 and 9 on West Coast. Native to central China. Introduced 1901 by E. H. Wilson.

Viburnum ×hillieri Stearn 'Winton'

This hybrid between *V. henryi* and *V. erubescens* is semi-evergreen to deciduous in Athens, developing an arching-spreading outline. Plants reach 10 to 12 feet in height and slightly wider at maturity. I witnessed an immense specimen at Hillier, 20 feet high and wide, 31 May 2006. The leaves are narrow-oval, serrated, bronze when emerging, lustrous dark green at maturity, turning purple-bronze-red in winter. Size ranges from 2 to 5 inches long, 1 to 2½

Viburnum ×hillieri 'Winton', habit, foliage and flower buds, and flowers

Viburnum ×hillieri
'Winton', fruits and
winter color (above)

Viburnum ×hillieri
'Winton' × *V.
awabuki*, foliage
(right)

inches wide, with an approximately 1-inch-long, reddish, pubescent petiole that is more prominently winged than that of *V. henryi*. Flowers, profuse, appear in broad panicles of foamy off-white after beginning green in bud. Flowers are at their best in June (England). The effect is potent. The ⅓- to ½-inch-long, oblong to obovate fruits turn red to deep maroon to black. Tolerates any well-drained soil and full sun to moderate shade. Pleasing as an edge of woodland or semi-shaded border plant. Certainly not well known in the United States, but performs well in Portland, Oregon, and plants I brought back from England have performed respectably in the Athens area (Zone 7) since 1999. Zones 7 and 8, 9 and 10 on the West Coast. Originated in 1950 at Hillier Nursery.

CULTIVARS & VARIETIES

I spotted a complex hybrid, *V. ×hillieri* 'Winton' × *V. awabuki* (*V. odoratissimum* var. *awabuki*, according to Hillier and Coombes 2002), the leaves with bronze new growth, maturing dark green, gray-green below, elliptic-ovate, acute, cuneate, 3 to 4 inches long, 1 to 1½ inches wide, irregularly toothed in upper two-thirds, 6 to 8 vein pairs, glabrous, and petiole ¼ to ½ inch long. Overall texture not as aesthetic as either parent. Plant observed was 3 to 4 feet high, reasonably dense, upright, with a modicum of ornamental appeal. This hybrid may be one for Ripley's Believe It or Not.

Viburnum hupehense Rehd.
HUBEI VIBURNUM

Although described as a unique species, the similarity to *V. dilatatum* in foliage, flower, and fruit provides pause for reflection. I initially identified the few plants that crossed my path as *V. dilatatum*, until I read the label. Kenyon (2001) noted that *V. hupehense* has stipules at the base of the leaf and orbicular-ovate leaves, while *V. dilatatum* does not. The herbarium specimen I examined did not have the stipules: leaves broad-ovate, obovate, acute, rounded, 5 to 7 vein pairs, dentate-serrate, pubescent, 2 to 4 inches long, 1½ to 3 inches wide, petiole ¾ to 1 inch long. I have assessed numerous *V. dilatatum*, and leaves that match perfectly with *V. hupehense* do occur. The habit was coarse on the 12-foot-high shrub at RHS Wisley (8 May 1999). A 4- by 5-foot shrub was irregular, loose, and open with clean foliage on 30 June 1999 at Hillier. Flowers, pink in bud, open white (June) and are stinky (malodorous), like *V. dilatatum*. In full flower 3 June 1999 at Hillier. Fruits are ⅓ inch long, oval, red, and hold the color into winter. With so many superior cultivars of *V. dilatatum*, there is minimal reason to grow *V. hupehense*, unless for collection purposes. Leaves, upper and lower, petiole, stem, and inflorescences have short, consistent pubescence, not

Viburnum hupehense, flower buds and foliage

as woolly as that of *V. dilatatum*. An 8- by 12-foot loose, arching specimen with
unopened green flower buds grew at Hillier, 31 May 2006. Zones 5 to 7. Native
to Hubei and Sichuan provinces in China. Introduced in 1908 by E. H. Wilson.

Viburnum ichangense Rehd.
ICHANG VIBURNUM

Related to *V. erosum*, but a planting at Longwood Gardens resembled *V. dilatatum*. Typically, a leggy, 5- to 10-foot-high, 4- to 6-foot-wide shrub with foul,
white flowers (late April–early May at Hillier) and clusters of red fruits. Dense,
compact, 6- by 7-foot plant with clean, dark blue-green foliage at Hillier, 1 July
1999. The Longwood plants were 8 to 10 feet high and upright-spreading. The
1- to 2¼-inch-long, ½- to 1-inch-wide, elliptic-ovate, sharply serrate, pubescent
leaves are dark yellow-green. Petiole, ¹⁄₁₆ to ⅛ inch long, is hairy. I have seen
bronze color on emerging leaves (27 April 1999). Foliage (Longwood) developed
muted red-purple hues in autumn. Culturally, treat like *V. dilatatum*. Zones 5
to 7(8). Native to Hubei, China. Introduced in 1901 by E. H. Wilson.

Viburnum japonicum (Thunb.) Spreng.
JAPANESE VIBURNUM

Viburnum japonicum is another confused species in the United States, often
equated with *V. odoratissimum* and *V. awabuki*. Evergreen, rounded, rather tidy
shrub, typically 6 to 8 feet high and wide. Have seen 10-foot-high plants in England; Lancaster (2000) noted 20-foot-high plants were recorded in Japan. The
foliage is lustrous dark green, coriaceous, glabrous, 3 to 6 inches long, 2 to 4

Viburnum ichangense, habit, flowers, and fruits

Viburnum japonicum

Viburnum japonicum, foliage, flowers, and fruits

Viburnum 'Chippewa'

inches wide, entire or slightly toothed near the apex, 5 to 8 pairs of veins; petiole ½ to 1¼ inch long, green (may be red-tinted) and deeply grooved above. Leaf has numerous, minute, brown glands on the lower surface which are visible with a hand-lens. Leaves have turned reddish green in winter in Zone 7. Flowers, white and fragrant, open in April–May (full flower on 26 April 2004 at the JC Raulston Arboretum, Raleigh, North Carolina) in 7-rayed cymes, 3 to 5 inches wide. Fruits are shiny red, ⅓ inch long, orbicular, flattened, and beautiful. Site in partial shade to full sun, protect from winter winds, and provide well-drained soil. Respectable specimens grow in Aiken, South Carolina, Atlanta, Georgia, and Raleigh, North Carolina. Very shade tolerant in Southeast. Use in shrub border. Zones 7 and 8, 9 on West Coast. Native to Japan and Taiwan; grows in coastal thickets and rocky areas at 16 to 1,600 feet above sea level, where it is quite common. Introduced about 1879 by Charles Maries from Japan.

CULTIVARS & VARIETIES

'Chippewa' is a hybrid (*V. japonicum* × *V. dilatatum*) with semi-evergreen to deciduous leaves and a densely branched, multi-stemmed nature. The parent plant was 8 feet high and 10 feet wide after ten years. Leaves are glossy, leathery dark green, 2 to 4½ inches long, 1½ to 3 inches wide, and turn dark maroon to bright red in autumn. The white flowers occur in 4- to 7½-inch-wide, 5- to 7-rayed cymes containing 200 to 300 flowers per inflorescence. Oblong dark red, ⅜-inch-long, ⅓-inch-wide fruits ripen in August and persist into winter. No winter damage has occurred at −10°F, but foliage is deciduous. A five-year-old plant is 6 feet high and 8 feet wide in the UGA trials. Generally, 'Chippewa' is more irregular and not as effective as the more compact 'Huron'. Flowers seven to ten days ahead of 'Huron'. Fruit set has been minimal. Remarkably good heat tolerance in Zone 7. The result of a backcross by Egolf utilizing embryo rescue to generate plants.

'Huron' (*V. lobophyllum* × *V. japonicum*) is a tardily deciduous (December, Zone 7), dense-branched, multi-stemmed shrub that grew 7¼ feet by 9¼ feet after 17 years. Leaves are leathery, dull dark green turning rich purple in late autumn. Holds leaves later than 'Chippewa'. White flowers occur in 4- to 6-inch-wide, 6- to 7-rayed cymes containing 250 to 400 florets per inflorescence. Flower buds just showing on 15 April 2006 at the Sarah P. Duke Gardens, Durham, North Carolina; in full flower 26 April 2003 in Athens, Georgia. Ovoid dark red, ¼- to ⅓-inch-long, ⅓-inch-wide fruits ripen in August and persist into winter. Hardy to at least −10°F, at which temperature it is deciduous. For additional information on both cultivars, see Egolf 1987. The plant in the Georgia

Viburnum
'Chippewa',
fall color

Viburnum
'Huron'

Viburnum
japonicum
'Variegatum'

trials is 4 feet high and wide after five years. Habit is more compact and dense than 'Chippewa'. Fruit set has not been heavy.

'Variegatum' is a marble-cake mix of cream and yellow on a bronze background as the leaves emerge, cream-yellow on glossy green with maturity. Slower growing than the species, and I have noticed reversions. A collector's plant. A 6-foot-high plant grew in the JC Raulston Arboretum. This plant had two variegated shoots remaining when observed 29 June 2006; all others green.

Viburnum ×juddii Rehd.
JUDD VIBURNUM

Judd viburnum is the result of a cross between *V. carlesii* and *V. bitchiuense*, with the best features of both parents. I feel it is superior to run-of-the-mill *V. carlesii* and is challenging it as the dominant semi-snowball, fragrant viburnum. The habit is full and rounded, with mature height approaching 6 to 8 feet. Leaves, broad-ovate, irregularly toothed, are dull green, almost blue-green above, grayish below, and pubescent on both surfaces, 1 to 3 inches long, 1 to 2½ inches wide, with a ¼-inch-long pubescent petiole. Seldom develops significant fall color, but I have observed muted red-purple. It is more resistant to bacterial leaf spot and roots much more readily from softwood cuttings. The inflorescence, pink in bud, maturing white, ranges from 2½ to 3¼ inches wide and when open is highly fragrant. I have heard people say that the fragrance of *V. ×juddii* is not as pronounced as that of *V. carlesii* but am hard-pressed to distinguish differences. This hybrid was raised at the Arnold Arboretum by William

Viburnum ×juddii

*Viburnum
×juddii*, flowers
and fall color
(above)

*Viburnum
kansuense* (right)

H. Judd, propagator, in 1920, flowered for the first time in 1929, when it was 6 feet high, and named in 1935. Has proven an adaptable and floriferous shrub in the UGA Botanical Garden. Located by a walk that leads from the parking area, and many people stop to sample its delicious perfume. The plants are over 10 feet high (2006). Flowers consistently in late March–early April in Athens. Observed in full flower on 13 April 1999 at Hillier. Zones 4 to 8.

Viburnum kansuense Batal.

Viburnum kansuense has been observed only once by this author, and I thought the plant was *V. opulus*. Grows 7 to 10 feet high with a similar spread. The dark green leaves, 3- to 5-lobed, are 1 to 2 inches long and wide with a ½- to 1-inch-long petiole. Leaves are broad-ovate to oblong-ovate, acuminate, broad-cuneate to subcordate, lobes acuminate to acute, coarsely toothed with mucronulate teeth, with tufts of hairs in the vein axils below. Leaves may color dark red in autumn. The pale pink-white flowers are borne in 1-inch or slightly wider 5- to 7-rayed cymes in May. There are no enlarged sterile flowers similar to those on *V. opulus*, *V. sargentii*, and *V. trilobum*. Fruits are ⅓ inch long, oval to rounded, and red. I am unsure of adaptability but suspect Zones 6 and 7 for starters, 8 to 10 on West Coast. Molecular taxonomy has shown this closely allied with the purple- to black-fruited *V. acerifolium*. Native to western China. Introduced by E. H. Wilson in 1908.

Viburnum koreanum Nakai

Like *V. kansuense*, a one-time sighting. Leaves with 3 lobes, white flowers with both fertile flowers and the enlarged sterile flowers on the periphery. *Flora of Korea* (1966) shows all fertile flowers. Fruits are red and oval-rounded. Crûg Farm describes the plant in the wild with yellow fall color and red fruits from their collection around Odaesan National Park, South Korea. Reaches 7 to 10 feet high and wide. Zones 6 and 7? Native to Korea.

Viburnum lantana L.
WAYFARINGTREE VIBURNUM

This was the crabgrass viburnum of the Midwest but has lost favor to the better cultivars ('Mohican', 'Rugosum') and the hybrid *V. ×rhytidophylloides*. A large, rounded, leggy shrub, 10 to 15 feet high and wide, it is quite coarse in texture, particularly through winter. The thick-textured, dark green leaves are grayish

Viburnum lantana

Viburnum lantana, foliage, flowers, and fruits (above and top left and right)

Viburnum lantana var. *discolor* (above right)

Viburnum lantana 'Aureum' (right)

pubescent on the lower surfaces, 10 to 15 vein pairs, 2 to 5 inches long, 1½ to 4 inches wide, acute, cordate, serrated, and seldom develop fall color; petiole is ½ to 1 inch long and woolly pubescent. Late April–early May brings the flowers: white with prominent yellow stamens, malodorous, in 7-rayed, 3- to 5-inch, flat-topped cymes. The fruits, ⅓ inch long, oblong, are beautiful—transitioning through yellow to red to black; often all colors in the infructescence at the same time—and ripen in August–September. Adaptable to sun and partial shade. Excellent screen, grouping, mixed-border plant. Zones (3)4 to 7. Does not prosper in the heat of the South. Wide distribution from Europe to North Africa and western Asia. Grows in the hedgerows of the English countryside. Terrifically well adapted to chalky (limestone) soils. Witnessed 15-foot-high plants along the Test Way, Hampshire, England. Long cultivated.

CULTIVARS & VARIETIES

'Aureum' has rather handsome golden yellow young shoots, later becoming green. I have seen this form on occasion, not too offensive. Reported to hold yellowish coloration when sited under some shade. Not as large as the species, to 8 feet high, and not as vigorous. Witnessed a 7- by 10-foot plant at Hillier in 1999. Leaf shape, size, and pubescence similar to the species. During a visit to England in late May 2006, I noted several plants with diminished yellow leaf color. Introduced in 1921 by Spaeth of Germany.

Variety *discolor* Huter has smaller, 1¾- to 2½-inch-long, 1- to 1½-inch-wide, serrated, firmer-textured leaves with dense woolly, almost white, pubescence below. Upper surface is lustrous dark green with short pubescence. Eight to 10 vein pairs. Habit is more compact than the species. Has potential for breeding improved foliage characteristics into *V. lantana* and related taxa. Noted a loose, open habit on a 3½- to 5-foot plant at Hillier on 1 July 1999.

'Macrophyllum', as I witnessed on 14 April 1999 at RHS Wisley, has larger leaves than the species, and the inflorescences are listed as much as 8 inches across.

'Mohican' is a seedling selected in 1956 from a population grown from *V. lantana* seed received from Poland. The plant, as a deciduous shrub, was selected for compact growth habit, thick dark green leaves, persistent orange-red fruits, and resistance to bacterial leaf spot. Leaves are 3½ to 4½ inches long, 1¾ to 2¼ inches wide, pubescent on both surfaces but not to the degree of typical *V. lantana*; in fact, the underside of the leaf is more green than the gray one would expect from *V. lantana*. The creamy white flowers and expanding pale green leaves appear together for a week in early May. The orange-red fruits begin to ripen in early July and remain effective for four or more weeks, whereas fruits on other *V. lantana* plants pass rapidly from red to black. The original spec-

Viburnum lantana 'Mohican', habit and fruits (below)

Viburnum lantana 'Variegatum' (above right)

Viburnum lantana 'Variifolium' (right)

imen in 15 years had grown to 8½ feet high and 9 feet wide. Witnessed a 10-by 8-foot, oval-rounded, dense specimen with clean foliage and heavy fruit at Hillier on 1 July 1999. An Egolf introduction and now extremely popular in the nursery trade.

'Rugosum' (var. *rugosum* Lange) is a leathery-leaf form with larger, darker green leaves that are more handsome than those of the species. Tends to become open and rather ragged with age.

'Variegatum' has yellow-variegated leaves.

'Variifolium' has spotted, speckled, and swooshed white, cream, and yellow variegation. New leaves emerge tinged pink-bronze. They average 3 inches by 2 to 2½ inches, appearing rounded. The variegation was stable and the plant more compact (5 feet) than the species. Have observed this twice, and it appears unique from 'Variegatum' and 'Versicolor', although the latter name has been used as a synonym for 'Variifolium'.

'Versicolor' has pale yellow young leaves, finally turning gold.

Viburnum lantanoides Michx.
HOBBLEBUSH

Viburnum lantanoides (formerly *V. alnifolium* Marsh.) is a straggling shrub that often develops a procumbent habit, and roots develop where the pendulous outer branches touch the ground. It reaches 9 to 12 feet in height. Hiking Monhegan Island, Maine, on 14 August 1998, I noticed a 15-foot-high by 18-foot-wide plant. The summer foliage is medium to dark green and develops reddish to deep claret in fall, although I saw plants in Maine in rather deep shade that were beautiful rose-gold, green-gold to pinkish purple. Leaves are broad-ovate to suborbicular, 4 to 8 inches long, nearly as wide, short acuminate, cordate, irregularly denticulate, stellate-pubescent above at first, later glabrous, more densely pubescent beneath, chiefly on the veins. Petiole is 1 to 2½ inches long and scurfy. Color or semblance of same develops early, and it is not unusual to experience blushed red to red-purple leaves in mid to late summer. Easy plant to identify because of the large leaves, premature fall coloration, and straggly habit. In the southern Appalachians, the plant grows in significant quantities above 3,000 feet. One of my favorite discoveries when hiking. The flowers are borne in flat-topped, 3- to 5-inch-wide cymes; the outer flowers are sterile, white, about 1 inch in diameter, and produced in mid May. The fruit, a red, finally purple-black, broad-oval drupe about ⅓ inch long, matures in September. Probably requires two seedlings to facilitate cross-pollination and heavy fruit set. This species is maximally adapted to shady, moist areas, and acid soils. This is a shrub one has to adapt to, for it lacks the symmetry of many viburnums.

*Viburnum
lantanoides*, habit,
foliage, flowers,
fruits, and fall color

Probably best utilized in naturalized situations. Native to New Brunswick and Michigan to North Carolina and Georgia in the mountains. Zones 3 to 5(6). Introduced 1820.

CULTIVARS & VARIETIES

'Praecox' is described as flowering three weeks before the typical species. I have yet to see this form.

'Serenity' is listed as being more restrained in habit. Eastern Plant Specialties, Georgetown, Maine, offered it in the past.

Viburnum lentago L.

NANNYBERRY VIBURNUM, SHEEPBERRY VIBURNUM

Nannyberry viburnum is typically a woodland and woodland-edge species that is tall and leggy, with foliage borne on the upper half. The bark—blackish, patterned scaly to blocky—is readily discernible on older plants. The species develops a suckering, multi-stemmed outline or that of a single-stemmed tree, 15 to 18 feet high. A dense, graceful, multi-stemmed specimen, 12 feet high and wide, grew at Hiller in 1999. The national champion, in Oakland County, Michigan, is 50 feet by 40 feet. The dark green, often lustrous leaves, 2 to 4 inches long, 1 to 2 inches wide, and sharply serrate, develop hues of yellow, red, and purple in autumn. Petiole, ½ to ¾ inches long, is ruffled and winged. Mildew can be a significant problem, but obvious resistance is evident in native populations. The white flowers with prominent yellow stamens occur in 3- to 5(7)-rayed, 3- to 4½-inch-wide cymes as the leaves are expanding and usually at full size. Abundant yellow stamens result in a cream-yellow color in mid May (Asheville, North Carolina). I am unable to detect any floral odor, and one of my field notes

Viburnum lentago, foliage and flowers

Viburnum lentago,
habit, fruits, bark, and
fall color (bottom left)

*Viburnum
lobophyllum*, foliage
(bottom right)

states, "No real fragrance." Bean (1981) called the flowers "agreeably fragrant." Fruits, oval, ½ inch long, green, yellow, pink, rose, and finally bluish black often with a grayish bloom, make for a great show. One of the most adaptable species inhabiting lowland, extremely moist soils as well as drier, woodland situations. Good naturalizing plant, particularly in shady situations. A natural hybrid, *V. ×jackii* Rehd. (*V. lentago* × *V. prunifolium*), is known. Intermediate in characteristics. Zones 3 to 7. Native to Canada and eastern North America to Georgia and Mississippi. Introduced 1761.

CULTIVARS & VARIETIES

'Deep Green' with thick glossy leaves, white flowers, and pink-rose to black fruits grows to 20 feet high. Listed by Fairweather Gardens, New Jersey.

'Pink Beauty' is described, but I have yet to see anything but a similarly named cultivar that belongs to *V. nudum*.

'Show Girl' (variegated) and 'Nanum' are also in the literature but doubtfully available.

Viburnum lobophyllum Graebn.

Another stinky white-flowered, red-fruited, 10- to 15-foot-high, 10- to 12-foot-wide shrub that resembles *V. betulifolium*, *V. hupehense*, and *V. dilatatum*. The one sighting (2 May 1999) at RHS Wisley confirmed the similarities. Leaves ovate to orbicular-ovate or broad obovate, 2 to 4 inches long and wide, acuminate, truncate or broad-cuneate, dentate with mucronate teeth, slightly hairy on midvein above and the veins below, 5 to 6 vein pairs; petiole ½ to 1 inch long. Egolf utilized this and *V. japonicum* to produce 'Huron' (see under *V. japonicum*). Zones 6 and 7. Native to central and western China. Introduced in 1901 by E. H. Wilson.

Viburnum luzonicum Rolfe

Virtually unknown in the United States, but a fine specimen of *V. luzonicum* at the JC Raulston Arboretum always piqued my interest. A five-year-old plant (8 feet by 6 feet) in our University of Georgia plant trials has performed magnificently. Performance in the South was verified with a call from Bobby Green, Fairhope, Alabama, asking about the species and relating how well it performed in Zone 8(9). Why has no one commercialized the species? A variable species over its native range, Southeast Asia, with at least five varieties described (Kenyon 2001). Habit is dense, terrifically so, no cat could penetrate, haystack (UGA) to broad-rounded (Raulston) with thickly set twiggy branches and leaves. The

Viburnum luzonicum, habit, foliage, flowers, and fall color

leaves emerge in late March, often dehiscing by late December (Athens). Fall color is consistent and long-persisting reddish purple. On 29 December 2005, 40 percent of the leaves were still present. I have not observed insect or disease problems and believe that, for Zones 7 to 9, here is a viburnum with promise. Lustrous dark green leaves, typically 1 to 3 inches long, ¾ to 2 inches wide, are on the small side with the UGA plant. Apex is acute, base rounded, margins with irregularly spaced, mucronate teeth, 4 to 6 vein pairs, and hairy below; petiole about ⅓ inch long. The white flowers open in April (Athens) in 1- to 2-inch-wide cymes; they are objectionably odoriferous (a 25 April 2002 field note states, "Off-fragrant," another from 26 April 2003, "Off-odor, similar to *V. dilatatum*"). Fruits, though sparse on the single plant, are red, ¼ inch long, and ovoid in shape. In the wild, it occurs in shady places, but the UGA plant is in full sun. Any well-drained soil appears suitable. The heat and drought tolerances displayed over the five years in the Georgia trials give hope that here is a worthy garden species. I have yet to have any visitor guess its identity. Listed as inhabiting the Philippines to south China, western China, Indo-China, and Taiwan. May reach 10 to 20 feet in height and width. Opportunities for breeding with this species are promising.

Viburnum macrocephalum Fort.
CHINESE SNOWBALL VIBURNUM

Viburnum macrocephalum is a dense, rounded shrub growing 6 to 10 feet high in northerly climes, larger in the South, 12 to 15 feet. The flowers are white, nonfragrant, each individual floret 1¼ inch across, and emerge in mid to late April (Athens) borne in 3- to 8-inch-wide, hemispherical cymes. Extremely showy in flower but requires a protected location and well-drained soil in Zone 5. I have seen it flowering in Columbus, Ohio, in a protected area. The foliage is semi-evergreen to deciduous, usually the latter in the South, ovate or ellip-

Viburnum macrocephalum

Viburnum macrocephalum, young foliage and flowers (above)

Viburnum macrocephalum f. *keteleeri*, habit, flowers, and fruits

tic to ovate-oblong, 2 to 4 inches long, 1¼ to 2½ inches wide, acute or obtusish, rounded at base, denticulate or entire, dark green and nearly glabrous above, stellate-pubescent beneath; petiole ½ to ¾ inch long and consistently pubescent. In the southern states the plant may grow 20 feet high and form a massive, rounded shrub. It tends to flower a second time in the fall during warm weather in the South. In full flower it is a spectacular shrub and certainly worthy of consideration in larger gardens. For 20 years, it was a staple in the entrance planting to our home. Every three or four years I cut it 18 inches from the ground because of its tendency to overgrow the surrounding vegetation. First year after cutting back there are no flowers, but in subsequent years unbelievable profusion. Interestingly, the showy florets are apple-green when emerging, finally white. People stop to ask the identity of the plant. Most ask, "What hydrangea is that?" I smile. Great for obtrusive show. Does not fruit, as the flowers are sterile. Zones 6 to 9. Native to China. Introduced in 1844 by Robert Fortune.

CULTIVARS & VARIETIES

Forma *keteleeri* (Carr.) Rehd. is the wild type with fertile and showy, nonfertile flowers in a lace-cap configuration. Foliage is similar to *V. macrocephalum*. The white, slightly off-odor flowers open in early April (Athens) in 4- to 5-inch-wide, flat-topped cymes. The shiny red to black, oblong, ½-inch-long fruits are beautiful. Easily 10 to 15 feet high and larger. Witnessed a 17- by 14-foot specimen at Hillier, 1 July 1999. Native to China. Introduced about 1860. This was used to produce *V.* ×*carlcephalum* (*V. carlesii* × *V. m.* f. *keteleeri*). Egolf crossed f. *keteleeri* with 'Eskimo', which resulted in a dense, broadleaf evergreen shrub with large white irregular, cloud-like inflorescences of fertile and sterile flowers in early to mid April (Athens). In full flower 6 April 2006 (Athens). This hybrid, National Arboretum 69852, has proven outstanding in the UGA tests and dis-

Viburnum National Arboretum 69852, habit and foliage

plays superior heat and drought tolerances. Has consistently (five years) maintained all its foliage through the winter. Grew to 6½ feet by 4 feet in five years.

In April 2003, I crossed *V. ×burkwoodii* 'Park Farm Hybrid' with f. *keteleeri*, and the resultant seedling population showed great introgression of traits from both parents. The goal was to incorporate the large, fragrant, semi-snowball flowers and superior foliage of 'Park Farm Hybrid' with the vigor and heat and drought tolerance of f. *keteleeri*. For anyone considering *Viburnum* breeding, f. *keteleeri* should be integrated where possible.

Viburnum molle Michx.
KENTUCKY VIBURNUM

Viburnum molle melds into the *V. dentatum* complex, and doubtfully, by leaf, could it be separated from the *V. dentatum* taxa. According to the molecular work of Winkworth and Donoghue (2005), it is more closely related to *V. ellipticum* from the West Coast than *V. dentatum*. The dark green leaves, 2 to 5 inches long and about as wide, 8 to 10 vein pairs, coarsely dentate, are soft pubescent on the lower surface (sometimes with reddish glandular hairs). The ½- to 2-inch-long, slender petioles are glabrous to glandular-hairy. Flowers, white, in 5- to 7-rayed, 2- to 3½-inch-wide cymes in May are followed in August–October by ⅜-inch-long, ellipsoidal, bluish black fruits. The species forms a rounded shrub, 8 to 12 feet high and wide, and resembles everyday *V. dentatum*. The major difference is the gray to brown exfoliating bark, which shreds in papery pieces not unlike *Acer griseum*, paperbark maple. Excellent naturalizing plant but seldom available in commerce. Grows in calcareous (limestone) soils on rocky hills and bluffs. Zones (5)6 to 8. Native to Pennsylvania to Arkansas and Missouri. Introduced 1923.

Viburnum molle, foliage and bark

RELATED SPECIES

Viburnum ozarkense Ashe was recently elevated to legitimate species status based on field work and morphological analysis. Now considered an endemic shrub species of the Interior Highlands of Arkansas, Missouri, and Oklahoma.

Viburnum mongolicum (Pall.) Rehd.

A rare species and, to date, every plant except two that I have witnessed has been incorrectly labeled. A plant at Mt. Airy Arboretum was grazed by deer; the small plant at the JC Raulston Arboretum matched the following leaf description. Attached to the Lantana section (Krüssmann 1985), the 1- to 2½-inch-long, 1- to 1¾-inch-wide, broad-ovate, acute, rounded, shallowly dentate, dull dark green leaves have the dense stellate pubescence of *V. lantana* on the lower surface. Petiole is ⅕ to ⅓ inch long. Grows 5 to 6 feet high and wide with stellate-pubescent branches. Malodorous white flowers open in April–May (24 April 2004 at Mt. Airy) in few-flowered, 1- to 2-inch-wide cymes, each floret ¼ inch wide. Fruit is a ¼-inch-long, ellipsoidal drupe, red maturing black. Treat like *V. lantana* as far as culture. Zones 4 to 7. Native to eastern Siberia and Inner Mongolia. Introduced 1785.

CULTIVARS & VARIETIES

Summer Reflection™ is a hybrid selected in the mid 1990s by Michael Yanny from open-pollinated *V. mongolicum* for its shiny dark green, 4- by 2-inch leathery leaves. Fall color may be rich wine-red. Flowering and fruiting are similar to *V. lantana*. Habit is oval-rounded, 9 feet high and 8 feet wide. *Viburnum* ×*rhytidophylloides* 'Alleghany' may be the pollen parent. Introduced by Johnson's Nursery, Menomonee Falls, Wisconsin.

Viburnum mullaha Buch.-Ham ex D. Don

This species was in the UGA trials but perished, and I am not sure why. A tall shrub, 10 to 18 feet high, 6 to 12 feet across, with ovate to round-ovate, long acuminate, medium green, 3½- to 6-inch-long leaves, glabrous above, pubescent below, with 6 to 9 vein pairs, deeply dentate in the upper half, petiole ½ to 1 inch long. The white flowers are held in 2- to 3-inch-wide cymes and open in May. The egg-shaped, ⅓-inch-long, drupaceous fruits initiate yellow, finally red with sparse pubescence. Zones 7 and 8. Native to Himalayas to Southeast Asia.

Viburnum mullaha
(above)

*Viburnum
nervosum* (above
right)

Viburnum nervosum D. Don

As my 16 April 1999 field notes state, "Looks like *V. lantana*" . . . and indeed the broad-ovate, fine-toothed, 2½- to 3¼-inch-long, 1¼- to 2½-inch-wide, medium green leaves, with 6 to 7 prominent lateral veins, grayish pubescent lower surface, and ⅓-inch-long, hairy petiole parallel leaves of *V. lantana*. Lancaster (1989) noted yellow to red fall color on a 15- to 20-foot-high plant in China. The Hillier shrub was 12 feet high and 10 to 12 feet wide. The flower buds are pink, opening white with purple anthers, sweet-scented according to Crûg Farm, in 4- to 5-inch-wide, slightly rounded cymes in April–May before or with the leaves (full flower on 16 April 1999 at Hillier). The fruits, ⅓ inch long, ellipsoidal, are red initially, maturing black. Like *V. lantana*, the species appears quite adaptable. I examined the herbarium specimen from Hillier, and my first thought was *V. lantana*. Leaves are smaller than *V. lantana*, but the variation in that species is enormous and could entertain the foliage of *V. nervosum*. Zones 6 and 7, 8 and 9 on West Coast. Native to western China, Himalayas, southeast Tibet, and northern Burma.

Viburnum nudum L.

SMOOTH WITHEROD

A superb native species of the eastern United States which is still underutilized in gardens, even with the advent of 'Winterthur', 'Earth Shade', 'Count Pulaski', and 'Pink Beauty' (the first two available in commerce). I have experienced many permutations of the species in the wild, from compact growth, almost rounded, glossy green leaves on a seedling along a creek in Chapel Hill, North Carolina, to leggy, open, sparse-foliage, less-than-aesthetic seedlings in the swamps of Weeks Bay Reserve, Alabama. All seedlings grew near or in water. Leaves are sensational, mirror-surface glossy and reflective, 3 to 6 inches long, 1 to 2½ inches wide, entire or slightly toothed; petiole about ½ inch long. Autumn colors are maddeningly schizophrenic from plant to plant: green, yellow, red, purple, and combinations. As the photograph (next page) shows, brilliant reds coupled with high leaf gloss are spectacular. Flowers, white with yellow stamens, stinky, in 2- to 4-inch-wide cymes, open mid to late May, Chapel Hill; mid May, Athens. Fruits, ⅓ inch long, oval, pink to robin's-egg blue ripen in September. Fruits have persisted longer into winter than many viburnums. Size ranges from 6 to 8(15) feet, usually not as wide. I grew this species in my Illinois garden, where it survived −20°F. This is a choice candidate for moist to wet areas. More high-pH sensitive than most viburnums, so performs best under acid soil conditions. Native to Connecticut, Long Island to Florida, west to Kentucky, Louisiana, and east Texas. Zones 5 to 9. Introduced in 1752.

'Pink Beauty' and an unnamed seedling grow contentedly in our Chapel Hill, North Carolina, garden. Both flowered at the same time (late May 2006), but only 'Pink Beauty' set abundant fruits. See Dirr 1998b for an expanded discussion of my emotional bonding with this and *V. cassinoides*. *Viburnum nudum* has been crossed with *V. lentago* to produce *V. ×vetteri* Zabel. Whole fruits were sown by Donna Heaton, director of the Center for Applied Nursery Research,

Viburnum nudum

Viburnum nudum,
foliage, flowers, and
fall color

Viburnum nudum
var. *angustifolium*,
fall color

Dearing, Georgia, with good germination the following spring. About half of the two-year-old seedlings produced great quantities of fruits, with one seedling covered with fruits at every node (fruits are usually produced at the terminals). Might be a selection that warrants introduction.

CULTIVARS & VARIETIES

Variety *angustifolium* Torrey and Gray has smaller, narrower leaves (2 to 3 inches by 1 inch) and smaller stature than the species. My initial reaction to the plants trialed at UGA was "Where's the beef?" Young plants were open, and the foliage was not as sheeny as that of the typical species. At five years of age, plants are more dense, and the red-purple, long-persisting fall color is a great bonus. Perhaps hasty in my judgment. Flowered later than the species and 'Pink Beauty'. Produced lovely pink to blue fruit in copious quantities. I walked my UGA viburnum trials on 8 June 2006 and was impressed with the 8- by 6-foot, densely foliaged specimen. The finer-textured leaves make it distinct from the species.

Brandywine™ ('Bulk') is described as a heavy-fruiting selection, 5 feet high and wide, from Mark Bulk in the Netherlands. The fruits are produced in shades of green, pink, and blue. I have yet to see the plant but have doubts about the 5 foot height. Also, the fruits on most *V. nudum* are the same color. Time will tell if it is unique. The plant is listed as PPAF. I have yet to witness a *V. nudum* produce more fruits than 'Pink Beauty'.

'Count Pulaski' is a multi-stemmed, loosely structured form with rapid growth. Larger leaf than typical, almost glossy. Extremely floriferous with white, musky-scented flowers. Fruits are borne in 6- to 10-inch-wide, flat-topped cymes in colors that range from green to exotic salmon-pink to shades of lavender, to blue and purplish black. A lone plant in the great garden of Coach Vince Dooley, Athens, Georgia, has grown tall, lanky, and open. Fruits have not paralleled the description above. 'Earth Shade', 'Pink Beauty', and 'Winterthur' are superior. The original plant was collected in Pulaski County, Arkansas, and introduced by Larry Lowman.

'Earth Shade' is a selection whose glossy dark green leaves take on hues of yellow, orange, and red in autumn. More compact than 'Winterthur' but in the 6- to 10-foot range. Typical cream-white flowers, pink to blue fruits of the species. Original plant was given to me by William Flemer of Earth Shade Nursery, Warne, North Carolina. I considered it superior to run of the mill seedlings and named it after Bill's nursery.

'Pink Beauty' has remained relatively compact in our Chapel Hill, North Carolina, garden and set abundant fruit without another pollinator. Leaves are

Viburnum nudum 'Earth Shade' (top left)

Viburnum nudum 'Pink Beauty' (top right)

Viburnum nudum 'Winterthur', foliage and flowers, fall color and fruits (above and right)

absolutely stunning, glossy dark green in summer, developing red-purple autumn hues. Flowers opened fully on 23 May 2006 in Chapel Hill. Fruits start pink, mature to blue-purple-black, and were still present on 4 April 1999 as the new bronzy leaves are pushing forth.

'Winterthur' is an improved form selected at the Winterthur Garden, Delaware. Killed the first one in Georgia, added another, and it grew well, with lustrous, waxy foliage, compact, 6 feet in ten years. A planting at Longwood Gardens was 10 feet high, rather open, in late April 2005. Red fall foliage and abundant blue fruits were evident on the Longwood plants on 29 September 2002.

Viburnum obovatum Walt.

SMALL VIBURNUM

Viburnum obovatum, small viburnum, is a densely twiggy, upright ascending, large shrub or small tree. Habit is rather wild and splaying; a ten-year-old plant in the UGA Botanical Garden is now 12 feet high and wide. National champion, in Suwannee River Water Management District, Florida, is 32 feet by 31 feet. The only thing small about this plant are the leaves, which are semi-evergreen to deciduous, oblanceolate to spatulate, some rounded-obovate, ¾ to 2 inches long, ⅓ to 1¼ inch wide, obtuse or rounded, cuneate, entire or finely serrate midway to apex, dark green, often lustrous, glabrous, with the lower surface brown dotted. They can be sessile or with a red petiole to ⅕ inch long. Leaves emerge early, often evident by mid February in Zone 7. The small leaves may turn bronze-purple in fall–winter and persist into the new year during mild winters (15°F and above). Small white flowers, nonfragrant or only slightly so, in 1¾- to 2¼-inch-wide cymes, open with the emerging leaves—April in Athens. All the compact cultivars were in full flower 6 April 2006 in Athens. Flowers are not in any sense spectacular but, en masse, they do pack a wallop. Fruits are ¼- to ⅓-inch-wide, ellipsoidal to spherical, red to shiny black drupes. My observations indicate that this is a remarkably heat and drought tolerant spe-

*Viburnum
obovatum*

Viburnum obovatum, foliage and flowers (above)

Viburnum obovatum 'Mrs. Schiller's Delight' (right)

Viburnum obovatum 'Reifler's Dwarf'

cies. Adapted to wet soils in the wild; supportive of drier situations under cultivation. Semi-shade to full sun for best growth. Have seen in Tampa, Florida, landscapes and utilized with great success in the Houston, Texas, area as a hedge, screen, and topiary. Safe to state, the species is tremendously heat tolerant and also drought resistant. I observed a hybrid of this and *V. rufidulum* in Houston that offers potential. Native to South Carolina to Florida and Alabama. Zones 6 to 9.

CULTIVARS & VARIETIES

Ten accessions of *V. obovatum* are growing in our UGA trials. I have yet to witness insects, diseases, or drought- or heat-related maladies. These cultivars range from compact, rounded shrubs like 'Reifler's Dwarf' to the upright, open 'St. Paul'. The compact clones would make great alternatives to the dwarf hollies like 'Carissa', 'Rotunda', 'Helleri', and 'Shillings'. Foliage on these compact forms has remained completely evergreen, with dark green to wine-red winter coloration. All produce abundant white flowers that froth the foliage. Truly amazing that the species has not been domesticated to any degree for everyday landscape use in Zones 6 to 9. In November 2006 I witnessed three new compact introductions, Bright 'n' Tight™, Snow Fury™, and Specmaker™, from Steve Reifler. All were growing in 3-gallon containers, and Snow Fury™ was the densest, with the most aesthetic, lustrous dark green foliage.

'Christmas Snow' grew 5½ feet by 4½ feet in three years. This form has an upright habit that is more open than most cultivars but tighter than the species.

'Lord Byron' is upright in habit, with larger leaves than the species. It is a hybrid with *V. rufidulum*. Flowers in hemispherical cymes, 3 to 3½ inches across, nonfragrant, extremely showy. Observed in full flower at Hawksridge Nursery, Hickory, North Carolina, 17 April 2007.

'Mrs. Schiller's Delight' was the most compact in the UGA trials, growing to 14 inches by 3 feet in three years. It produced abundant flowers and lustrous dark green foliage. Would make a great grouping or mass planting.

'Reifler's Dwarf' was one of the first in the UGA collection, reaching 3½ feet by 4½ feet after five years. It has lustrous dark green foliage that is sometimes red-purple in winter and abundant white flowers. Certainly an eye-catcher, and many visitors ask about its identity.

'St. Paul' is a rather loose, open selection, attaining 12 feet by 8 feet in five years. Foliage and flowers are sparse compared to 'Reifler's Dwarf'. Flowers open earlier than the dwarf types, late March 2006 at the JC Raulston Arboretum, Raleigh, North Carolina. Perhaps more attractive than the species, which can grow larger and is open and splaying.

Viburnum obovatum 'Reifler's Dwarf', winter color

'Whorled Class' is unique by virtue of the 3 leaves per node—hence the name. Growth habit is dense, compact, 2½ feet by 3½ feet after three years. Lustrous dark green leaves. The white flowers are not as abundant as on 'Reifler's Dwarf' and 'Mrs. Schiller's Delight'. 'Best Densa' is similar, if not the same.

Viburnum odoratissimum Ker-Gawler

Viburnum odoratissimum is confused with *V. awabuki* in the Southeast but clearly is not as cold hardy, and its leaves are a duller green, with a fetid green-pepper odor evident when crushed. Plants show up at Atlanta garden centers but seldom survive for any time in the landscape. Habit is quite dense, with height ranging from 10 to 20(30) feet. In 1987, I witnessed a 25-foot-high plant in a container at Herrenhausen Gardens, in Hanover, Germany. At Louisiana Nursery, a 15- to 20-foot-high screen convinced me that the species grows larger than usually advertised. At Leu Gardens, Orlando, Florida, a 40-foot-high tree reminded me that plants do not read books. Leaves are variable in shape and size, from 3 to 8 inches long, 1½ to 4 inches wide. The typical U.S. type has dull olive-green leaves, with 4 to 6 vein pairs, and is elliptic-ovate in shape. As mentioned, the odor of the leaves is a telltale sign. The fragrant, cream-white flowers occur in 3- to 6-inch-long, 2½- to 5-inch-wide pyramidal panicles in late April–early May, Dearing, Georgia. Fruits are red maturing purple-black, ¼ inch long, and ovoid. The species is adaptable to full sun, moderate shade, and well-drained soil. Tolerates heat and drought and is quite salt tolerant. Useful

Viburnum odoratissimum, habit, foliage, and emerging flowers

for screens, hedges, groupings. Cold is the limiting factor: 20°F or lower will result in some foliage injury. Zones 8 to 10(11). Kenyon (2001) cites native habitat from northeast India, Southeast Asia, Japan, Taiwan, Java, Philippines, and Celebes (Sulawesi). Grows as an understory tree in broadleaved-evergreen forests near the coast, even under gloomy (shady) environments.

CULTIVARS & VARIETIES

Several questionable varieties and the species *V. hasseltii* Miq., *V. arboricolum* Hayata, *V. liukiuense* Nakai, and *V. zambalence* may prove synonymous with *V. odoratissimum*. Crûg Farm lists *V. arboricolum* as a distinct species that they collected in Taiwan. Apparently, *V. odoratissimum* is polymorphic and like *V. dentatum* in the United States displays minor vegetative differences.

'Emerald Lustre' has pink-tinged new shoots, the leaves maturing lustrous green.

'Red Tip' produces reddish green new shoots that mature to green. A plant in Athens, Georgia, was killed outright by the cold.

Viburnum opulus L.
EUROPEAN CRANBERRYBUSH VIBURNUM

Viburnum opulus is termed the "guelder rose" in Europe (for its origins in the province of Gelderland, Netherlands), but this name is also applied to the cultivar 'Roseum'. An immense shrub, typically 10 to 15 feet high and wide, I recorded an 18- by 18-foot behemoth on 29 April 1999 at Hillier; a 15- by 20-foot plant at Wakehurst, 27 May 2006. In actuality, not preferable to *V. trilobum*, although it is slightly more heat tolerant. Develops a thicket of stems, rather coarse, finally rounded in outline. The 3-lobed leaves, irregularly serrated, lustrous dark green, 2 to 4 inches long and wide (wider), glabrous above, pubescent below, may develop yellow, red, and purple collages in fall, but this seasonal display is unreliable and green is about as good as they turn (stay). Petiole is ½ to ¾ inch long with concave raised glands. The flat, lacecap-type inflorescences, 2 to 3(4) inches across, with fertile (slightly off-odor) inner flowers and showy nonfertile outer flowers, open in mid May (Boston; 28 May 2006, southern England). The bright red fruits ripen in September–October and may persist through winter. I have observed ripening (coloring) fruits in mid August at Spring Grove in Cincinnati, Ohio. In the latter stages, during winter, they assume the form of withered raisins. Each fruit ranges from ¼ to ⅓ inch wide and is globose in shape. Extremely adaptable to moist and wet soils and is native in such situations. Any moist, well-drained soil, acid to neutral, supports adequate performance. Full sun to partial shade. For whatever reason, 'Roseum', the snowball form, is common in the Piedmont of Georgia and has persisted and performed well over the garden ages. Aphids and the viburnum beetle are common pests (see chapter 5). The species and cultivars are used for shrub borders, screens, groupings, masses, and even hedges; they are a common element in the famed hedgerows of England. Bonnie and I walked the Test Way in Hampshire, and in damp, moist areas, hedgerows, and open areas, plants were everywhere in flower, 28 May 2006. Zones (3)4 to 7(8). Native to Europe, northwest Africa, Asia Minor, Caucasus, and central Asia.

CULTIVARS & VARIETIES

'Apricot' is listed in the 2006 *RHS Plant Finder*. Possibly refers to fruit color.

'Aureum' has new growth that is a reasonably good yellow but soon fades to rather sickly yellow-green; the color is either lost (to green), or the foliage may burn in hot climates. Slower growing than the species, it has a rather limited landscape appeal. Flowers and fruits are like the species. Grows to 12 feet high and 10 feet wide and requires some shade. There was a 10- by 8-foot, dense,

Viburnum opulus, habit, flowers, and fruits

compact shrub at Hillier, 30 June 1999, with aphid damage on young growth. The yellow color was only on the young growth.

'Bulliton' is listed by the Dawes Arboretum, Newark, Ohio, without supporting information.

Variety *calvescens* is almost glabrous in all its parts, the petiole longer than the species, 1¼ to 1½ inches, and the anthers dark purple. I observed two plants at the JC Raulston Arboretum, Raleigh, North Carolina, that are performing well. I see little difference between this and the variable species. Certainly the anthers were not purple on plants I observed. The fruits are red. Flowers open early to mid May at the JC Raulston Arboretum. Appears to be smaller than straight species. A forma *flavum* of this variety, with yellow anthers and fruits, is known. Variety *calvescens* is often listed as a variety of *V. sargentii*. The leaf characteristics, however, parallel those of *V. opulus*.

'Compactum' is an excellent plant where space is limited, as it matures to one-half the size of the species in height and is extremely dense in habit. I witnessed many plants that were 6 feet high in England. Excellent in flower and fruit; the red fruits make a brilliant show. Fall color is often a formidable red. Excellent in masses. Probably should be considered over the species in the smaller, more restricted planting areas of the modern landscape. I have been told that stem borers can be a problem. This is an excellent plant when properly grown. I witnessed a plant at Hillier, 10 feet high and wide, on 31 May 2006 with the flowers just opening. Appears to be slightly later than the species. Some question in my mind if this plant was a true 'Compactum'.

'Cream Puff' is a small form I witnessed at Bailey Nurseries, St. Paul, Minnesota.

'Eliksir' and 'Krasnaya Grozd' are the most promising selections of a Russian breeding program to increase fruit yield and content of biologically active substances as well as to reduce the bitter taste of the fruit.

'Fructuluteo' ('Fructo-Luteo') has pale yellow fruits turning rich yellow-tinted pink. This is a large form, growing to 10 feet high. Known in cultivation from about 1901 (Kenyon 2001).

'Harvest Gold' has leaves that are richer yellow than 'Aureum', but it is not much different otherwise. I observed this form at Hillier.

'Leonard's Dwarf' I have only seen described in Forest Farm's 1997 fall catalog. Reads like 'Compactum' and/or 'Nanum'.

'Losely's Compact' is listed by Dawes Arboretum, Newark, Ohio.

'Nanum' is a dwarf form, much-branched and dense, 18 to 24 inches in height and one-and-a-half times that in spread. I have seen specimens between 4 and 5 feet high and wide. Supposedly never flowers or fruits, but, again, I have seen several isolated flowering and fruiting specimens. Makes a good filler or facer

*Viburnum
opulus*
'Aureum'

*Viburnum
opulus* var.
calvescens

*Viburnum
opulus*
'Compactum'

Viburnum opulus
'Compactum', fruits

Viburnum opulus 'Nanum'

Viburnum opulus 'Notcutt's Variety', deer damage on lower third plant; can be used for low hedges. Will not withstand wet, poorly drained conditions, and in wet weather contracts significant leaf spot. Leaves range from ¾ to 1½ inches in width. Eugene W. Coffman, Ridge Road Nursery, Bellevue, Iowa, reports a branch sport of 'Nanum' that is slower growing and more compact. Listed as originating about 1841 in France.

'Notcutt's Variety' ('Notcutt') is more vigorous (to 12 feet) than the species with larger flowers and fruits and excellent maroon-red fall color.

'Park Harvest' was new to me until 1999, when I witnessed a large plant (10 feet) at Hillier. Leaves are yellow initially, greening with time, possibly not as potent as those of 'Aureum'. 'Park Harvest' is akin to 'Harvest Gold'.

'Pohjan Neito', a clone of the species, offers abundant inflorescences and significant cold hardiness. Selection and naming resulted from comparative field trials at five sites in Finland from 1989 to 1993.

'Roseum' ('Sterile') is commonly known as the European snowball or guelder rose. This form has sterile flowers and is extremely showy in flower; the 2½- to 3-inch-wide inflorescences literally cover the shrub in mid to late April (Athens). It was in full flower 12 May 2006 at the 3,000 foot elevation in Fancy Gap, Virginia; likewise on 29 May 2006 at Hinton Ampner near Winchester, England. This is an heirloom favorite, more apt to be located around older residences. Aphids infest this form quite heavily and often distort the young leaves and stems. The flowers are an apple-green in the early stages and change to white, remaining effective for a long period. A 20-year-old specimen in Fargo, North Dakota, showed no dieback although temperatures dropped as low as −30°F. A pink-flowered form is reported, but this I have not observed; however, the aging inflorescence sometimes assumes a slight pink tinge. Known since the 16th century. Grows 10 to 12 feet high and is a vigorous form. I recorded an 8- by 10-foot, dense, broad-mounded shrub with leaf spot at Hillier, 1 July 1999.

Viburnum opulus 'Park Harvest'

Viburnum opulus 'Roseum', habit, flowers, and fall color

Viburnum opulus 'Xanthocarpum' (below right)

'Variegatum'. Several cream- and white-variegated ('Tatteri') forms with unusual names are listed in English literature.

'Xanthocarpum' has yellowish gold fruits that are quite attractive and often persistent, becoming translucent golden-yellow after frosts; a nice color complement to the red-fruited type. I have seen in England on several occasions. Worth considering! Will grow 8 to 10 feet high. Most mature plants I observed were smaller, in the 6- to 8-foot range. Habit is much more compact and rounded than 'Fructuluteo' and more aesthetic. There was a 7- by 8-foot, rounded, dense plant at Hillier, 1 July 1999. A plant at Hillier was 12 feet by 15 feet in full flower, odor not offensive, on 31 May 2006. Introduced in 1910 by Spaeth of Germany.

Viburnum orientale Pall.

Observed only once by the author, *V. orientale* is somewhat similar to *V. acerifolium* in habit but larger in stature, to 8 feet in height. Leaves are rich dark green, 3-lobed, 3 to 5 inches long and about that wide, with a base that is rounded to subcordate. No black dots on lower surface, which separates it from *V. acerifolium*. The petioles have glands like *V. opulus*, *V. trilobum*, and *V. sargentii*. Stems are pubescent. Flowers are white in 2-inch-wide cymes, in May–June. The red fruits mature black. The herbarium specimen collected from Hillier had red fruits. Native to the Caucasus. The one plant in the United States that I observed came from Turkish seed. Zone 6. Introduced 1827.

Viburnum phlebotricum Sieb. & Zucc.

Another red-fruited species, *V. phlebotricum* is more closely aligned with *V. setigerum*, tea viburnum, but differs in smaller leaves, shorter petiole, and smaller, more slender habit. I was given an unidentified viburnum by David Parks, Camellia Forest Nursery, Chapel Hill, North Carolina, that approximates this

Viburnum orientale (below left)

Viburnum phlebotricum (below)

description. Another seedling from the same source had bright red fruits. The initial plant developed cream-yellow to coral and finally bright red fruits over a four- to six-week period in late September–October; the fruits, then dark red and raisin-like, persisted into winter. Leaves, lustrous dark green, orange-red in autumn, 6 to 9 vein pairs, 1 to 3 inches long, 1 to 1¾ inches wide, are silky pubescent below. The petioles average about ½ inch long. Flowers, white, nonfragrant, open in 1- to 1¾-inch-wide cymes in April–May (Athens). In full flower 23 May 1991 at the Arnold Arboretum. They are sheltered among the leaves and do not overwhelm. The ⅓-inch-long, broad-ovoid, red drupes, are long persistent. Has performed well in North Carolina and Georgia. Wonderful for summer and fall foliage. Particularly outstanding fruits. Grows 6 to 8 feet high and wide. Best in groupings and masses. I speculate that the reason for terrific fruit set in Georgia trials is the presence of two seedlings for effective cross-pollination. Zones 6 to 8. Native to the mountains of Japan. Grows naturally in rather dry sites along ridges in the cool to warm-temperate regions of Japan.

In 2006, my technician, Vickie Waters, germinated a large seedling population from the yellow-, coral-, and red-fruited plant and the red-fruited seedling. Obviously, the fruit coloration of the former is under different genetic control than the typical species. The objectives are to develop cultivars with unique, stable fruit colors (such as pure yellow) and improved habit (denser foliage, more compact branching). The seedlings are similar in foliage to the parent plant.

I am convinced that this species is inadequately represented in American gardens. On 31 May 2006, John Wood and Darren Andrews, gardeners at Hinton Ampner, England, found a label on a specimen that two days earlier had piqued my curiosity and rattled the brain. The metal label said "*V. phlebotricum*"! Ten feet by 8 feet, full flower, light pink buds opening white, nonfragrant, abundant, 2 inches across. Leaf did not look like what is described above: more ovate, pubescent, and strongly serrate.

CULTIVARS & VARIETIES
Forma *xanthocarpum* Hayashi has yellow fruits.

Fruits of a Camellia Forest Nursery seedling

Viburnum plicatum f. *plicatum* Thunb.
JAPANESE SNOWBALL VIBURNUM

To admit taxonomic defeat, especially to botanists who labor in broom closets, is embarrassing. In brief, f. *plicatum* umbrellas all the sterile snowball types of *V. plicatum*, while f. *tomentosum* harbors the lacecap, fertile-flowered, fruit-producing taxa. Culture is similar and adequately addressed under f. *tomentosum*. Forma *plicatum* produces 2- to 3-inch-wide, rounded, white, sterile, non-fragrant inflorescences that open green and turn white with the petals abscising during senescence. Flowers open two to three weeks later than f. *tomentosum* and remain effective longer. In full flower late April–early May, Athens, Georgia. Numerous forms, from compact Newport® ('Newzam') to typical f. *plicatum* (15 feet high and wide with horizontally stratified branches) offer great architecture and aesthetics for the garden. I have observed and grown most, and rank 'Popcorn', from David Leach, at the pinnacle for its heat and drought tolerance in the UGA trials. Forma *plicatum* was introduced by Fortune in 1846 but known since 1712. Zones 5 to 7, 8 and 9 on West Coast.

CULTIVARS & VARIETIES

'Chyverton' has a low, wide-spreading habit. Flowers all sterile as in typical f. *plicatum*. A mature plant grew 4 feet high and 20 feet wide in 24 years. At Stourhead, England, there was a relatively low-growing, wide-spreading form with abundant flowers. This form might be welcome in American gardens since the principal type in cultivation is upright, large, and coarse. Introduced by Nigel Holman in 1964 from cuttings he collected from the garden of Lionel Fortescue.

'Grandiflorum' is a fine form with abundant, slightly larger flower heads than f. *plicatum* and leaves that are wider, more rounded, with veins tinted red below.

Viburnum plicatum f. *plicatum*

Viburnum plicatum
f. *plicatum*, flowers,
opening green and
matured white
(above)

Viburnum plicatum
f. *plicatum*
'Grandiflorum'
(right)

Viburnum plicatum
f. *plicatum* 'Mary
Milton' (below)

Viburnum plicatum
f. *plicatum*
Newport® (below
right)

White flowers are occasionally tinted pink at petal edges. Earlier flowering than most f. *plicatum* types, the plants I have seen showed an accentuated horizontal branching pattern. This form is worth seeking out. Witnessed plants 12 feet high, 10 to 12 feet wide at Hillier, 31 May 2006. Introduced by Hesse Nurseries, Germany, in the late 1800s.

'Leach's Compacta' is a dwarf form that grows 4 feet by 3 feet with double, white flowers in snowball inflorescences. Foliage is red-burgundy in fall. I have not witnessed this in cultivation.

'Mary Milton' ('Mary Melton') is akin to 'Rosace' with consistent pink, snowball flowers. Starting to make the garden rounds. Matures 8 to 10 feet high. I have read descriptions that flowers open white and age to pink. The lone flowering plant I witnessed (23 April 1998, Athens, Georgia) was green-pink in bud, opening light pink and fading white; it looked different from 'Rosace'. I know several gardeners who have purchased this cultivar, and all have flowered white. Not as vigorous as 'Rosace'.

Newport® ('Newzam') I have seen in a number of places in the Midwest. The habit is extremely dense, mounded, with smaller dark green leaves than the species that turn burgundy in fall. Five to 6 feet high and wide; 4 feet by 4 feet in five years in the University of Georgia trials. Initially, I did not think much of flower quality, but reasonably mature plants at Spring Grove, in Ohio, flowered profusely. Flowers are a looser, snowball type that are nestled among the foliage, and since the plant is so dense, their effect is reduced compared to f. *plicatum*, but still appreciable. Survived −20 to −30°F in Bellevue, Iowa. Plants that were severely killed back (not eliminated) at −25°F in Spring Grove in January 1994 had grown back to 3 to 4 feet high by January 1998. Flowered later than 'Popcorn' by seven to ten days in the Georgia trials. A Lake County Nursery introduction.

'Pink Dawn' is described by Kinsey Gardens, Knoxville, Tennessee, as a hot-

Viburnum plicatum f. *plicatum* Newport® ('Newzam')

pink, early-flowering type with flowers 2½ inches across. New foliage is bronzy-purple; as the leaves mature, they hold some of this color. Vigorous upright habit. Although listed as f. *plicatum* may be a form of *V. farreri*. This could be a rename of 'Rosace'.

'Pink Sensation' has pink-emerging snowball flowers that turn white with maturity. Leaves bronze-tinted maturing green. Opens mid April in Raleigh, North Carolina, with white inflorescences mixed with pink, reflecting reversion. Flowered 1 May 2006 at the JC Raulston Arboretum, where I first observed this form in 2005. Might be another rename for 'Rosace'.

'Popcorn' is an introduction from David Leach, North Madison, Ohio, and the best of the f. *plicatum* litter. Vigorous but tight in habit with leathery, dark green leaves that are more heat and drought resistant than the species. The 3-inch or slightly larger, white snowball flowers appear in profusion in April (13 April 2005, Athens). Earlier to flower than the other f. *plicatum* cultivars. I can look down the row of f. *plicatum* types, and in late summer this is the most pristine. Probably 8 to 10 feet high. Has not spread as much as 'Grandiflorum' and 'Rotundifolium'. Hardy to −23°F. Nine feet by 9 feet in five years in Georgia trials.

'Rosace' was selected and introduced around 1953 (1957, according to Kenyon 2001) by Carl Kern of Wyoming Nursery, Cincinnati, Ohio, for its medium-pink flower and bronze tinged foliage. I believe this is the same as 'Kern's Pink', 'Pink Sensation', and possibly others; as I saw 'Kern's Pink' the color was on/off-pink with some inflorescences pink, others white, and still others mixed. Don Shadow has grown 'Rosace' for years and tried to stabilize the chimera, i.e., pink flowers. The plants are beautiful in flower, with pink being genetic and not environmentally or culturally regulated. In fact, the mix of pink and white inflorescences on the same plant is beautiful. In full flower 25 April 1994 at Winchester, Tennessee. This form has reasonable vigor and plants should mature between 6 to 10 feet.

'Rotundifolium' is a form with round leaves that are 1 to 2 inches long and 1 to 1½ inches wide. It is more refined than f. *plicatum* and grows 7 to 8 feet high and wider at maturity.

Viburnum plicatum f. *plicatum* 'Pink Sensation', foliage and flowers, opening pink

Viburnum plicatum f. *plicatum* 'Popcorn' (left)

Viburnum plicatum f. *plicatum* 'Rosace', flowers and foliage (below left and below)

Viburnum plicatum f. *plicatum* 'Rotundifolium' (bottom left)

Viburnum plicatum f. *plicatum* Triumph® ('Trizam') (bottom right)

'Sawtooth', like f. *plicatum*, has large, coarsely toothed, dark green leaves and large, snowball flowers. It has not performed well in UGA trials: it grows next to 'Popcorn', and the greatness of its neighbor is easily understood. 'Sawtooth' has been a weak grower and really languished in the heat.

Triumph® ('Trizam') is a rounded, dense, compact form—5 to 6 feet high and 6 to 8 feet wide—with thick, quilted dark green foliage, white typical snowball flowers, and few fruits. Derived from Newport® and described as prolific flowering. As I observed the plant in proximity to Newport®, it was taller and less dense. A Lake County Nursery introduction.

Viburnum plicatum f. *tomentosum* (Thunb.) Rehd.
DOUBLEFILE VIBURNUM

Doublefile viburnum is a classy shrub, horizontally branched, with white lacecap flowers marching two by two along each branch's length. Flowers rise on 2-inch-high peduncles, showcasing their beauty above the deeply pleated, dark green foliage. Does it get any better than this? Yes, if the potpourri of cultivars are considered. In its finest forms, broad-spreading, horizontal branches fill an 8- to 10-foot-high space, extending wider. Great plant to soften vertical elements and upright plants in shrub borders. The eyes follow the horizontal lines. Leaves, 2 to 5 inches long, 1 to 2½ inches wide, veins deeply impressed, 8 to 12 pairs, margins dentate-serrate, dark green, stellate-pubescent below, develop red-purple in fall. Petiole is ⅓ to ⅔ inches long and pubescent. The 2- to 4(6)-inch-wide, flat-topped inflorescences, with white outer, irregularly shaped, sterile flowers, fertile inner, open in April (Athens; late May 2006 in much of southern England). Flowers are borne along the length of the branches and are spectacular. Fertile flowers have no fragrance. The red fruits ripen in June (Athens) and mature black if the birds do not descend. Fruits bright red on 14 June 2006, Chapel Hill, North Carolina. Fruits are relished by the birds and ripen ahead of many fruiting shrubs. Easy to culture if soils are consistently moist, laden with organic matter, and slightly acid. Consistent drought and high heat result in bedraggled specimens. In the South, best site in some shade and mulch. Extremely shade tolerant and floriferous specimens thrive as understory plants. Every garden has a spot for a doublefile. Occasionally a branch will die, and I am not sure of the reason. Tired, overgrown plants can be rejuvenated by cutting to 12 to 18 inches of the soil in late winter. Zones 5 to 7(8), 9 on West Coast. See cultivar descriptions for specific hardiness ratings. Native to China, Taiwan, and Japan. Widely distributed in cool and warm temperate zones of the three countries. Found at its best in moderately moist sites along streams. Introduced about 1865.

Viburnum plicatum f. *tomentosum*, habit, foliage, flowers, fruits, and fall color

CULTIVARS & VARIETIES

Many and varied. For example, 'Shasta', originally described as 6 feet high, has grown over 12 feet high in Georgia. Certainly beautiful but too big for most gardens. The moral: choose wisely from the cultivars.

'Cascade' is a seedling of 'Rowallane', selected in 1971 in the Netherlands, with wide-spreading branches. Inflorescences are umbrella-shaped, 2½ to 4 inches across, with large, showy sterile outer flowers that arch slightly at the middle, creating a cascading effect. Red fruits are produced in abundance. Good burgundy fall color. I witnessed in flower at Crathes Castle Garden, Scotland, in late June 1995, and it is actually better than the text: a must-have for serious doublefile junkies. On 25 May 2006, Bonnie and I were assessing the *Viburnum* collection at RHS Wisley, and the only doublefile that was easy to identify from a distance was this selection; that plant was 6 to 7 feet in height. I have serious qualms about 'Cascade' ultimately growing taller than 'Mariesii', even though the literature states it so, having observed greater than 15-foot-high 'Mariesii'.

'Dart's Red Robin' is broad-spreading to 5 feet (probably more like 6 to 10 feet high), with dark green leaves, profuse, white-tinged pink flowers in umbrella-shaped inflorescences, and deep red fruits, profusely borne. Inflorescences are smaller (about 3 inches) than the typical f. *tomentosum*. I have observed in heavy fruit at RHS Wisley in late July; Wisley plant was 9 feet high, straggly and leggy, on 25 May 2006. Have seen plants labeled 'Dart's Red Robin' that appeared to be 'Lanarth'.

'Everblooming' is listed, but I have not observed. I suspect may be the same as 'Summer Snowflake'.

'Fireworks' produces 6-inch white flowers on an 8- by 6-foot shrub that is hardy to −23°F. Fertile flowers and pedicels are reddish and surrounded by the pure white, outer, sterile flowers. Developed by David Leach, North Madison, Ohio.

'Igloo' originated as a chance seedling at Winterthur Garden, Delaware. The plant develops a wide-spreading, mounded habit, 6 feet by 12 feet, that resembles an igloo in outline. Lacecap flowers occur in 4- to 5-inch-wide, flat-topped cymes in May and are followed by dark red fruits in July. Ken Day of Winterthur's nursery speculates that 'Mariesii' is the parent. Selected in 1991. Survived −20 to −30°F in Bellevue, Iowa.

'Lanarth' is a larger-flowered form than typical doublefile, with ray flowers up to 2 inches in diameter and larger. It is probably confused with 'Mariesii'. As I have observed it, a very beautiful selection, 12 to 14 feet high and wide; a wonderful plant at the Arnold Arboretum was 8 feet by 10 to 12 feet. Habit is flat-topped, with a strong, distinctly horizontal branch architecture. One of the best forms. Introduced before 1930 from Lanarth, Cornwall, England.

Viburnum plicatum f. *tomentosum* 'Cascade', habit and flowers (left and below left)

Viburnum plicatum f. *tomentosum* 'Dart's Red Robin' (below)

Viburnum plicatum f. *tomentosum* 'Lanarth'

Viburnum plicatum f. *tomentosum* 'Mariesii'

Viburnum plicatum f. *tomentosum* 'Molly Schroeder'

Viburnum plicatum f. *tomentosum* 'Pink Beauty'

'Magic Puff' has a compact, rounded habit, 4 feet high and 5 feet wide, typical lacecap flowers, red to black fruits, clean dark green leaves, and wine-red fall color. Best in Zone 5, although listed as 4. Introduced by Willoway Nurseries, Avon, Ohio.

'Mariesii' has large ray flowers, up to 1¾ inches in diameter, raised on a 2½-inch-high peduncle that brings the flowers above the foliage. Habit is distinctly horizontal, and a plant in full flower is a magnificent sight. The leaves may turn reddish purple in fall. I have read conflicting accounts; some state 'Mariesii' is the best fruiting form, others that fruit is sparsely set. I have not resolved this discrepancy in my own mind—as with many viburnums, lack of fruit set may be due to absence of a cross-pollinator. Leaves perhaps lighter green in summer than other types. Many plants offered as 'Mariesii' are, in fact, something else. 'Mariesii' bears leaves that have extended apices (long-acuminate) with a slight drooping tendency. Plants over 10 feet high in England are common. Although cited as lower-growing than 'Lanarth', this is not absolute. I have observed 15-foot-high 'Mariesii' in England; witnessed a 12- by 14-foot plant at RHS Wisley, 25 May 2006. Introduced about 1877 from Japan by Maries. Killed in Bellevue, Iowa, after −20 to −30°F, while 'Igloo', 'Shasta', and 'Shoshoni' survived.

'Molly Schroeder' is described by Dan Hinkley as a dependably pink-flowered selection with persistent blooming throughout the summer. Grows 8 feet high and 5 feet wide with horizontal branches. I witnessed this for the first time on 19 April 2007 at Dudley Nursery, Thomson, Georgia. Flowers light pink, inflorescence and foliage smaller than typical. Appeared to be a branch sport of 'Summer Snowflake' or 'Pink Beauty'.

'Nanum Semperflorens' ('Watanabei', 'Watanabe Nanum') is a compact form introduced from Wada's Nursery in Japan. Habit is dense, flowers smaller than the type but making a good display. May grow 5 to 6 feet high. Flowers on and off through summer. Sparse fruit set. Supposedly grows very dwarf; some literature states less than 2 feet high, but I don't buy this designation. Discovered by Mr. Watanabe in the foothills of Mount Fuji and propagated by his firm in the 1950s. A plant at the JC Raulston Arboretum is 6 to 7 feet high, 8 to 10 feet wide. Not the same as 'Summer Snowflake'.

'Pink Beauty' is a handsome form with pink flowers. Specimens I have observed had leaves and flowers slightly smaller than typical doublefile, but the deep pink petal color was outstanding. Somewhat upright in habit, generally smaller in all its parts. Flower color develops as petals age; this pink coloration is variable over my traveling years. I observed a plant at Sissinghurst that one season was outstanding pink; on later visits, flowers were white, and I was not sure if it was the same plant. I have on occasion discovered heavily red-fruited specimens. Fruits ripened on 3 June 2004 at the JC Raulston Arboretum; not

Viburnum plicatum f. *tomentosum* 'Pink Beauty', fruits

Viburnum plicatum f. *tomentosum* 'Rowallane'

Viburnum plicatum f. *tomentosum* 'Shasta'

as pubescent on the lower surface as typical f. *tomentosum*. In the 6- to 10-foot range, less in spread. A 10- by 7-foot plant at Hillier in 1999. Appears that temperature affects petal color, and there is no absolute that 'Pink Beauty' will be just that. In fact, on 31 May 2006 at Hillier, two specimens of 'Pink Beauty' were snow-white, and the English spring was cool and moist.

'Roseum' has sterile flowers that open white and gradually fade to an excellent deep pink. It also has smaller leaves and is less vigorous than the type. In several respects 'Pink Beauty' and 'Roseum' are similar and may be one and the same. From the Brooklyn Botanic Garden.

'Rowallane' is less vigorous than 'Lanarth' and 'Mariesii', with smaller, broadly ovate, short acuminate leaves. Flowers are not as wide but the ray-florets are still large and form a uniform circle around the sparse, fertile inner flowers. Supposedly fruits heavier than 'Mariesii'; I witnessed in flower in late June at Rowallane. Best description is haystack-shaped. Inflorescences smaller than typical but produced in wondrous quantities—an amazing show. Plant was 8 to 10 feet high, 6 to 8 feet wide. Selected and distributed before 1942 in Rowallane Gardens, Northern Ireland, but possibly raised at Rostrevor from seed collected by E. H. Wilson.

'Shasta' is a tremendous 1979 introduction from the U.S. National Arboretum and Don Egolf's breeding program. It is a broad, horizontally branched shrub, originally described as 6 feet high by 10 to 12 feet wide at maturity. The abundant, 4- to 6-inch-wide inflorescences have sterile, marginal, pure white florets about 1¼ to 2 inches wide; the 5 to 15 inner florets, ½ to 1½ inches wide, are dispersed among the fertile flowers. The flowers are followed in July by bright red, maturing to black fruits. This excellent plant is now embedded in the psyche of American gardeners. I nurtured a supposed specimen of 'Shasta' into a 7-foot by 8-foot specimen, only to decide it was just the species or a cheap imitation. My garden heart was broken, especially when I saw the real McCoy with wide-spreading, horizontally accentuated branches and immense inflorescences that literally smothered the leaves. Will become a large plant—easily 10 feet or more high and wider at maturity. Plants in the UGA Botanical Garden are over 12 feet high. Survived −20 to −30°F in Bellevue, Iowa. In 1954 a select *V. plicatum* f. *tomentosum* was crossed with 'Mariesii'; from the second generation of this hybrid population, a superior plant was selected in 1968, named and released in 1978, as 'Shasta'. See Egolf 1979 for additional information.

'Shasta Variegated' has leaves that resemble 'Shasta' in shape and size, with yellow-green marbling; some are heavily yellow-marbled. A branch sport found by George Krauth, Estill Springs, Tennessee. Apparently an unstable chimera and never fully introduced into cultivation.

Viburnum plicatum f.
tomentosum 'Shasta',
fruits and fall color
(top left and right)

Viburnum plicatum f.
tomentosum 'Shoshoni'
(above)

Viburnum plicatum f.
tomentosum 'Summer
Snowflake' (right)

'Shoshoni', a seedling of 'Shasta' bred by Egolf, has performed well in UGA trials and is one-third to half the size of 'Shasta', with all the attributes of that form on a smaller scale. I noted prodigious fruit set on the trial plants: probably related to prevalence of pollinators. The parent plant was 5 feet high and 8 feet wide in 17 years; 7 feet high and wide in five years in the UGA trials. The dark green leaves are 2½ to 6 inches long, 1¼ to 2½ inches wide, and turn dull purplish red in fall. The flowers occur in 3- to 5-inch-wide, flat-topped cymes in April–May; full flower on 27 April 2004, Chapel Hill, North Carolina. The 5 to 7 outer, sterile, showy florets average ¾ to 1¼ inch long and 1 to 1¾ inches wide with 50 to 130, greenish white, perfect flowers in the center. The ovoid, ⅓-inch-long, ⅕-inch-wide drupe ripens red and matures to black. Fruits coloring 1 to 15 June 2006 in Athens. Never really jumped out of the starting blocks, but I have seen this at the National Arboretum and, indeed, it is worthy of consideration for the smaller garden. An Egolf/U.S. National Arboretum introduction (see Egolf 1986 for additional information). Survived −20 to −30°F in Bellevue, Iowa.

'St. Keverne' is a large form—10 to 12 feet high and wide. Inflorescences are umbrella-shaped, and it seldom produces fruits. Better than typical species.

'Summer Snowflake' ('Fujisanensis', 'Mt. Fuji') is a tall-growing, rather narrow selection with smaller leaves, flowers, and fruits than the species. The ability to flower prominently in spring (April in Athens), then sporadically into November distinguishes it from other doublefile cultivars. Have observed plants 15 feet high and greater, with an 18-foot-tall specimen still flowering on 30 July 1999 at Burncoose Nursery, Cornwall, England. I estimate plants will mature two to three times taller than wide. Has picked up steam in the U.S. nursery industry because it flowers over a long period. Not as cold hardy as 'Igloo', 'Shasta', 'Shoshoni', and Newport® ('Newzam'). Flattened to ground after −22°F in Louisville, Kentucky.

'Weeping Magic' has pendulous branches, which produce a low-mounding habit. It is wider than high at maturity, approximately 4 feet high by 6 feet wide; young container plants develop the shape of a bird's-nest spruce (*Picea abies* 'Nidiformis'). Leaves are light green; defoliation occurs before any fall color. Typical lacecap flowers and fruits. The smaller size and habit are unique. Introduced by Willoway Nurseries, Avon, Ohio.

'White Delight' is described by Kenyon (2001) as a dense, upright plant, not as wide-spreading as 'Shasta'.

Viburnum 'Pragense'

PRAGUE VIBURNUM

Prague viburnum (*V. ×pragense* Hujek & Kroutman), the result of a cross between *V. rhytidophyllum* and *V. utile*, was raised by Joseph Vik in Prague Municipal Gardens in 1955 and named in 1959. It is an attractive evergreen shrub with lustrous dark green, 2- to 4-inch-long, 1- to 1½-inch-wide, elliptic leaves that are gray tomentose below; petiole ½ to 1 inch long. The flowers are pink in bud, opening creamy white, slightly fragrant, and produced in terminal, 3- to 6(8)-inch-wide, slightly convex cymes in mid April in Athens. The fruit, which I have yet to see on cultivated plants, is described as ⅓ inch long, oval, red to glossy black. This hybrid is extremely hardy. There was a plant in the woody plant test plots at the University of Illinois which held up well under the rigors of Midwestern winters. It survived −6°F in the Arnold Arboretum without foliage discoloration. I observed severe leaf burn (no stem or bud damage) at Spring Grove after exposure to –17°F. It will grow 10 feet or more and is suited to culture in Zones 5 to 8. Dense, full specimen at Hillier, 12 feet high and wide, 1 July 1999. It is easily propagated from softwood cuttings. The habit is upright, oval to oval-rounded. The growth extensions are so vigorous that they must be pruned to achieve reasonable density. Extremely fast growing and makes a good screen, grouping, or accent plant. Has much more ornamental charm than *V. rhytidophyllum* and based on my observations is hardier than either parent. In fact, in the Arnold Arboretum's *Viburnum* collection, *V.* 'Pragense' was 8 to 10

Viburnum 'Pragense', habit, foliage, and flowers

feet high, *V. rhytidophyllum* a dieback shrub, and *V. utile* did not exist. Fruits were sent to me from Illinois in 2005; they have been through the stratification process. The progeny is an F_2 population and should prove exciting!

CULTIVARS & VARIETIES

'Decker' was selected by Decker Nursery, Ohio, for lustrous dark green leaves and pink-budded flowers that open white. Supposed quite hardy. Looks like typical *V.* 'Pragense' to me. In January 2006, while visiting Piedmont Carolina Nursery near Greensboro, North Carolina, I looked over a number of 'Decker' and simply could not tell an iota of difference between this and 'Pragense'.

Viburnum propinquum Hemsl.

Viburnum propinquum, scarcely known in the eastern United States, is typically described as a small, shrubby evergreen, 3 feet high and 3 to 5 feet wide. In England, I measured a 10-foot-high plant; another was 12 feet by 8 feet. A small

Viburnum propinquum, habit, foliage, and flowers

plant grows at the JC Raulston Arboretum, Raleigh, North Carolina (2006). A gigantic 18- by 12-foot, haystack-shaped specimen, with tiered branches, was observed 31 May 2006 at Hillier. The shiny dark green, leathery, 3-nerved leaves, 2 to 3 inches long, 1 to 1½ inch wide, irregularly finely serrated, essentially glabrous, hold color through the winter. Petiole about ½ inch long, red-purple. The new shoots emerge bronze and contrast with the older foliage. The greenish white, nonfragrant flowers, in 1½- to 3-inch-wide terminal inflorescences, open in mid May (Hillier) without fanfare. Have seen emerging flower buds on 6 February 2006 at the JC Raulston Arboretum. In full flower 2 April 2003, Aiken, South Carolina. The fruits are egg-shaped, ⅕-inch-long, blue-black drupes. Any well-drained soil, sun to moderate shade, and wind protection serve it well. My plant "friends" have quizzed me on this plant several times. The 3-nerved leaves with scattered serrations and the red-brown, lenticellate stems are clues. A plant for the collector. Zones 7 and 8, 9 and 10 on West Coast. Performs well in Portland, Oregon. Native to central and western China, Taiwan, and the Philippines. Introduced in 1901 by E. H. Wilson.

Viburnum prunifolium L.
BLACKHAW VIBURNUM

Blackhaw viburnum is a worthwhile native shrub or small tree, often suckering and forming thickets. Early leafing and flowering as evidenced by a full-flowered, 15-foot-tall specimen in Silk Hope, North Carolina, that I jumped from a (moving) car to photograph on 1 April 2006. New foliage growth is about half normal size when flowers open. For size comparisons, co-champions in Virginia are 24 feet by 33 feet and 24 feet by 28 feet. A tree form at Hillier was 20 feet by 12 feet in 1999. The 1½- to 3½-inch-long, 1- to 2-inch-wide, dull dark green, finely toothed leaves have a narrow (unwinged), ⅓- to ¾-inch-long, reddish petiole. The latter trait separates it from the wavy, prominently winged petiole of *V. lentago*. Fall color is variable from dull bronze-red to shining red. Flowers, not offensive in odor, white with yellow stamens, are carried in 2- to 4-inch-wide cymes in April (Athens). The fruit, up to ½-inch-long and oval, transitions pinkish rose to bluish black with a pruinose bloom (wax), September into fall. Colors are beautiful. Listed as sweet and edible. The author suggests tiny bites . . . Adaptable species that grows in low areas along streams and drier woodlands. Displays full-sun to almost full-shade tolerance. Tends to leaf out two to three weeks before the overstory trees and may gain a competitive advantage by storing photosynthates early. Excellent native with iron-clad resiliency. Bark is unique, becoming black and blocky, similar to *Diospyros virginiana* and *Nyssa sylvatica*. Smaller cultivars could endear it to gardeners and de-

Viburnum prunifolium, habit, foliage, flowers, fruits, and fall color

signers. Zones 3 to 9. Native from Connecticut to Florida, west to Michigan and Texas. Introduced 1727.

CULTIVARS & VARIETIES

Kenyon (2001) lists 'Gladwyne', 'Holden', and 'Mrs. Henry Large'; none probably in commerce.

'Early Red' has new leaves emerging subdued red and developing burgundy in autumn. Offered by Fairweather Gardens, New Jersey.

Guardian™ ('Guazam') was selected for the crisp, healthy green foliage that persists until fall (when it turns brilliant crimson-red), white flowers, blue-black fruits, and strong vigorous upright habit. Grows 10 to 12 feet high, 6 to 8 feet wide. A Lake County Nursery introduction, part of their Shepherd's Series™.

'McRouge' has a uniform habit, typical cream-white flat-topped inflorescences, and blue-black fruits. Deep glossy green foliage turns purple-red in autumn. Introduced by Dan Moore, McKay Nursery, Waterloo, Wisconsin.

Ovation™ ('Ovazam') is columnar, 10 feet by 4 feet. New leaves are rosy pink and mature crisp celery-green. Self-scaffolding branches, good for hedging and limited space use. Hardy to Zone 3. Another member of Lake County Nursery's Shepherd's Series™.

'Summer Magic' produces red to pink new growth, leathery dark green mature leaves, and yellow to red fall colors on an upright habit, 8 to 10 feet high by 6 to 8 feet wide. Zone 5. Introduced by Willoway Nurseries, Avon, Ohio.

Viburnum rafinesquianum Schultes
RAFINESQUE VIBURNUM, DOWNY ARROWWOOD VIBURNUM

I knew little about this native, relatively compact, finely twiggy species that inhabits Canada (Quebec and Manitoba) and much of the eastern United States (to Arkansas, Missouri, and Kentucky). I observed thriving specimens at the Minnesota Landscape Arboretum (Zone 4) and the UGA Botanical Garden (Zone 7). These specimens were compact, 5 to 6 feet high, 6 to 8 feet wide, and densely clothed with 1- to 2½-inch-long, 1- to 1¾-inch-wide, dark green, 4- to 6-veined, coarsely toothed leaves. I noticed mildew on a plant at the Minnesota Landscape Arboretum on 20 July 2005. Leaves emerge early, generally mid to late April in the Chapel Hill, North Carolina, area, where the species is abundant in the understory. Fall color is muted red to russet-red, and I continue to look for a bright red, fall-coloring seedling. The white, malodorous flowers are held in 1½- to 3-inch-wide, 5- to 7-rayed terminal cymes in late April–early May (Chapel Hill). Flower abundance is prominent in shade, even more so in sun. Fruits are black, not particularly showy, ⅓ inch long, ellipsoidal, lost among the

Viburnum rafinesquianum, habit, foliage, flowers, and fall color

foliage, ripening by July. Have observed some fruits transitioning from red to black. Adaptable to extremes of soil and climate, full sun and shade, and tolerant of heat and drought. In 2005, extreme drought conditions prevailed from early July to early October in Chapel Hill. Although showing some effects of stress, I did not see a brown (dead) plant among the extensive native populations. Many years past, Mark Griffith, a former student, propagated liners and offered same through Griffith Propagation Nursery. I think Mark still has some for sale . . . A utilitarian plant for native landscapes. Beautiful in woodland settings. Usually found in calcareous soils of dry slopes and woods. Zones (3)4 to 7.

CULTIVARS & VARIETIES

'Louise's Sunbeam' is a yellow-foliage shrub, discovered in North Carolina by the author in May 2005. Compact, dense, 4 feet high and wide, it is named after Louise Quinlan, our youngest daughter's, Susy's, organ donor. The noble and memorable story of its discovery brings me to tears. In mid April 2006, I returned to the original location and walked the site, discovering two additional yellow-leaf seedlings. I suspect that seeds from the original plant gave rise to these color variants. All are safely ensconced in an undisclosed location as I evaluate the three for potential release into commerce. Our goal is to give any royalties to the Sweet Melissa Fund at the University of North Carolina–Chapel Hill, which supports lung transplant patients and their families.

Viburnum
rafinesquianum
'Louise's
Sunbeam'

Viburnum recognitum Fern

Tangentially a subset of *V. dentatum* but given species status, *V. recognitum* is a large shrub, listed as 10 to 15 feet high and almost as wide, but my sightings of cultivated plants reflect 5 to 6 feet by 5 to 8 feet, and 8 feet high and wide. Further field notes state, "Much like *V. dentatum* in habit, leaf, and flower" (1 July 1999 at Hillier). Hillier plant was broad-rounded, extremely dense, 10 feet by 12 feet, with lustrous dark green foliage. The typical thinnish, lighter green leaves are 2 to 4 inches long and as wide or wider, with 10 to 15 pairs of coarse marginal teeth and 6 to 8 vein pairs. Leaves on the herbarium specimens varied from ovate to rounded, typically longer than wide. The leaf underside and petiole are prominently pubescent; likewise the buds and stems. Bean (1981) stated that the parts are essentially glabrous. The flowers, white, open in June in 3- to 5-inch-wide cymes. Blue-black, ⅓-inch-long, oval-round fruits mature in late summer. Like *V. dentatum*, very adaptable but better suited to cold-climate areas. Zones 4 to 6. From a landscape viewpoint, not sufficiently distinct

Viburnum recognitum, habit, foliage, and flowers

from the better adapted and superior *V. dentatum* cultivars. Native to eastern North America. Typically more northerly distribution than *V. dentatum*. Introduced in the 18th century.

Viburnum ×rhytidocarpum Lemoine

In my estimation, *V. ×rhytidocarpum* is more a curiosity than everyday garden shrub. The habit is akin to *V. ×rhytidophylloides*, upright, spreading, 10 to 12 feet high, with semi-evergreen foliage. An open and coarse plant, 15 feet high and wide, grew in the Hillier Arboretum, 22 May 2006. Typically in Zone 7, only the leaves toward the terminals of the branches are retained. The 6- to 8-inch-long, approximately 2- to 3-inch-wide leaves are glossy dark green above, densely gray pubescent below, almost like those of *Buddleia davidii*. Petiole is ½ to 1 inch long with gray to brown pubescence. The white flowers, anthers yellow, similar in fragrance to *V. rhytidophyllum*, open in late April–May, borne in 2- to 4-inch-wide, 7-rayed cymes. Flowers on the plants I witnessed do not excite. Fruits are red maturing black, oval, and ⅓ inch long. Parentage is *V. buddleifolium* × *V. rhytidophyllum*. Raised by Lemoine and introduced to commerce in 1936. Zones 6 and 7, higher on West Coast.

Viburnum ×rhytidocarpum, habit, foliage, and flowers

Viburnum ×rhytidophylloides Suringar

LANTANAPHYLLUM VIBURNUM

A hybrid between *V. rhytidophyllum* and *V. lantana* that first occurred about 1925 in the Netherlands and has since been reconstituted several times with *V. rhytidophyllum* as the seed parent. Large, to some degree oafy, spreading, rounded, but commonly grown, particularly 'Alleghany'. Leaves favor *V. rhytidophyllum*, ranging from 4 to 8 inches long, 2 to 4 inches wide, finely toothed, rugose and leathery, dark green above, gray pubescent below, with an approximately 1-inch-long petiole. Many times the hybrid is confused with *V. rhytidophyllum*, but the leaf of the former is wider (i.e., elliptic-ovate). Also, the hybrid is completely deciduous in the North, with variable leaf retention in Zone 7(8). Flowers, unpleasantly scented, in 3- to 4-inch-wide, flat-topped cymes, white with yellow stamens, open in mid April (Athens) and are followed by red, changing to black, ⅓-inch-long, oval fruits in late August–September. Beautiful when the red and black are mixed in the ripening infructescences. Fruit abundance depends on the presence of a suitable pollinator. Culturally, tougher than nails: any reasonably drained soil and sun to partial shade. Use in groupings, masses, for screens and blended with broadleaf evergreens. Falls in the range of 10 to 15 feet high and wide, although I cataloged an 18- by 18-foot specimen at Hillier (22 April 1999). Plants may look the worse-for-wear after a difficult winter as the persisting leaves become increasingly tatty. Much more cold-hardy than *V. rhytidophyllum*. Zones (4)5 to 8, 9 on the West Coast.

Viburnum ×rhytidophylloides, habit, foliage, and flowers

*Viburnum
×rhytidophylloides*,
fruits

*Viburnum
×rhytidophylloides*
'Alleghany', habit
and foliage (below)

*Viburnum
×rhytidophylloides*
'Willowwood'
(below right)

CULTIVARS & VARIETIES

'Alleghany' is an Egolf/U.S. National Arboretum introduction selected from an F$_2$ *V. rhytidophyllum* × *V. lantana* 'Mohican' seedling population in 1958 (1953 cross). Named and released in 1966. Actual 'Alleghany' resulted from a selfed seedling that produced the F$_2$ population resulting in 'Alleghany'. Plants have very dark green, leathery leaves; abundant inflorescences; resistance to bacterial leaf spot; hardiness; and vigorous, dense, globose growth habit. The foliage, which tends to be deciduous to semi-persistent, is intermediate between the parental species (33 percent evergreen at Hillier on 3 March 1999). It is smaller than *V. rhytidophyllum*, and is more leathery than *V. lantana*. The rugose, coriaceous leaves are resistant to leaf spot and are highly ornamental. The abundant, yellowish white inflorescences in May are effectively displayed above the dark green foliage. For several weeks in September and October the fruits become brilliant red as ripening advances to black at maturity. In 13 years the original plant attained a height of 10½ feet and a spread of 11 feet. This has proven to be an outstanding selection and is being successfully grown as far north as the Minnesota Landscape Arboretum, although it is not perfectly cold hardy. Has been a stalwart in Zone 7 but little known or grown. It is so superior to *V. lantana* that I do not understand the reasons for planting that species. 'Alleghany' was used by Pellett to develop 'Emerald Triumph' (see under *V. burejaeticum*).

Dart's Duke™ ('Interduke') has large, leathery dark green foliage, 6 to 8 inches in length, and white flowers in 6-inch-wide cymes. Often flowers in the fall like 'Willowwood'. Grows 8 to 10 feet high and wide. From Darthuizer nursery in the Netherlands.

'Holland' is presented here only for historical purposes: it was apparently one of the first named hybrids between the two species, raised about 1925.

'Willowwood' is a form with excellent lustrous, rugose, dark green foliage and an arching habit. Has performed admirably in the Midwest, at times coming through the winter with foliage in good condition. A 15- by 10-foot plant at Hillier was 75 percent evergreen on 26 April 1999. I have seen this cultivar flowering in October on the Purdue University campus, West Lafayette, Indiana. It is the result of a cross made in 1928 by Henry Tubbs of Willowwood Farm, Gladstone, New Jersey. In Georgia, flowers in October–November and again in spring.

Viburnum rhytidophyllum Hemsl.
LEATHERLEAF VIBURNUM

Leatherleaf viburnum is a boldly textured, evergreen shrub with large, leathery, 4- to 8-inch-long, 1- to 2½-inch-wide leaves that are lustrous above, covered with gray pubescence below with a petiole about 1 inch long with brown stellate pubescence. Gigantic in proportions, easily 10 to 15 feet high and wide. I charted 18-foot-high specimens in Europe; 10- by 12-foot plant at Hillier in 1999. Bean (1981) mentioned a 20- by 30-foot plant that grew at Borde Hall, Sussex, England. Habit is eventually rounded, so space is the issue, especially in modern-day gardens. In winter, leaves droop like those of an admonished puppy and appear desiccated. In our Georgia garden, a plant grew in a corner of the fence until Bonnie said, "I hate that plant." Removal ensued. The moral: the texture affects people in myriad ways. Safe to state the flowers are slightly fragrant, white with prominent yellow stamens, emerging in April (Athens) in 7- to 11-rayed, 4- to 8-inch-wide, flat-topped cymes. Flowers emerge from the exposed brownish pubescent naked buds—ornamental in a quirky way. Fruits follow the color pattern of *V. lantana* and *V.* ×*rhytidophylloides*, coloring red, finally black, both colors often mixed in the infructescence. Definitely requires another seedling or clone for cross-pollination. Any well-drained soil, sun or shade, and wind protection provide best success. Dark and somewhat frightening presence! Not for the small garden. Use in groupings, screening, and the shrub border. Temperatures of –10 to –15°F result in stem kill. Zones (5)6 and 7, 8 and 9 on the West Coast. Native to central and western China. Introduced in 1900 by E. H. Wilson.

CULTIVARS & VARIETIES

'Aldenham' ('Aldenhamensis') did not appear much different from the species, at least the RHS Hyde Hall specimen I photographed 1 May 1999 did not. Pink-budded flowers open white in large cymes.

'Cree' is more compact than the species, oval-rounded, with lustrous dark green leaves that are 6 inches by 2 inches. I have observed at the U.S. National Arboretum and the Sarah P. Duke Gardens and was not overwhelmed. A small plant in my evaluation tests is traveling nowhere—better than run-of-the-mill *V. rhytidophyllum*, but no reason to rejoice. Grew 8½ feet by 8 feet in 14 years. Leaves in winter do not curl or roll as profoundly as the species. Possibly more cold hardy. Produces abundant white flowers and red, maturing to black fruits. Introduced in 1994.

'Green Trump' is a darker green, more compact form of leatherleaf from the Netherlands.

Viburnum rhytidophyllum, habit, flower buds, flowers, and foliage

'Roseum' (also listed as forma *roseum*) has pink flower buds that open yellowish white. I have seen this form in England and indeed the buds are an attractive pink, not overwhelming. Dense 8- by 8-foot plant at Hillier, 1 July 1999.

'Variegatum'. I had high hopes for this creamy white, irregularly variegated shrub but, after seeing it in England a few times, came away disappointed. The plant reverts, and it is often difficult to locate the variegated leaves. For the collector who has time to prune away the green shoots. A 10-foot-high plant at Hillier had about 15 variegated leaves and 300 green leaves on 31 May 2006, some a mix of green-yellow-cream, a few yellow, and one or two cream.

Viburnum rhytidophyllum, fruits (above)

Viburnum rhytidophyllum 'Roseum', flower buds (above right)

Viburnum rhytidophyllum 'Variegatum' (right)

Viburnum rufidulum Raf.

RUSTY BLACKHAW VIBURNUM, SOUTHERN BLACKHAW VIBURNUM

Truly one of the most beautiful viburnums for foliage . . . lustrous, waxy, dark green with sheeny maroon to deep burgundy fall color. Has more pubescent plant parts and is slightly less hardy than *V. lentago* and *V. prunifolium*. Leaves, oval, ovate to obovate, 2 to 4 inches long, 1 to 1½ inches wide, sometimes almost as wide as long, obtuse, or short acuminate, broad cuneate to almost rounded, leathery, serrulate, lustrous dark green above, pubescent below initially, finally glabrous, with a petiole ¼ to ½ inch long, more or less winged, with rusty pubescence. Flowers, cream-white, slightly fragrant to no fragrance, kind of neutral, bloom early to mid April (Athens), each floret ⅓ inch across, in up to 5-inch-wide cymes. The buds are covered with a deep rich rusty brown pubescence which distinguishes it from any viburnum in this book. Fruit is a ½- to ⅔-inch-long, ellipsoidal, bloomy dark blue drupe. The habit can be shrubby or tree-like, and larger branches develop a blocky-black, *Cornus florida*–like bark. Excellent plant and should be used more widely where it can be grown. I have

Viburnum rufidulum, habit, bark, and foliage

Viburnum rufidulum, flower buds, flowers, fruits, and fall color

Viburnum sargentii (right)

developed a real fondness for this species and found it wild in the Athens, Georgia, environs. Will grow 10 to 20 feet high under typical landscape conditions but may reach 30 to 40 feet in the wild. National champion, in Knox County, Tennessee, is 30 feet by 23 feet. Witnessed a 20- by 15-foot plant at Hillier in 1999. Occurs as an understory plant in the Piedmont of Georgia and tends toward an open habit in such locations. In full sun, it becomes more dense. An upland species in well-drained woodlands, hedgerows, and fencerows. Also grows in river bottom areas. Displays excellent drought tolerance and has withstood −25°F in the Midwest without damage. A compact form would be a tremendous garden addition. On the Georgia campus, a group of seedlings was planted in 1993. They are now 6 to 10 feet high, and each is different. I have propagated the most dense, lustrous dark green leaf form, but it is the largest, now about 10 feet high. Native from Virginia to Florida, west to Illinois and Texas. Zones 5 to 9. Introduced 1883.

CULTIVARS & VARIETIES

Emerald Charm™ ('Morton') has glossy dark green leaves, burgundy in fall, and is cold hardy. Matures 10 to 12 feet high by 8 to 10 feet wide. Originated from seed collected in Webb City, Missouri, by the Morton Arboretum and introduced through Chicagoland Grows.

'Royal Guard' has excellent glossy dark green foliage that turns rich burgundy to deep maroon in autumn. Supposedly grows 12 feet by 6 feet, although I have read spreads of 10 to 20 feet. Flowers and fruits are similar to the species. Hardiness is often debated, but 15-foot-high specimens have withstood −20 to −25°F at the Morton Arboretum. A 10-foot-high plant at the JC Raulston Arboretum flowered 24 April 2005; it did not impress any more than the average species seedling I see at woodland edges in the Southeast.

Viburnum sargentii Koehne
SARGENT VIBURNUM, SARGENT CRANBERRYBUSH

Uncommon in everyday commerce, taking a back seat to *V. opulus* and *V. trilobum*, with which it is often confused, *V. sargentii* is a vigorous and robust grower—more so than *V. opulus*. Forms a 12- to 15-foot-high and -wide rounded shrub of coarse stems and branches. The 2- to 5-inch-long, 3-lobed leaves are firmer textured with a longer central lobe than *V. opulus*. Also, the central lobe is not as toothed or incised as that of *V. opulus*. Young shoots are often bronze-purple, while fall colors range from yellow to red. The 1-inch-long petiole has concave glands similar to those of *V. opulus*. Leaves were one-third their full size by late March 2004 at the JC Raulston Arboretum. Very early leafing and

Viburnum sargentii, foliage, flowers, fruits, and fall color

Viburnum sargentii 'Onondaga' (right)

may be damaged by late spring frosts. The lacecap inflorescences bear white, sterile, showy outer florets, inner white and fertile, with purple anthers. The purple anthers are not consistent, and I have seen more plants with yellow than purple. Fertile flowers are stinky, perhaps several degrees more so than *V. opulus*. Inflorescences are 3- to 4-inch-wide cymes on 1- to 2-inch-long peduncles. In full flower 14 May 2004 in Chapel Hill, North Carolina. The scarlet, ⅓- to ½-inch-long, globose, berry-like drupe is effective in August through October. Fruits are spectacular but not always borne in great numbers; the lack of fruits is probably attributable to the need for another pollinator. Best suited to cold climate use; definitely not heat tolerant. More aphid resistant than *V. opulus*. Have observed slight viburnum beetle feeding. Grows in wet and watery places with willows. Use in groupings and borders. One of the largest and best-fruiting specimens resides in the Lyle E. Littlefield Ornamental Gardens at the University of Maine, Orono. Zones (3)4 to 7. Native to northeastern Asia. Introduced by C. S. Sargent in 1892.

CULTIVARS & VARIETIES

'Chiquita' is a compact, 5- to 6-foot-high and -wide selection. Flowers and fruits similar to the species. Medium green leaves turn yellow in autumn. Introduced by McKay Nursery, Waterloo, Wisconsin.

'Flavum' (f. *flavum* Rehd., 'Fructolutea') has yellow anthers and golden-yellow translucent fruits. Wyman has an interesting anecdote concerning a trial he conducted growing seedlings from the yellow-fruited form. He noted that many seedlings showed yellowish leaf petioles and others reddish. The seedlings with yellowish petioles turned yellowish green in fall; those with reddish petioles colored red. Obviously the fruits will follow the same trends exhibited in petiole color.

Forma *lutescens* is listed, presumably a reference to the yellow fruit color, but it could be the foliage color that is meant.

'Onondaga' is an Egolf/U.S. National Arboretum introduction distinguished by the velvety, fine-textured, dark maroon young foliage that maintains a maroon tinge when mature. Leaves are smaller than species, still with the long central lobe. Flower buds are maroon-red, opening creamy-white with a trace of pink, in 2- to 4-inch-wide, flat-topped cymes, with 10 to 17 outer, 1¼- to 1¾-inch-wide, sterile florets. The red fruits are sparsely produced. Usually forms a globose shrub 6 feet high and wide but will grow larger. I have seen 8- to 10-foot-high specimens and, at Hillier Arboretum, I experienced a 12-foot-high plant on 1 July 1999. Typically, 'Onondaga' is more upright in habit than the species. Introduced in 1966.

Viburnum sargentii 'Onondaga', foliage and flowers

Viburnum sargentii 'Susquehanna' (right)

'Puberlosum' has smaller flowers and pubescent parts. Taxonomically, I don't know whether this designation is justified.

'Puberulum' looks suspiciously like 'Puberlosum'. A 15- by 15-foot plant with terrible leaf spot grew at Hillier in 1999. I examined herbarium specimens of both and saw no differences.

Forma *sterile* is a semi-snowball form that, from the photo I witnessed, is striking.

'Susquehanna' is an Egolf/U.S. National Arboretum introduction from 1966 best described as a select *V. sargentii* with a heavy-branched, corky trunk; coriaceous, dark green foliage; abundant flowers and fruits; and upright growth habit. Leaves, up to 5½ inches long, central lobe more than half the length of the leaf, not as pubescent as species, 'Onondaga', 'Puberlosum', and 'Puberulum'. New growth emerges green in April, a reasonable way to separate it from 'Onondaga'. Appeared as a seedling in a population of 209 raised from seed obtained from Matsu, Hondo, Japan. It becomes a large shrub, 12 to 15 feet high, approximating the species in size. I have seen it in fruit, and the effect is striking. Flowers are stinky. Probably too large for the average landscape but good for parks, campuses, and large areas. A 15- by 15-foot specimen noted at Hillier, 31 May 2006.

Viburnum schensianum Maxim.
SHENSI VIBURNUM

I see little difference between this species and *V. lantana*. Size, 10 to 12 feet high and wide; leaves, 1 to 2 inches long, ½ to 1¼ inch wide, with 5 to 6 vein pairs; serrations, dentate; flowers, off-white in 5-rayed, 2- to 3-inch-wide cymes in May; and fruits, ⅓ inch long, ellipsoidal, red turning black at maturity—all reflect close affiliation with *V. lantana*. Nearest ally among the Lantana section (Krüssmann 1985) is considered to be *V. burejaeticum*. Collected by Roy Lancaster at 6,300 feet. Zones 6 and 7. Native to northwest China. Introduced in 1910.

Viburnum sempervirens K. Koch

Robert McCartney, Woodlanders, Aiken, South Carolina, showed me this beautifully foliaged species with the bronze-green young shoots and glossy dark green mature leaves. The young stems are 4-sided (quadrangular) and pale yellow, maturing red-brown and cylindrical in the second year. The rich dark green leaves, 1½ to 4 inches long, 1 to 1½ inches wide, are leathery, elliptic-lanceolate, toothed toward the apex or entire with glandular markings on the lighter-colored lower surface. Petiole is about ⅓ inch long. The white flowers appear in approximately 2-inch-wide cymes (May) and are followed by red fruits. Adapted to heat, drought, and sandy, acid soils. Again, a collector's plant with potential for breeding and use in the lower South. Listed as Zone 9, but grows in Zones 7 and 8 in the Southeast. Native to Yunnan Province, China.

Viburnum setigerum Hance
TEA VIBURNUM

For fruit display, *V. setigerum* is among the Top 5 *Viburnum* species. The bright red fruits sometimes mingle among the muted red fall-coloring leaves—absolutely as good as a gardener could wish! The one mini-liability is the habit—leggy, open, with foliage in the upper one-third to half. The branches splay, and the foliage has a nodding tendency. If plant breeders could tighten habit, increase foliage density, and keep fruit size and abundance, then the market would grow exponentially. The flat, soft blue-green to dark green, ovate-lanceolate leaves are 3 to 6 inches long, 1¼ to 2½ inches wide, with remote denticulate teeth. The petiole ranges from ½ to 1 inch long. The fall color, though subdued red, is quite effective and long-persistent. The white, slightly fragrant to nonfragrant flowers, on short, lateral, 2-leafed twigs, in 5-rayed, 1- to 2-inch-wide cymes, open in early April (Athens), May (Boston) with the emerging leaves. In full flower 20 April 2004 at the JC Raulston Arboretum with a slight unpleasant odor. The principal ornamental asset is the egg-shaped, ⅓- to ½-inch-long, bright red, drupaceous fruits. Adaptable species with sun and partial-shade tolerance. Best in a shrub border, where the lower branches can be masked. The leaves were used for making tea and have medicinal properties. Related to *V. phlebotricum* but has consistently larger, longer leaves. Eight to 12 feet high, 6 to 10 feet wide. Zones 5 to 7(8). Native to central and western China. Introduced by Wilson in 1901.

CULTIVARS & VARIETIES
'Aurantiacum' is an orange-fruited form, quite distinct in color from that of the species. All other characteristics are similar. Arnold Arboretum introduction from seed Wilson collected in Hubei, China, in 1907.

Viburnum setigerum

Viburnum setigerum,
flowers and fruits (top
left and right) and in
December (left)

Viburnum setigerum
'Aurantiacum' (above)

Viburnum sieboldii Miq.
SIEBOLD VIBURNUM

During an August 2005 tour of J. F. Schmidt & Son Nursery, Boring, Oregon, horticulturist Keith Warren showed me a row of seedling *V. sieboldii* with remarkable variation. Phenomenal fruit production was the signature statement, but the pyramidal-columnar form with dense foliage begged for introduction (see photo). A large species, 15 to 20(30) feet, Siebold viburnum makes a reasonable tree but is most often grown as a multi-stemmed shrub. Recorded a large, low-branched tree, 18-inch-wide trunk, 25 feet by 30 feet at Hillier, 2 July 1999. The shining dark green, 2- to 6-inch-long, 1½- to 3-inch-wide, essentially glabrous leaves, have 7 to 10 pairs of impressed veins and are coarsely crenate-serrate. Petiole ½ to ¾ inches long. When crushed, the foliage smells like green peppers. Foliage emerges early (1 March 1999 at Hillier, according to my field notes). Leaves hold late, often into December, and in my experience seldom color, although the literature gives red-purple as a possibility. The best I witnessed was ashy purple on a plant at the University of Maine. The fragrant (lemon-scented), cream-white flowers occur in large, 3- to 4-inch-wide, cymose-paniculate inflorescences in April–May (full flower on 20 April 2004 at the JC Raulston Arboretum). The oval, ⅓- to ½-inch-long, pink, rose-red, red to black fruits ripen in August–October. Birds devour the fruits, *but* the rose-red pedicels and peduncle of the infructescence remain an effective ornamental display for two to four weeks. Another adaptable species—sun and moderate shade—but requires moisture in hot, dry situations. Have observed significant leaf scorch under the latter conditions. Notable as a single specimen, grouping, and against expanse of brick. Another species where breeders need to reduce size but keep the terrifically showy flowers and fruits. Zones 4 to 7(8). Native to Japan. Scattered distribution in the warm-temperate area of central and south-

Viburnum sieboldii, pyramidal-columnar form in a row of seedlings

Viburnum sieboldii, habit, flowers, fruits, and fall color

ern Japan. Abundant around Mount Fuji, central Honshu. Introduced by the Arnold Arboretum in 1880.

CULTIVARS & VARIETIES

Ironclad™ ('KLMfour') from Roy Klehm at Beaver Creek Nursery. This selection was dubbed Ironclad™ when it was the only survivor of a seedling planting. Listed as a heavy-flowering form with creamy white cymes; clean, rugose, shiny green summer foliage; green-burgundy fall color; and red fruits that age black. Matures 15 feet high by 12 feet wide. True Zone 4.

Varieties *longifolium* Satake and *reticulatum* (Yamagita) Sugimoto are listed by Kenyon (2001). I have not observed them.

Variety *obovatifolum* (Yamagita) Sugimoto has obovate to broad-rounded, serrate leaves to 10 inches long. Every plant I'd ever witnessed at three gardens in England had smaller leaves; then on 27 May 2006, I experienced a 12- by 10-foot plant with obovate, 10-inch leaves at Wakehurst Place. Fit the botanical description like an old shoe. Good-looking plant but unique only by virtue of the foliage. Found on the Sea of Japan side of Honshu.

'Seneca' resulted from a self-pollination of *V. sieboldii*. The plant was selected for the abundant, large, pendulant inflorescences of firm red fruits on red pedicels, which persist on the plant up to three months before turning black and falling. The massive, creamy white panicles are produced in May–early June as the young foliage unfolds. The panicles are supported on stout, spreading branches that are picturesque in all seasons. The multi-colored clusters of orange-red ripening to blood-red fruits are spectacularly displayed above the coriaceous, green foliage. Birds normally eat the fruits of *V. sieboldii* before it has matured; the fruits of 'Seneca', however, are very firm and are not devoured by birds even when fully ripe (countering this claim, Lanny Rawdon, Arborvillage, Holt, Missouri, reports Midwest birds love 'Seneca' fruits). 'Seneca' is tree-like

Viburnum sieboldii var. *obovatifolium* (left)

Viburnum sieboldii 'Seneca' (right)

and will undoubtedly equal plants of the species in size; it can be as much as 30 feet high with a gnarled trunk and has attained a width of 13½ feet. This cultivar can also be trained with several branches from the base and kept as a large spreading shrub. An Egolf/U.S. National Arboretum introduction in 1966.

'Wavecrest' is a vigorous grower with brick-red fall color and large leaves and flowers. From Eugene W. Coffman, Ridge Road Nursery, Bellevue, Iowa, who received a seedling from Robert Tomayer, Wavecrest Nursery, Fennville, Michigan, with larger, thicker leaves. In a letter to me, Coffman reports the abundant fruits are orange, and the pedicels bright scarlet; he describes fall color as barn-red. His original plant was 7 to 8 feet high and 4 feet across after five years in Zone 4.

Viburnum suspensum Lindl.
SANDANKWA VIBURNUM

Viburnum suspensum is a 6- to 12-foot-high, evergreen shrub that is used in the Coastal Plain and on the West Coast, and frequently seen in Florida gardens. Leaves, evergreen, ovate to oval, 2 to 5 inches long, 1½ to 3 inches wide, pointed, rounded or broadly wedge-shaped, toothed in the upper two-thirds or scarcely at all, leathery lustrous green, glabrous, with 4 to 5 vein pairs and a petiole that is ¼ to ½ inch long. The white, faintly tinged pink, fragrant (I noted off-odor) flowers occur in a 2½- to 4-inch-long and -wide, corymbose panicle in late winter. Flowers fully open, 25 February 2002 at the JC Raulston Arboretum. The globose, ¼-inch-wide fruits are red maturing to black. I have yet to see mature fruit, and several references state only red coloration. It prefers a hot, dry climate and also seems well-suited to sandy soils. Excellent in full sun and shade. I see the species everywhere in Florida, all the way to Key West, where it is used for screens, specimens, and the ubiquitous hedge. Interestingly, sizeable

Viburnum suspensum

plants were killed to the ground or outright on the Georgia coast at 11°F. A single plant has survived in Raleigh, North Carolina, but is knocked back by low temperatures. Leaves emerge early and late spring frosts may do as much damage as winter lows. Bob McCartney, Woodlanders, Aiken, South Carolina, told me there are immense specimens in Florida but, as I said, almost every plant I experienced was hedged or pruned. Ryukyu Islands, Japan. Zones 8 to 11. Introduced 1850.

Viburnum tinus L.

LAURUSTINUS

Laurustinus is a fine upright-oval to rounded evergreen species that reaches 6 to 12 feet in height and usually less in spread. There was a 15- by 15-foot plant and an 18- by 20-foot plant at Hillier in 1999. The lustrous dark green leaves are handsome throughout the year. They are narrowly ovate to oblong, 1½ to 4 inches long, ¾ to 1½ inches wide, entire, lustrous dark green above, paler beneath, axillary tufts below; petiole is ⅓ to ¾ inch long and usually pubescent. The pink-budded, 2- to 4-inch-wide flowers open to white and often flower in January–February into April in the South. Flowers are slightly fragrant. The flowers are followed by ovoid, metallic blue fruits that mature blue-black to black. Species is reported to be self-incompatible, so another seedling or clone must be in proximity to induce good fruit set. It is an excellent plant for screening and hedging, and withstands full sun and considerable shade as well as salt spray. It is hardy to 0°F once established and appears to be insect- and disease-free. This is a variable species in degree of pubescence, leaf size, etc. It is not common in the South but does make a handsome evergreen shrub. It can be used for screening, hedging, and massing. I noticed the plant was frequently

Viburnum tinus, habit, foliage, flowers, and fruits

used in England. It is a serviceable evergreen shrub for Mediterranean climates or where winter temperatures seldom drop below 10°F. Witnessed viburnum beetle damage on plants in England in 2006. Over my 28 years in Athens, Georgia, I have watched a 7-foot-high specimen disappear to its root tips. The University grounds department tried several plants of 'Spring Bouquet' in a protected area, only to have them succumb to the vagaries of a southern winter. I do not believe the plant hardens off early enough in fall to avoid the early fall freezes. In Washington, Georgia, 40 miles southeast of Athens, I discovered two 8- to 10-foot specimens that survived the mid 1980s and 1994 cold. Perhaps five degrees Fahrenheit difference between Athens and Washington. The species and cultivars continue to expand into southeastern gardens and are frequently available at garden centers. I noticed a screen (dense) in full flower on 2 April 2006 in Chapel Hill. Plants were growing under a large shade tree, yet were clothed with foliage and dense as green brick. Deer will feed on the species. Native to southern Europe, primarily in the Mediterranean region, northern Africa. Cultivated since the 16th century in England. Zones (7)8 to 10.

CULTIVARS & VARIETIES

'Bewley's Variegated' has significantly variegated pale cream to soft yellow leaves, dense bushy habit, 6 to 7 feet high and wide. A small plant in our shop has been impressive. Larger plants I observed in England are similar to 'Variegatum'. Less cold hardy than the species. Flower buds are pink, opening white.

'Clyne Castle' has large, glossy leaves and improved hardiness.

'Compactum' will grow one-half to three-quarters the size of the species and has slightly smaller leaves than the species. A respectable specimen grew in the White Garden, JC Raulston Arboretum, for many years.

'Eve Price' is a compact form with smaller leaves than the species and attractive red buds and pink-tinged flowers. Plant at Hillier was 15 feet by 10 feet with a strongly upright vase shape.

'French White' is a strong-growing form with large, white flower heads. Eighteen feet by 10 feet at Hillier in 1999.

'Froebelii' is compact with light green leaves and snow-white flowers.

'Gwenllian' grows 10 feet high and wide. Leaves are dark green. Flowers rich pink in bud, opening blush.

'Israel' has large leaves and waxy, clear white flowers.

'Little Bognor' is a compact selection that appeared to be the real deal when observed in a container at Wyevale Garden Center in England. Have not observed the plant since that 1999 sighting.

'Lucidum' is larger in all its parts, extremely lustrous dark green leaves, full and dense to ground, 12 feet high and wide at Hiller in 1999.

Viburnum tinus 'Bewley's Variegated' (above left)

Viburnum tinus 'Gwenllian' (above)

Viburnum tinus 'Compactum' (left)

Viburnum tinus 'Eve Price'

Viburnum tinus
'Israel' (right)

Viburnum tinus
'Lucidum' (below)

*Viburnum
tinus* 'Lucidum
Variegatum' (below
right)

Viburnum tinus
'Pink Prelude'
(bottom left)

Viburnum tinus
'Purpureum'
(bottom right)

'Lucidum Variegatum' has marble-like swirled green and white foliage but is unstable and will revert to green.

'Nutsy' is described as having deep green leaves, pink buds opening to pink-white flowers in late winter–early spring, and metallic deep blue fruits. Who named this?

'Pink Prelude' produces white flowers that age pink, 10 feet by 12 feet, dense, rounded with finer leaf texture.

'Purpureum' has purple young leaves that mature green, tinted red.

Subspecies *rigidum* (Vent.) P. Silva is the robust, large-leaf, quite hairy variation from the Canary Islands. Distinguished from *V. tinus* by the larger (up to 4 inches long), dull green, hairy leaves and more open habit. Also treated as a species, *V. rigidum* Vent.

'Robustum' is larger in its upright dense habit (15 feet) and leaf (4 inches), has deep green leaves, and blush-white flowers.

'Spectrum' ('Pyramidale') is erect, narrow-conical in habit. Witnessed an 8-by 8-foot plant, dense, rounded, healthy foliage, fine to medium texture at Hillier, 1 July 1999.

'Spirit' looks good in leaf with red-purple flower buds, opening white. More compact growth habit and earlier to flower than 'Spring Bouquet'. Supposedly grows *only* to 5 feet high, but is already larger than this in several southeastern gardens.

'Spring Bouquet' may be the same as 'Compactum' and offers dark red flower buds that open to white on a 5- to 6-foot-high and -wide compact plant.

Viburnum tinus 'Spectrum'

'Variegatum' is a handsome clone with conspicuous creamy yellow variegation. Not as cold hardy as the species. A 6- by 5-foot dense plant grew at Hillier in 1999.

Viburnum trilobum Marsh.
AMERICAN CRANBERRYBUSH VIBURNUM

Viburnum trilobum (or, as new nomenclature lists it, *V. opulus* L. var. *americanum* Ait.) is similar to *V. opulus* and frequently confused with that species. The singular *best* identification characteristic is the thinnish matchstick glands on the petiole of *V. trilobum*; those of *V. opulus* are squat and concave. Typically, aphids are less troublesome on *V. trilobum*, but this is a strange way to separate the two. Have the aphids sit at your dinner table, and unbeknownst to the little critters provide unmarked *V. trilobum* and *V. opulus* salads. You know where this is going . . .

Viburnum trilobum forms a 10-foot-high and -wide, rounded, multi-stem shrub. National champion, in Westcroft Gardens, Michigan, is 32 feet by 31 feet. The 3-lobed, 3- to 5-inch-long and -wide leaves, petiole ½ to 1 inch long, lustrous medium to dark green, develop yellow to red-purple fall color. Leaf undersides are not as pubescent as any *V. opulus* I examined. The young shoots are bronzy-red. Lacecap, 3- to 4½-inch-wide, flat-topped cymes, outer flowers sterile and showy, inner fertile, typically nonoffensive in odor, open in May. In full flower 20 April 2004 at the JC Raulston Arboretum, off-odor from the fertile flowers. Fruits like its European cousin, ripen yellow to red, and persist into winter. The nearly globose, ⅓-inch-wide drupes are bright red and are used for making jams and jellies. Culture is similar to that of *V. opulus*. I have observed

*Viburnum
trilobum*,
habit, flowers,
fruits, and fall
color

plants growing in water in Maine and Massachusetts. I cannot remember a thriving specimen in lower Zone 7 of the Southeast. Excellent plant for groupings, screens, shrub border. Leaves emerge early, often by early April in Chapel Hill, North Carolina. The compact cultivars are better suited to contemporary landscapes. Zones 3 to 7. Broad natural distribution from New Brunswick to British Columbia, south to New York, Michigan, South Dakota, and Oregon. Growing in wooded lakeshores; low, wet woods; moist, springy, rocky, brushy hillsides. Introduced 1812.

CULTIVARS & VARIETIES

'Andrews', 'Hahs', and 'Wentworth' have been selected for larger fruits. The story goes deeper than that, for in the early 1900s A. E. Morgan assembled over 3,000 seedlings from North America in Lee, Massachusetts. In 1921, the USDA took over the study and released the three just mentioned in 1922. They are early, mid, and late ripening, respectively, and were selected for edibility. I have observed 'Wentworth', and it is beautiful as the fruits pass from a yellow-red to bright red but, in my mind, is no better than other plants I have seen in various locations. It may have the best red fall color. 'Hahs' has large fruits and is popular in the Chicago region. 'Hahs' matures at a smaller size than the species, 6 to 8 feet high and wide, and produces 2- to 4-inch-wide cymes and attractive, neat, dark green foliage. Noted a 6-foot, compact specimen with more abundant fruit than 'Wentworth' at the Minnesota Landscape Arboretum on 20 July 2005. Listed as hardy to Zone 2. 'Wentworth', of the three, is the most available in commerce and grows 10 to 12 feet high and wide. Large, wild, loose, open, 15- by 15-foot specimen at Hillier, 2 July 1999.

'Alfredo' is similar to 'Compactum' but with a denser, broader habit, 5 to 6 feet high and wide, good summer foliage, and excellent red fall color. Supposedly quite aphid resistant. Selected by Alfredo Garcia, Bailey Nurseries, St. Paul, Minnesota. Flower and fruit set are sparse. Unfortunately, I have read literature that said fruit set was good.

'Bailey Compact' is another selection from Bailey Nurseries, with compact habit, 5 to 6 feet high and wide, deep red fall foliage, and moderate fruit.

'Compactum' is an excellent compact, dwarf form with good flowering and fruiting habit. The stems are much more slender and uniformly upright-spreading than its counterpart, *V. opulus* 'Compactum', and it grows about half the size of the species (6 feet). Fall color is not particularly good and is usually yellow at best. The entire taxonomy of this group is rather confusing, and I am not sure I can "unconfuse" it. True 'Compactum' is alternately listed as virtually sterile and heavy flowering and fruiting. In my Illinois garden, 'Compactum' grew with passion and flowered and fruited without any significant fall color. I

Viburnum trilobum 'Hahs' (top left)

Viburnum trilobum 'Wentworth' (above)

Viburnum trilobum 'Alfredo' (left)

Viburnum trilobum 'Bailey Compact'

Viburnum trilobum 'Compactum'

Viburnum trilobum 'Compactum', flowers

have a suspicion that lack of fruit set on 'Compactum' may be the result of the lack of a suitable cross-pollinator.

'Garry Pink' has pink flowers in cool, moist weather; if hot and dry, flowers are white. Discovered in 1962 in Fort Garry, Manitoba, Canada.

'Jewell Box' has a dwarf, compact habit described as resembling a cushion mum, 18 inches high by 24 to 30 inches wide. New foliage emerges red, then dark green, with a burgundy fall color. Flowering is virtually nil, but a few inflorescences were observed. Considered less susceptible to leaf spot than *V. opulus* 'Nanum'. Introduced by John Lindmeyer, formerly with Jewell Nursery, Wisconsin.

Leelanau Germplasm, from seed collected in 1981 in Leelanau County, Michigan, is offered by Rose Lake Plant Material Center, East Lansing, Michigan.

'Leonard's Dwarf' I have seen placed under *V. opulus*. It is vigorous and compact with broom-like branches. How different it is from other compact forms, I do not know.

'Manito' ('Manitou Pembina' by Dawes Arboretum, Newark, Ohio) was selected for large fruit size and named in 1947. Original plant grew by Lake Manitoba.

'Phillips' has deep wine-red fruits. This form flowers and fruits abundantly and free of the odor and flavor of the species, making it useful for jelly. Grows 8 to 10 feet high and wide on an upright habit with clean foliage. Zone 2 hardy. Introduced in 1956 by E. M. Meader, University of New Hampshire, Durham, who introduced many useful plants.

Redwing™ ('J. N. Select') produces a strong red flush of new growth and offers a neat, dense habit. The dark green leaves turn bright red in autumn. Three- to 4-inch-wide, white inflorescences and bright red, persistent fruits are also colorful. Matures 8 to 12 feet high and wide. Viburnum crown borer can be a problem. Selected by Michael Yanny in 1983 and introduced by Johnson's Nursery, Menomonee Falls, Wisconsin.

'Spring Green Compact' is more refined than the species in flower, foliage, and fruit. It produces excellent red fruits and orange-red fall color on a 3- to 4-foot-high shrub.

'Spring Red Compact' has new reddish growth that turns green at maturity, good orange-red fall color, and a limited fruit set. It is somewhat upright in growth habit, maturing 3 to 5 feet high.

Viburnum utile Hemsl.
SERVICE VIBURNUM

Seldom available in commerce, *V. utile* is nevertheless one of the most important evergreen species for breeding: the fine glossy character of its superior dark green foliage often appears in its offspring. Consider *V. ×burkwoodii* (*V. utile* × *V. carlesii*) and its many cultivars; 'Cayuga' × *V. utile* and the resultant 'Chesapeake' and 'Eskimo'; *V. utile* × *V. ×burkwoodii* 'Park Farm Hybrid' and the beautiful 'Conoy' to fully comprehend the opportunity for viburnum improvement via *V. utile* input. I collected two forms, both with silvery undersided leaves. One had 2- to 2½-inch-long, ½-inch-wide leaves; the other had 3½-inch-long, 1½-inch-wide leaves. Difficult to believe they are from the same species.

Service viburnum is a small evergreen shrub, 4 to 6 feet high and wide, of rather straggly habit. There was a 4- by 5-foot, wispy shrub at Hillier, 1 July 1999.

Viburnum utile,
habit, foliage,
flowers, and
immature fruits

Viburnum veitchii
(bottom right)

The leaves have a rather wavy and at times almost inrolled (revolute) appearance. They are ovate to oblong, 1 to 3 inches long, ¼ to 1¼ inch wide, obtuse, rarely acutish, broad-cuneate or rounded, entire, leathery, lustrous dark green and glabrous above, prominently veined (5 to 6 pairs) and white beneath with a dense covering of stellate hairs; petiole is ⅙ to ⅓ inch long. The pink-budded, slightly fragrant, white flowers occur in early to mid April (Athens) in 5-rayed, 2- to 3-inch-wide, rounded cymes. In full flower, late April 1999 at Hillier, with slight to no fragrance. Flowers occur in great profusion, a genetic characteristic that can be utilized to enhance flowering potential of hybrids. I see this increase in floral quantity in *V.* 'Pragense'. The fruit is a ¼-inch-long, bluish black drupe. Fruits on our two Georgia accessions have started red, a deep red, before maturing black.

The species is seldom seen in gardens and is not the handsomest of plants, owing to the open habit, small leaves, and rather nondescript flowers; however, it carries genes for heat tolerance, and old plants at Callaway Gardens, Pine Mountain, Georgia, and in Aiken, South Carolina, attest to this. Lancaster (1989) reported the species growing among scrubby vegetation in China, and a small plant in the Dirr garden reminded of the power of the great plant breeders: our gardens are blessed because certain individuals see and seize the future. I notice that hybrids involving *V. utile* are more resistant to deer browsing; and *V.* ×*burkwoodii* and *V.* 'Pragense' are more resistant to the viburnum beetle (Weston 2004; see chapter 5). Grows on limestone in its native habitat, a fact that explains its and its progeny's tolerance to calcareous and high pH soils. Zones 6 to 8. Native to central China. Introduced in 1901 by E. H. Wilson.

Viburnum veitchii C. H. Wright
VEITCH VIBURNUM

Observed at Kew Gardens on 14 June 1999 with the field note that the 8-foot-high plant looked like *V. lantana*, *V. veitchii* is considered more ornamental and smaller in stature at maturity. Upright, vase-shaped, coarse plant, 10 feet by 6 feet, with clean foliage at Hillier, 2 July 1999. The dark green, ovate leaves, 3 to 5 inches long, 2 to 3 inches wide, sharply and remotely serrated, are grayish and densely pubescent below, with a ½-inch-long, pubescent petiole. The white flowers are borne in 3- to 5-inch-wide, approximately 7-rayed, flat-topped cymes in May. The ellipsoidal, ⅓-inch-long fruit begins red and matures black. Treat like *V. lantana* in the garden. Differs from *V. lantana* in the more remote marginal serrations. Zones 6 and 7. Native to China. Introduced in 1901 by E. H. Wilson.

Viburnum wilsonii Rehd.

WILSON VIBURNUM

In deference to the great plant explorer E. H. Wilson, I include this species, which I've sighted only twice in English gardens. A 10-foot-high plant at RHS Hyde Hall piqued my interest; however, the sharply toothed, ovate leaves created some doubt about authenticity. Typically a loose, open, 7- to 10-foot-high and -wide shrub; 8- by 8-foot plant at Hillier in 1999, two 12-foot-high plants at Hillier, 31 May 2006. The dark green leaves, 2 to 3½ inches long, 1 to 1¾ inches wide, 6 to 7 vein pairs, are toothed along the margin. Essentially glabrous (non-hairy) below except for pubescence on the veins. Petiole hairy, about ½ inch long. The white flowers are held in 2- to 3-inch-wide, 5- to 6-rayed cymes on an approximately 1-inch-long, yellowish, pubescent peduncle in May–June. The ⅓-inch-long, oval fruits are bright red and pubescent. The young shoots are bronze-brown, quite pubescent, becoming dark purple with age. Appears adaptable. Zones 5 and 6. Native to central and western China. Introduced in 1908 from Sichuan by E. H. Wilson.

Viburnum wrightii Miq.

WRIGHT VIBURNUM

Wright viburnum is similar to *V. dilatatum* but differs in its larger leaves and the relative absence of pubescence on the stem and inflorescence. The leaves are simple, ovate or broad-ovate, 3 to 5 inches long, 2 to 3 inches wide, abruptly acuminate, rounded or broad-cuneate at base, coarsely dentate, dark green and glabrous above, and essentially glabrous beneath except for tufts of hairs in axils of veins, with 6 to 10 vein pairs and a petiole that is ¼ to ¾ inch long. I have seen true *V. wrightii* enough times to be able to separate it from *V. dilatatum*. The habit is upright-rounded, 6 to 10 feet high. The white flowers occur in 5-rayed, 2- to 4-inch-wide, flat-topped cymes in late April–May, and are subtended by the dark green foliage. The round-ovoid red fruits average about ⅓ inch in length and are quite showy, ripening in August and persisting. The dark metallic green leaves may turn a good red in fall. Might add that what is sold or labeled as *V. wrightii* is in most situations *V. dilatatum*. Zones 5 to 7. Possibly, slightly more cold hardy than *V. dilatatum*. Native to China, Korea, and Japan. Introduced in 1892 by C. S. Sargent.

CULTIVARS & VARIETIES

Varieties *eglandulosum* Nakai and *stipellatum* Nakai are listed.

'Hessei' [var. *hessei* (Koehne) Rehd.] is a compact form with attractive dark

Viburnum wilsonii

Viburnum wrightii, habit, foliage, and fruits

green summer and red fall foliage and sealing-wax red fruits. Flowers, white, are produced in 2-inch-wide cymes. In full flower 26 April 1999 at Hillier and my field notes state, "Actually fragrant." Apparently many plants were grown from seed collected by C. S. Sargent, Arnold Arboretum, by Hesse Nurseries, Germany. 'Hessei' has occasionally been listed as superior, but one person's 'Hessei' may not be the same as another's. 'Hessei' was 7 feet by 8 feet, dense, with clean foliage and a heavy fruit set on 30 June 1999 at Hillier. Appears to have less pubescence than the species. Japan and Korea. Introduced 1909.

Viburnum wrightii 'Hessei', foliage and flowers

CHAPTER 3

Breeding

DON EGOLF OPENED the wide window of opportunity for viburnum improvement with his 1956 dissertation work at Cornell and throughout his distinguished career at the U.S. National Arboretum. He released 18 viburnums, some resulting from open-pollinated seedling material, others from controlled crosses. A table of his viburnum introductions and available literature citations (for those seeking in-depth botanical descriptions), concludes this chapter, along with another table, after his 1956 dissertation, on *Viburnum* chromosome numbers. The article by Kathleen Fisher (1989) is required reading.

I read Egolf's Ph.D. dissertation and wondered how one man could accomplish so much with a difficult-to-breed and -germinate (= time-consuming evaluation), taxonomically variable genus. Most seedlings from Egolf's crosses were generated via embryo rescue, which involved extracting embryos, often immature, and culturing them on an agar-based medium with supplements (he noted that the addition of adenine sulfate to the medium yielded the greatest regeneration of whole plants). A list of Egolf's successful crosses (i.e., those resulting in fruits and, more importantly, plants) follows. Anyone pondering *Viburnum* breeding should reflect on his successes (and failures). The greatest successes were achieved among closely related *Viburnum* taxa (species and varieties).

Viburnum acerifolium × *V. acerifolium*
Viburnum ×*burkwoodii* × *V. carlesii*
Viburnum ×*burkwoodii* × *V. farreri*
Viburnum ×*burkwoodii* × *V. suspensum*

Viburnum carlesii × *V. bitchiuense*
Viburnum carlesii × *V.* ×*burkwoodii*
Viburnum carlesii × *V.* ×*carlcephalum*
Viburnum carlesii × *V. farreri*

Viburnum cassinoides × *V. cassinoides*
Viburnum cassinoides × *V. dentatum*
Viburnum cassinoides × *V. opulus*
Viburnum cassinoides × *V. rafinesquianum*
Viburnum cassinoides × *V. setigerum*
Viburnum dentatum × *V. dentatum*
Viburnum dentatum × *V. dentatum* var.
   pubescens
Viburnum dentatum × *V. rafinesquianum*
Viburnum dentatum × *V. setigerum*
Viburnum dentatum var. *pubescens* ×
   V. dentatum var. *pubescens*
Viburnum dentatum var. *pubescens* ×
   V. rafinesquianum
Viburnum dilatatum × *V. acerifolium*
Viburnum dilatatum × *V. dentatum*
Viburnum dilatatum × *V. dilatatum*
Viburnum dilatatum × *V. lobophyllum*
Viburnum dilatatum × *V. setigerum*
Viburnum dilatatum × *V. wrightii*
Viburnum farreri × *V. carlesii*
Viburnum farreri × *V. plicatum* f.
   tomentosum
Viburnum lantana × *V. lantana*
Viburnum lantana × *V. rhytidophyllum*
Viburnum lentago × *V. lantana*
Viburnum lentago × *V. lentago*
Viburnum lentago × *V. prunifolium*
Viburnum lentago × *V. rhytidophyllum*
Viburnum molle × *V. molle*
Viburnum opulus × *V. opulus*
Viburnum opulus × *V. trilobum*

Viburnum plicatum f. *tomentosum* ×
   V. lantanoides
Viburnum prunifolium × *V. carlesii*
Viburnum prunifolium × *V. farreri*
Viburnum prunifolium × *V. prunifolium*
Viburnum rhytidophyllum × *V. lantana*
Viburnum setigerum × *V. farreri*
Viburnum setigerum × *V. prunifolium*
Viburnum setigerum × *V. rhytidophyllum*
Viburnum setigerum × *V. setigerum*
Viburnum sieboldii × *V.* ×*burkwoodii*
Viburnum sieboldii × *V. carlesii*
Viburnum sieboldii × *V. farreri*
Viburnum sieboldii × *V. lantana*
Viburnum sieboldii × *V. lentago*
Viburnum sieboldii × *V. plicatum* f.
   tomentosum
Viburnum sieboldii × *V. prunifolium*
Viburnum sieboldii × *V. setigerum*
Viburnum sieboldii × *V. sieboldii*
Viburnum suspensum × *V.* ×*burkwoodii*
Viburnum suspensum × *V. carlesii*
Viburnum suspensum × *V. farreri*
Viburnum tinus × *V.* ×*burkwoodii*
Viburnum tinus × *V. cinnamomifolium*
Viburnum tinus × *V. farreri*
Viburnum tinus × *V. lantana*
Viburnum tinus × *V. tinus*
Viburnum trilobum × *V. opulus*
Viburnum trilobum × *V. orientale*
Viburnum trilobum × *V. trilobum*

I had often wondered why Egolf was one of the few to develop viburnum improvement programs. The answer is *time*. Evaluation time for making selections is five to ten years, often longer. From our work, now in the fifth year from germination, we have targeted two open-pollinated seedlings of 'Mohawk' and one of 'Eskimo'. Another two to three years of parallel evaluation and stock increase; a final decision to release and market; and then into commerce.

In April 2003, I successfully crossed (controlled) *V. ×burkwoodii* 'Park Farm Hybrid' ('PFH') (female) with *V. macrocephalum* f. *keteleeri*. Fruits were harvested in the fall, cleaned, warm stratified for three months (followed by cold), and sown. Twenty-two seedlings were grown to transplanting size and outplanted in November 2005. The plants show a range of foliage types intermediate in foliage but without flower buds. Their first winter (low of 15°F), some were totally deciduous; others completely evergreen. I wait for flowers! Taking these a generation further (F$_2$) would yield even greater variation than the controlled F$_1$. Segregation of traits (characteristics) is greater in the F$_2$, yielding seedlings with untold promise. At times it is advisable to backcross to the original parents to incorporate more of the characteristics for fragrance ('PFH'), evergreenness ('PFH'), and size of flower (f. *keteleeri*). All this crossing increases the years before new viburnums will find their way into our gardens. Egolf carried some of

Viburnum ×burkwoodii 'Mohawk' seedlings, October 2002 (above)

Viburnum ×burkwoodii 'Mohawk' seedlings, five months later (left)

Viburnum ×burk-woodii 'Mohawk' seedlings flowering in March 2006, 3½ years old (above)

Viburnum ×burk-woodii 'Park Farm Hybrid' × *V. macro-cephalum* f. *keteleeri* seedlings, showing re-markable variation in foliage (right)

the Cornell germplasm to the U.S. National Arboretum, with some of the resultant introductions consuming 20 or more years. I doubt whether another Egolf will surface because of the current penchant for instant gratification. Great viburnums cannot be hurried!

Others bred viburnums but not with the sustained effort of Egolf. *Viburnum ×burkwoodii* was developed by Albert Burkwood and Geoffrey Skipwith in England; the cross was made in 1914, and the plant introduced in 1924. 'Anne Russell' resulted from a backcross of *V. carlesii* × *V. ×burkwoodii* in 1951 at L. R. Russell, Ltd., England. *Viburnum ×juddii* was raised at the Arnold Arboretum by propagator William H. Judd in 1920; the plant flowered for the first time in 1929 and was named in 1935. Leslie Slinger, Slieve Donard Nursery, Ireland, using imported seed of *V. carlesii* from Japan, selected and hybridized, finally introducing 'Aurora', 'Charis', and 'Diana' in 1958.

Harold Pellett, University of Minnesota, crossed *V. ×rhytidophylloides* 'Alleghany' with *V. burejaeticum*, which resulted in the 1994 introduction of 'Emerald Triumph'. Brent McCown, University of Wisconsin, reports that he is in the final stages for about ten releases; plants were selected from a segregating population produced by intermating F_1 hybrids resulting from successful *V. lantana* × *V. carlesii* crosses.

Many nurseries (Lake County, Beaver Creek, Johnson's, Shadow) have made selections of open-pollinated seedlings and introduced new *Viburnum* cultivars. Margaret Pooler, U.S. National Arboretum, continues to evaluate Egolf's seedlings as well as her own viburnum crosses. Margaret and I plan to evaluate the material in 2007 for possible release. Certainly, thresholds for viburnum improvement have yet to be crossed. Opportunities abound for the adventuresome—and patient—plant breeder.

VIBURNUM BREEDING PROTOCOLS

My expertise in making crosses is limited, but observation and the literature point to several key approaches. Many viburnums are self-sterile and require another seedling, clone, or closely related species to promote abundant fruit set. Certainly, cultivars within *V. dilatatum* require the outside pollen source. Conversely, *V. bracteatum* sets great quantities of blue fruits with no pollinator in sight. I assume the species is self-fertile, a condition that appears to apply to the *V. dentatum* complex.

We learned from our work with *Hydrangea* species that it is always wise to remove the stamens from flowers that will be pollinated. Do this before anthers reach anthesis (pollen shedding). Pollen from the male source can then be applied to the stigma of the female with a fine camel-hair brush or simply by touching the stamen to the stigma. Crosses should be done reciprocally, with each plant serving as the maternal and paternal parent. For various reasons, a cross will succeed in one direction but not the other. Inflorescences, after crossing, can be covered with a bag or mesh material and labeled with a string tag using pencil. We used the mesh to keep birds from taking the fruits. If pollinations are made in the field, this is a must; if in the greenhouse or screen cages, then the problem of fruit loss is minimized.

Egolf covered ten unemasculated (stamens still present) inflorescences of each species with protective bags, and no fruits resulted. A small percentage of seed was obtained by self-pollination of these same species. He concluded that viburnums are more frequently cross-pollinated and usually require insects or wind to transfer the pollen from the anther to the short style in the base of each flower.

To synchronize pollen availability with female receptivity (and flowering), it is possible to store pollen in a viable state for six months. Also, branches of later-flowering species can be forced in a warm environment to advance viable pollen to coincide with the early-flowering species.

Fruit and seed collection, cleaning, and germination requirements are discussed in the propagation chapter, chapter 6.

TABLE 1. Egolf introductions.

SELECTION	ORIGIN	RELEASED	INTRODUCED
'Alleghany'	Selection from an F$_2$ *V. rhytidophyllum* × *V. lantana* 'Mohican' seedling population	1966	Egolf 1966b
'Catskill'	Open-pollinated seedling selection from Japanese seed	1966	Egolf 1966b
'Cayuga'	*V. carlesii* × *V.* ×*carlcephalum*	1966	Egolf 1966a
'Chesapeake'	'Cayuga' × *V. utile*	1980	Egolf 1981a
'Chippewa'	*V. japonicum* × *V. dilatatum* 'Catskill'	1986	Egolf 1987
'Conoy'	*V. utile* × *V.* ×*burkwoodii* 'Park Farm Hybrid'	1988	Egolf 1988
'Cree'	From *V. rhytidophyllum*; a result of Egolf's pioneering work but a USNA introduction	1994	1994
'Erie'	From *V. dilatatum*; open-pollinated seed from Japan	1970	Egolf 1971
'Eskimo'	'Cayuga' × *V. utile*	1980	Egolf 1981b
'Huron'	*V. lobophyllum* × *V. japonicum*	1986	Egolf 1987
'Iroquois'	Cross between two *V. dilatatum* selections	1966	Egolf 1966b
'Mohawk'	*V.* ×*burkwoodii* × *V. carlesii*	1966	Egolf 1966a
'Mohican'	Seedling selected from open-pollinated *V. lantana* from Poland	1966	Egolf 1966b
'Oneida'	*V. dilatatum* × *V. lobophyllum*	1966	Egolf 1966b
'Onondaga'	From *V. sargentii* (self)	1966	Egolf 1966b
'Seneca'	Self-pollination of *V. sieboldii*	1966	Egolf 1966b
'Shasta'	F$_2$ *V. plicatum* f. *tomentosum* × *V. plicatum* f. *tomentosum* 'Mariesii'	1978	Egolf 1979
'Shoshoni'	Seedling of 'Shasta' (self)	1986	Egolf 1986
'Susquehanna'	Open-pollinated seedling of *V. sargentii* from Province Matsu, Hondo, Japan	1966	Egolf 1966b

TABLE 2. *Viburnum* chromosome numbers from Egolf 1956. Diploid: 2n = 18.

TAXA	NUMBER OF CHROMOSOMES	TAXA	NUMBER OF CHROMOSOMES
Viburnum acerifolium	18	*Viburnum farreri*	16
Viburnum atrocyaneum	18	*Viburnum farreri* 'Candidissimum'	16
Viburnum betulifolium	18	*Viburnum farreri* 'Nanum'	16
Viburnum bitchiuense	18	*Viburnum foetidum*	18
Viburnum ×*bodnantense*	16	*Viburnum foetidum* var. rectangulatum	18
Viburnum bracteatum	72	*Viburnum furcatum*	18
Viburnum buddleifolium	18	*Viburnum grandiflorum*	16
Viburnum burejaeticum	18	*Viburnum grandiflorum* f. *foetens*	16
Viburnum ×*burkwoodii*	18	*Viburnum harryanum*	18
Viburnum ×*burkwoodii* 'Carlotta'	18	*Viburnum hartwegii*	18
Viburnum ×*burkwoodii* 'Chenaultii'	18	*Viburnum henryi*	32
Viburnum ×*burkwoodii* 'Park Farm Hybrid'	18	*Viburnum hupehense*	18
Viburnum calvum	18	*Viburnum ichangense*	18
Viburnum ×*carlcephalum*	18	*Viburnum* ×*jackii*	18
Viburnum carlesii	18, 20, 22 depending on seed source	*Viburnum japonicum*	18
		Viburnum ×*juddii*	18
Viburnum cassinoides	18	*Viburnum kansuense*	18
Viburnum cassinoides 'Nanum'	18	*Viburnum lantana* and cultivars	18
Viburnum cinnamomifolium	18	*Viburnum lantanoides*	18
Viburnum cotinifolium	18	*Viburnum lentago*	18
Viburnum cylindricum	18	*Viburnum lobophyllum*	18, 27
Viburnum davidii	18	*Viburnum macrocephalum*	18
Viburnum dentatum	36	*Viburnum macrocephalum* f. *keteleeri*	18
Viburnum dentatum var. *deamii*	72		
Viburnum dentatum var. *pubescens*	72, 36	*Viburnum molle*	36
Viburnum dentatum var. *scabrellum*	72	*Viburnum mongolicum*	18
		Viburnum nudum	18
Viburnum dilatatum	18	*Viburnum odoratissimum*	32, 40
Viburnum dilatatum f. *hispidum*	18	*Viburnum opulus* and cultivars	18
Viburnum dilatatum f. *pilosum*	18	*Viburnum orientale*	18
Viburnum dilatatum 'Xanthocarpum'	18	*Viburnum phlebotricum*	36
Viburnum edule	18	*Viburnum plicatum*	16
Viburnum ellipticum	18	*Viburnum plicatum* 'Grandiflorum'	16
Viburnum erosum	18	*Viburnum plicatum* 'Rotundifolium'	16
Viburnum erubescens	32	*Viburnum plicatum* f. *tomentosum*	16, 18
Viburnum erubescens var. *gracilipes*	32	*Viburnum plicatum* f. *tomentosum* 'Lanarth'	16

TAXA	NUMBER OF CHROMOSOMES	TAXA	NUMBER OF CHROMOSOMES
Viburnum plicatum f. *tomentosum* 'Mariesii'	16	*Viburnum sempervirens*	18
Viburnum plicatum f. *tomentosum* 'Roseum'	16	*Viburnum setigerum*	36, 18 listed once
		Viburnum setigerum 'Aurantiacum'	36
Viburnum plicatum f. *tomentosum* 'Rowallane'	16	*Viburnum sieboldii*	32, 16 listed once
Viburnum plicatum f. *tomentosum* 'St. Keverne'	16	*Viburnum suspensum*	16
Viburnum propinquum	18	*Viburnum sympodiale*	18
Viburnum prunifolium	18	*Viburnum tinus*	36
Viburnum rafinesquianum	36	*Viburnum tinus* 'French White'	36
Viburnum recognitum	18	*Viburnum tinus* 'Lucidum'	72
Viburnum ×*rhytidocarpum*	18	*Viburnum tinus* 'Lucidum Variegatum'	72
Viburnum ×*rhytidophylloides*	18	*Viburnum tinus* 'Purpureum'	36
Viburnum rhytidophyllum	18	*Viburnum tinus* 'Variegatum'	36
Viburnum rigidum	18	*Viburnum trilobum* and cultivars	18
Viburnum rufidulum	18	*Viburnum urceolatum*	18
Viburnum sargentii	18	*Viburnum utile*	18
Viburnum sargentii var. *calvescens*	18	*Viburnum veitchii*	18
Viburnum sargentii 'Flavum'	18	*Viburnum wilsonii*	18
Viburnum sargentii 'Puberulum'	18	*Viburnum wrightii*	18
Viburnum schensianum	18		

Viburnum plicatum f. *tomentosum* 'Lanarth'

CHAPTER 4

Planting, Pruning, Fertilization, and Landscape Uses

Viburnums are remarkably adaptable garden plants, more so (from a soil standpoint) than most woody shrubs. Well-drained, slightly acid, moist soils support the growth of most species. Several—*V. cassinoides, V. nudum, V. opulus, V. trilobum*—grow on wet soils in nature but are at home in the situation just described. *Viburnum lantana, V. opulus*, and others grow on chalk (i.e., high pH) soils. Viburnums, in general, possess a greater tolerance to higher pH soils than many shrub genera. Best flowering and fruiting typically occur in full sun to partial shade, but, again, there are exceptions: *V. acerifolium, V. lantanoides, V. nudum, V. prunifolium*, and *V. rafinesquianum* are native to shady, understory woodlands, either on the edges or under the canopy. Plants in shade are more open, becoming more restrained in habit in sun.

PLANTING

Viburnums are better transplanted from containers or as balled-and-burlapped larger material. Container-grown plants can be transplanted year-round, with spring and fall most ideal. Balled-and-burlapped plants are best moved when dormant, although plants pre-dug and stored in organic matter can be transplanted later.

Viburnums do not respond well to high rootball temperatures, and container plants should be installed immediately. Nurseries successfully grow viburnums in containers but do not carry them over for long periods. Also, the larger the growing container, the greater the protection against extreme heat and also cold. Look for white roots on the outside of the container medium. Simply removing the ball from the plastic container will tell a tale about the health of the root system. The more white roots, the better. If roots are matted, make five or six vertical slits around the rootball, running top to bottom, before planting.

Always plant with the top of the rootball at or slightly above the surface of the soil. Water thoroughly and mulch with 2 to 3 inches of organic compost. Small amounts of fertilizer can be applied at time of planting, but I usually wait a month or so after. Remember—less is more. Too much fertilizer can burn or kill, particularly young plants.

PRUNING

Pruning is straightforward on viburnums since almost all flower on previous year's wood. This means flower buds are formed in summer–fall, opening the following spring. The naked flower buds of *V. bitchiuense*, *V. ×burkwoodii*, *V. carlesii*, and related taxa are evident by late May–early June in Athens. *Viburnum farreri*, *V. grandiflorum*, and *V. ×bodnantense* spit flowers from fall into early spring, depending on temperatures. *Viburnum plicatum* f. *tomentosum* 'Summer Snowflake' shows a remontant (reblooming) propensity and will flower heavily in April–May and then sporadically into summer–early fall. *Viburnum macrocephalum* flowers magnificently in April (Athens) and again in October with a respectable show.

Viburnums do not require heavy-handed, butcher-shop type pruning. Tidying and shaping with hand pruners is best. I shorten (to the nodes) extended shoots, and the buds below are then released and form new shoots. With *V. macrocephalum*, I utilize a bow-saw, cutting the large branches to 18 inches from the ground (winter), with abundant new growth the following year and *no* flowers; in the second year following pruning, flowers again are formed in profusion.

My take on the best timing for pruning is after flowering. This allows sufficient time for the resultant regrowth to form new flower buds. Late pruning, September–October, should be avoided because the new growth may not properly harden by the time freezing temperatures occur.

Several viburnums (see the section on landscape uses, later in this chapter) serve as functional blocks of green. Traditional hedge shears, hand or powered, can be utilized, but may result in browned edges. Feather pruning with a hand pruner is best but time-consuming, as it involves removal of every other shoot, every other year; this results in a more aesthetic, not-as-blocky hedge.

The fragrant-flowered viburnums and several nonfragrant species—*V. bitchiuense*, *V. ×burkwoodii*, *V. ×carlcephalum*, *V. carlesii*, *V. ×juddii*, *V. lantana*, *V. rhytidophyllum*, *V. ×rhytidophylloides*, *V.* 'Pragense'—develop naked flower buds that look like small gray to brown cauliflowers, usually with a pair of strap-shaped leaves subtending the flower. When pruning, it is easy to recognize the flower buds. *Viburnum cassinoides*, *V. lentago*, *V. nudum*, *V. prunifolium*, *V. rufidulum*, and other species have bulbous flower buds with two extended, acuminate scales covering their parts. In *V. dentatum* and related species, *V. opulus* and related species, and *V. plicatum*, flower and vegetative buds are similar with both flower and shoot (leaf and stem) originating from the same bud. These are covered by two or more scales.

Pruning viburnums should be an exercise in restraint. Again, as with so many things, less is more. The species and cultivars are genetically well-mannered and groomed. Proper viburnum selection for the allotted garden space eliminates the need for heavy-handed pruning.

FERTILIZATION

Viburnums prosper quite well on a restricted fertilization diet. Most appear healthy under everyday garden conditions. As I pen this, I am trying, and failing, to recall truly lousy viburnums in the landscape. If plants are kept in containers too long, they become stunted, thin, and scraggly, with off-color (yellow) foliage.

In my garden, viburnums and other shrubs are fertilized in late winter with the recommended rate of 10-10-10 plus minor elements. Depending on the species or cultivar, the new spring growth extensions should average 6 to 12 inches in length. Viburnums will continue to grow into summer when provided moisture and fertilizer. A second application (one-half recommended rate) can be applied after flowering. If fruit set is heavy, considerable leaf tissue nitrogen is translocated to the maturing fruits. This can induce off-color (lighter) green leaves that subtend the fruit clusters. I have observed this with *V. lantana*, *V. rhytidophyllum* and *V. ×rhytidophylloides*.

Certainly, slow-release fertilizers like Osmocote® (The Scotts Company, www.scottsprohort.com/products/fertilizers/osmocote.cfm) and Nutricote® (Sun Gro Horticulture, www.sungro.com/products_displayProBrand.php?brand_id=6) are suitable as well, or water-soluble formulations like Miracle-Gro® (also from The Scotts Company, www.miraclegro.com). Always follow the rates, and never *overapply* any fertilizer.

Soils enriched with rotted and composted manures and other organic materials provide ideal havens for viburnums and reduce the need for supplemental fertilizer. Mulches of composted leaves also hold moisture, suppress weeds, and provide nutrients through chemical decomposition.

LANDSCAPE USES

Viburnums run the gamut as far as landscape applications. A specimen like *V. plicatum* f. *tomentosum*, aesthetically situated, holds court. This plant excels in sun and shade, becoming more open in the latter *but* still producing great quantities of flowers.

My affection for *V. ×burkwoodii* and the spicy-fragrant taxa is well documented. Any location where gardeners (and normal human beings) pass is perfect. The sweet perfume is similar to the best *Daphne odora*. I often pinch a flower and take an occasional (okay, prolonged) whiff when walking the garden. These viburnums are ideal shrub border plants and are easy to mesh in sunny borders and woodland edges.

In recent years, 'Conoy' and 'Eskimo' have been utilized in large groupings and massings. Sarah P. Duke Gardens, Durham, North Carolina, has a large mass of 'Eskimo' that has flowered spectacularly.

Although I dislike seeing viburnums chopped into hedges, certain species (*V. awabuki*, *V. dentatum*, *V. obovatum*, *V. odoratissimum*, *V. suspensum*, *V. tinus*) do make great hedging plants. Obviously, flowers and fruits are minimized or lost because of the repetitive pruning. In England, *V. tinus* is commonly utilized for screening and hedging. I have observed this species in full sun and deep shade, forming solid hedges; I have not observed many hedging plants that produce a more beautiful structure.

For wildlife, particularly birds, viburnums have few equals. *Viburnum plicatum* f. *tomentosum* fruits ripen in June, *V. dentatum* in summer–fall, with *V. dilatatum* persisting into winter. The birds are treated to a buffet of fruits. In cultivated areas, seedlings of *V. plicatum* f. *tomentosum* are common, resulting from bird planting.

Viburnums, like hydrangeas, cast a spell over collector gardeners. One is never enough. Eugene W. Coffman, Ridge Road Nursery, Bellevue, Iowa, reports testing 60 viburnums with 40 surviving (Zone 4). Lake County Nursery, Perry, Ohio, offers 31 types in the 2007–08 wholesale catalog. Wonderful collections of viburnums are displayed at the Arnold Arboretum, Jamaica Plain, Massachusetts; Minnesota Landscape Arboretum, Chanhassen; Dawes Arboretum, Newark, Ohio; U.S. National Arboretum, Washington, D.C.; University of Washington Arboretum, Seattle; Spring Grove and Mt. Airy Arboreta, Cincinnati, Ohio; and the Bernheim Arboretum, Clermont, Kentucky. These and many other collections around the United States provide the opportunities to appreciate and study the genus.

One, several, or many viburnums are primed for inclusion in your garden. Peruse the plants, whether in the landscape or in text and photographs, and allow your garden heart to choose. Then the adventure begins . . . Enjoy!

CHAPTER 5

Diseases, Insects, and Pests

For the greatest part, viburnums are trouble-free flowering shrubs, with few debilitating pests. Consider *Rosa* and the numerous diseases and insects afflicting the genus. Then consider *Viburnum*, and ask the question: does any gardener ever comment about keeping viburnums clean? The answer is No!

DISEASES

Viburnums, blessedly, are largely free of diseases. Bacterial leaf spot (black lesions on leaves) usually initiates on older leaves, causing leaves to drop prematurely; I see minimal examples of this.

Sudden oak death (SOD), caused by *Phytophthora ramorum*, also infects *Viburnum* species, although, again, I have yet to see it on viburnums. Diseased plants show wilting symptoms. Leaves are often affected first at their tips, and the brown discoloration spreads toward the base of the leaf in a V-shaped pattern. At later stages, individual stems die; death of the entire plant may occur within several days of the initial infection. *Viburnum* species known to be infected by SOD include *V. ×bodnantense*, *V. farreri*, *V. plicatum*, and *V. tinus*. The greatest threat is not to *Viburnum* but its capacity as a host and the subsequent transfer of the disease to the forests, where the red oak group is particularly susceptible. Approximately 23 species in 12 plant families have been naturally infected by SOD. Species in the Ericaceae (*Arctostaphylos*, *Pieris*, *Rhododendron*) and Fagaceae (*Quercus*) are especially prone to infection.

Other diseases that occasionally affect viburnums are crown gall, rusts, spot anthracnose, and verticillium wilt. Diseases specific to viburnums are presented in the table that follows.

TABLE 3. *Viburnum* diseases as compiled by Gary Moorman,
Pennsylvania State University, www.ppath.cas.psu.edu.

DISEASE	SYMPTOMS	PATHOGEN/CAUSE	MANAGEMENT
Botryosphaeria canker	Leaves on affected branches wilt and die. Branches die back and become covered with dark brown to black pimple-like fungal fruiting structures. Wood under the bark is dark brown.	*Botryosphaeria*	Plants most susceptible are those under drought stress. Therefore, provide sufficient water. Prune infected branches.
Downy mildew	Angular spots limited in shape by the leaf veins form blotches that die and shrivel in the spring when the weather is wet. Severely affected leaves fall. Light-colored fungal growth sparsely covers the spots on the underside of the leaf.	*Plasmopara viburni*	Rake and destroy fallen leaves in the autumn. Avoid overhead irrigation in the spring.
Powdery mildew	White fungal growth forms on the upper surface of leaves.	*Erysiphe* or *Phyllactinia*	No control is recommended since little damage occurs.

INSECTS

Viburnum aphid is common on *V. opulus*, particularly the new shoots. Have seen on *V. carlesii* in Maine. Causes curling, stunting, and malformation, and reduces flower impact. Other insects that may affect viburnums include the following:

- Asiatic garden beetle
- citrus flatid planthopper
- dogwood twig borer
- potato flea beetle
- scales
- tarnished plant bug
- thrips

The viburnum beetle (*Pyrrhalta viburni*) is a serious problem in upstate New York and New England, and I observed the deleterious effects on various *Viburnum* species in the Rochester parks. The larvae and adult beetles feed on leaves and can kill a shrub in as little as two to three years. Paul Weston, Cornell University, Ithaca, New York, has studied this pest and published the best information on biology, host resistance, and environmental effects. His work is reproduced and cited herein (Weston 2004); see http://www.hort.cornell.edu/vlb/.

A European native, the beetle was sighted in Canada in 1947 and first reached U.S. soil in 1994, in Maine, whence it has spread, fluidly, moving south and west with nursery stock.

Severe aphid infestation on *Viburnum opulus* (above left)

Pyrrhalta viburni larvae feeding on lower surface of *Viburnum opulus* 'Park Harvest' (above)

Viburnum beetle damage on *Viburnum dentatum* (left)

In North America, *Pyrrhalta viburni* overwinters in the egg stage. From July to October, adult females chew holes in small stems/branches and oviposit eggs, up to 500 by a single insect. Eggs hatch the next year in May, and the larvae feed on the underside of the tender leaves, leaving only midribs and major veins intact. By late June, larvae drop to the soil and pupate, with adults emerging in July to feed on the foliage and start the cycle. Eggs require a significant chilling period before they hatch. Eggs held at 41°F are not capable of hatching if the chilling period is less than four months. This may preclude the spread of the viburnum beetle into the southern states.

Control involves planting resistant species, removing infested stems after egg-laying has ceased, or chemical pesticides. Check with your local extension agent for the best and safest chemicals, if you choose this route. See Weston et al. 2002 for an evaluation of insecticides.

The following are viburnum beetle resistance/susceptibility ratings as compiled by Paul Weston (2004); those marked with an asterisk are based on observations at the Van Dusen Botanical Garden, Vancouver, B.C.

Highly susceptible	*V. dentatum, V. nudum, V. opulus, V. propinquum*, V. rafinesquianum, V. trilobum* (*V. opulus* var. *americanum*)
Susceptible	*V. acerifolium, V. lantana, V. rufidulum, V. sargentii, V. wrightii*
Moderately susceptible	*V.* ×*burkwoodii, V.* ×*carlcephalum, V. cassinoides, V. dilatatum, V. farreri* (except 'Nanum', which is highly susceptible), *V. lantanoides* (*V. alnifolium*), *V. lentago, V. macrocephalum, V.* 'Pragense' (*V.* ×*pragense*), *V. prunifolium, V.* ×*rhytidophylloides, V. tinus**
Resistant	*V.* ×*bodnantense, V. carlesii, V. davidii*, V.* ×*juddii, V.* 'Oneida', *V. plicatum* f. *plicatum, V. plicatum* f. *tomentosum, V. rhytidophyllum, V. setigerum, V. sieboldii*

Viburnum tinus is reported as susceptible by Royal Horticultural Society; I witnessed feeding on plants of this species in England during a late May 2006 visit.

Highly susceptible species are the first to be attacked and are generally destroyed in the first two to three years following infestation. Susceptible species are eventually destroyed but usually are not heavily fed upon until the most susceptible species are eliminated. Moderately susceptible species show varying degrees of susceptibility but usually are not destroyed by the beetle. Resistant species show little or no feeding damage and survive infestations rather well. *Most species in all susceptibility groups exhibit more feeding damage when grown in the shade.*

Viburnum borers are problematic on *V. lantana, V. opulus, V. trilobum,* and other species. Heavily infested plants lack vigor and show cracks and holes at their bases. Viburnum clearwing borer (*Synanthedon viburni*) and lesser viburnum borer (*S. fatifera*) infect from the ground level to about 18 inches up. Gnarled and scarred stems with sawdust (frass) are positive indications of infestation. During summer, the adults emerge from infected plants and deposit eggs around wounded tissue. The larvae tunnel in the bark and cambium but do not typically enter the wood. Vigorous, healthy plants are more resistant to borers and likely to survive infestation. I read a comment from Michael Yanny, Johnson's Nursery, that *V. trilobum* planted in wet soils is more borer prone. This may portend a bleak future for the species, since it grows in wet soils in the wild.

A recent report (Hartman and Parsons 2006) sheds new illumination on the biology of the borer. The work was conducted in the Green Bay, Wisconsin, area with *V. carlesii*, *V. dentatum*, *V. lantana*, *V. lentago*, *V. opulus*, *V. ×rhytidophylloides*, *V. sargentii*, and *V. trilobum*. All but *V. dentatum* were susceptible to borer activity. The researchers discovered injury (feeding) in both wood and bark, and activity in the root systems. *Synanthedon viburni* adults are in a mating cycle most of the growing season. Plants that are hosts to the larvae will support future generations until the plant dies. Chemical controls are available, but check with your local extension agent or a nearby nursery for the best strategy.

PESTS

I considered viburnums deer resistant until venturing through Mt. Airy Arboretum, Cincinnati, Ohio, and seeing the damage firsthand; the table I include here is based on my May 2002 observations of same (Dirr 2002). Breeders and gardeners alike should note the strong trends toward deer resistance within the genus. Any taxa with *V. utile* and *V. carlesii* in their parentage (e.g., *V. ×burkwoodii*, *V. ×carlcephalum* 'Chesapeake') are resistant to deer feeding. *Viburnum lantana*, *V. rhytidophyllum*, and their hybrids display reasonable resistance. The *V. plicatum* group (both f. *plicatum* and f. *tomentosum*) shows variable but in general quite good resistance. The *V. opulus* cultivars were among the most heavily browsed, along with *V. cassinoides*, *V. dentatum*, *V. lentago*, *V. nudum*, *V. rufidulum*, *V. setigerum*, and *V. wrightii*. Mt. Airy is an approximately 1,500-acre reserve that is surrounded by humans; the deer have retreated to this habitat, so the pressure on the vegetation is greater than normal. On the many occasions I have driven or walked the Arboretum since, I have noticed the deer exhibit minimal trepidation of human activity. They look up, then go back to feeding.

Deer damage
on *Viburnum
dentatum*, Mt.
Airy Arboretum,
May 2002

Deer
decimation
of *Viburnum
dilatatum*
'Erie', Mt. Airy
Arboretum,
April 2004

TABLE 4. Observations on *Viburnum* and deer feeding,
Mt. Airy Arboretum, May 2002.

TAXA	NOTES ON DEER FEEDING
Viburnum burejaeticum	Light feeding
Viburnum ×burkwoodii 'Chenaultii'	No damage
Viburnum ×burkwoodii 'Conoy'	Not eaten, 3 feet high and 4½ feet wide, beautiful foliage
Viburnum ×burkwoodii 'Mohawk'	Eaten
Viburnum ×carlcephalum	Minimal browsing on 12- to 14-foot-high plant
Viburnum ×carlcephalum 'Cayuga'	Minimal damage, 6-foot-tall specimen with leaves to ground
Viburnum ×carlcephalum 'Chesapeake'	No damage on 6-foot-tall plant growing next to *V. lantana* 'Rugosum'
Viburnum ×carlcephalum 'Eskimo'	Not eaten; I examined this 6-foot-tall plant top to bottom, side to side, and could not find a single shoot that was removed
Viburnum carlesii	Slight browsing
Viburnum carlesii 'Aurora'	No damage
Viburnum cassinoides	Heavy feeding, plants eaten down to 2 feet above ground
Viburnum dentatum	Heavily browsed
Viburnum dilatatum	Minimal browsing on 3 plants, each 10 to 12 feet high
Viburnum dilatatum 'Asian Beauty'	Heavy feeding
Viburnum dilatatum 'Erie'	Voraciously eaten
Viburnum dilatatum 'Iroquois'	Obviously browsed outside protective fence
Viburnum 'Emerald Triumph'	Eaten
Viburnum farreri	Minimal browsing on an 8- to 10-foot-high specimen
Viburnum ×juddii	No damage
Viburnum lantana	Resistant
Viburnum lantana 'Mohican'	Resistant
Viburnum lantana 'Rugosum'	Heavy feeding
Viburnum lentago	Protected by fence, obviously browsed outside fence

TABLE 4, continued

TAXA	NOTES ON DEER FEEDING
Viburnum macrocephalum	Minimal browsing on a 15-foot-high specimen
Viburnum nudum	Heavy feeding
Viburnum 'Oneida'	No damage
Viburnum opulus 'Nanum'	3 of 5 plants growing together were heavily browsed, 2 were without damage; how can this be explained?
Viburnum opulus 'Notcutt's Variety'	Heavy feeding, 3 plants browsed clean as high as deer reach
Viburnum opulus 'Xanthocarpum'	Heavy browse
Viburnum plicatum f. *plicatum*	Eaten
Viburnum plicatum f. *plicatum* 'Popcorn'	A few young shoots nibbled, but plant with leaves and branches to ground
Viburnum plicatum f. *plicatum* 'Rosace'	Slight browse
Viburnum plicatum f. *tomentosum* 'Shasta'	No feeding on 12-foot-high and -wide specimen
Viburnum plicatum f. *tomentosum* 'Shoshoni'	Heavy feeding
Viburnum plicatum f. *tomentosum* 'Summer Snowflake'	Eaten
Viburnum prunifolium	15 to 20 feet high, browsed at base
Viburnum ×*rhytidophylloides*	Light feeding
Viburnum rhytidophyllum	Slight damage
Viburnum rufidulum	Heavy feeding; extremely disappointing as this is a favorite viburnum, abundant in Dirr garden and in the wild around Athens; yet to witness deer damage in the wild
Viburnum setigerum	Devastated; the worst for wear in the entire collection
Viburnum sieboldii	Light feeding on a 14-foot-high specimen
Viburnum wrightii	Severely browsed, second to *V. setigerum* for damage

CHAPTER 6

Propagation

SEEDS

In a world of instant gratification, viburnum seed propagation should not be the first pursuit. Seeds may require two to three years for germination—a cycle of warm stratification followed by cold, other similar cycles, and then germination . . . possibly. This is the extreme, and in recent years our UGA protocol involves harvesting fruits when they ripen (start to color); soaking and removing the fleshy fruit wall; placing the seeds in warm stratification for three months, followed by cold stratification for three months; then sowing the seeds and waiting for germination. Be patient: seeds do not germinate immediately, and seedlings have emerged after three or more months in the greenhouse. The flats are returned to the cold (three months) if germination does not ensue within four to five months; this provides the second cycle of warm (while in greenhouse) and then cold. When returned to the warmth of the greenhouse for the third time, now with two cycles of warm/cold behind them, seeds should germinate.

Before this tortuous process, conduct a cut test to ensure that the seeds are not hollow (void). If the inside of the stone is not solid and green to cream in color, then the seed is nonviable. This will save considerable work! Often abundant seeds are not available, especially with controlled crosses. In this case, the extra work is necessary to preserve what could be the next great hybrid.

Seeds are often planted outside in fall in ground beds or frames. The natural cycles of warm/cold result in germination, possibly the first spring, often the second. Protect seeds from birds, mice, chipmunks, and pests of similar ilk. For the home gardener: plant seeds in a container, plunge in the ground, cover with mesh screen, and wait until germination. We have used this technique with complexly dormant Asiatic maple seed with good success.

Quick tips for success:

- Collect fruits as they start to color. Birds are prominent gleaners. Also, seeds are often "less dormant" at that time than when collected later.
- Soak fruits for 24 to 48 hours, perhaps longer, to soften exterior. Rub over a screen, or use a seed cleaner (macerator) or blender (mask blades with tape or tubing) to remove fleshy coat.
- Dry seeds on newspaper and place in dry cold storage (34 to 38°F) if either stratification or planting are delayed. Viability of air-dried seeds can be maintained for ten years at 34 to 38°F and as low as 0°F if seeds are stored in sealed, moisture-proof containers.
- Place seeds in a moist medium like peat, vermiculite, or sand in poly bags. For warm stratification, keep out of direct light at temperature of 68°F and above. Cold stratification is best at 41°F. Check the bags in the warm part of cycle periodically for root radical emergence. If they are present, move bag to cold for epicotyl (shoot) dormancy breaking.
- Always utilize well-drained seedling mix or soil for sowing the seeds. Maintain even moisture and a medium temperature of 70 to 75°F.

GRAFTING

Grafting is almost a lost art for increasing *Viburnum* cultivars. When I was on sabbatical in 1999, the great Hillier Nursery was still side-grafting a few of the *V. carlesii* group. Ian Hobbs, the propagator there, told me that the cost approached £2.50, which at that time was about $3.75 (cuttings, in contrast, can be rooted for $0.40 or less). *Viburnum lantana* is the preferred understock; it will sucker, mingling with and at times overtaking the scion. Labor, time, handling, and aftercare limit grafting as an economical method to increase stock of viburnums.

CUTTINGS

Cutting or vegetative propagation is the most common and economical method in the nursery industry for reproducing the best cultivars. The quality traits are captured *in toto*, ensuring trueness to type, genetic replicas of the original clones/cultivars. Softwood cuttings of *V. bracteatum*, *V. dentatum*, and related taxa root readily and are easy to overwinter. *Viburnum carlesii*, *V. bitchiuense*, *V. ×carlcephalum*, *V. ×juddii*, *V. macrocephalum* and some of the hybrids with *V. utile* may require extra care and manipulation after rooting to successfully overwinter and grow off.

More explicit information on cutting propagation is given in the appendix. The information serves as a guide; it is not a cake recipe, so be forewarned. With vegetative propagation of *Viburnum*, the species, cultivar, age of stock plant, timing, hormone, medium, and post-rooting handling of cuttings impact success.

Here, I have included a table of UGA cutting propagation activities over 14 years, from 1991 to 2005. From year to year, successes have been variable and are seldom comparable. Viburnums ideally require a mist system, well-drained medium, removal from mist as soon as rooted, and, possibly, an extended (24-hour) photoperiod (60-watt bulb, 3 feet above plants) to induce growth after rooting. We apply minimal levels of slow-release fertilizer like Nutricote®. Rooted cuttings should be properly hardened in late summer–early fall and overwintered in a polyhouse. After growth ensues the following spring, the cuttings can be transplanted.

Note that in the table, data are grouped by species and cultivars, with multiple years' data under each. These results sometimes represent different sources. From year to year, and within the same year, rooting results seldom jibe. For all cuttings, the medium was perlite:peat, 3:1 by volume, with a hormone (growth regulator) concentration (potassium salt of indolebutyric acid, or KIBA) of either 0.1 = 1000 ppm, 0.3 = 3000 ppm, 0.5 = 5000 ppm, or 0.8 = 8000 ppm. The data serve as a guide: a cutting collected on 1 May in Athens, Georgia, would be about the same growth stage as a 1 June cutting in Boston or a late June cutting in Minneapolis.

TABLE 5. Dirr cutting propagation data, 1991–2005.

TAXA	DATE COLLECTED	HORMONE (KIBA) CONCEN-TRATION	NUMBER OF CUT-TINGS TREATED	DATE SAMPLED FOR ROOTING	NUMBER ROOTED	PERCENTAGE ROOTED
Viburnum acerifolium	7/9/2003	0.5	8	8/28/2003	3	37%
Viburnum atrocyaneum	6/21/2002	0.5	8	8/9/2002	3	37%
Viburnum awabuki	6/8/2000	0.5	16	7/12/2000	16	100%
Viburnum awabuki	6/13/2002	0.5	8	7/10/2002	8	100%
Viburnum awabuki	7/9/2003	0.5	8	8/6/2003	6	75%
Viburnum bitchiuense	6/13/2002	0.5	8	7/26/2002	6	75%
Viburnum bitchiuense	5/31/2003	0.5	16	7/11/2003	14	87%
Viburnum bitchiuense	7/9/2003	0.5	8	8/28/2003	4	50%
Viburnum bracteatum	6/19/1992	0.5	16	8/7/1992	16	100%
Viburnum bracteatum	7/28/1992	0.5	48	9/9/1992	46	96%
Viburnum bracteatum	7/20/1995	0.3	16	8/17/1995	16	100%

TABLE 5, continued

TAXA	DATE COLLECTED	HORMONE (KIBA) CONCEN-TRATION	NUMBER OF CUT-TINGS TREATED	DATE SAMPLED FOR ROOTING	NUMBER ROOTED	PERCENTAGE ROOTED
Viburnum bracteatum	9/3/1996	0.3	22	10/8/1996	18	82%
Viburnum bracteatum	6/8/2000	0.5	17	7/12/2000	13	76%
Viburnum bracteatum	6/8/2000	0.5	16	7/12/2000	16	100%
Viburnum bracteatum	6/13/2002	0.5	8	7/10/2002	8	100%
Viburnum bracteatum	7/9/2003	0.5	8	8/6/2003	8	100%
Viburnum bracteatum 'Emerald Luster'	5/27/1994	0.1	32	6/24/1994	31	97%
Viburnum bracteatum 'Emerald Luster'	6/18/1998	0.3	18	7/15/1998	18	100%
Viburnum bracteatum 'Emerald Luster'	7/14/1998	0.5	18	8/11/1998	18	100%
Viburnum bracteatum 'Emerald Luster'	6/8/2000	0.5	26	7/12/2000	25	96%
Viburnum bracteatum 'Emerald Luster'	6/13/2002	0.5	8	7/10/2002	8	100%
Viburnum bracteatum 'Emerald Luster'	7/9/2003	0.5	8	8/6/2003	8	100%
Viburnum ×burkwoodii	7/5/2002	0.5	9	7/31/2002	7	78%
Viburnum ×burkwoodii	7/9/2003	0.5	8	8/6/2003	7	87%
Viburnum ×burkwoodii 'Conoy'	7/24/1992	0.1	32	9/9/1992	31	97%
Viburnum ×burkwoodii 'Conoy'	5/27/1994	0.3	26	7/1/1994	22	85%
Viburnum ×burkwoodii 'Conoy'	7/12/1995	0.3	16	8/17/1995	15	94%
Viburnum ×burkwoodii 'Conoy'	6/10/1996	0.3	16	7/9/1996	15	94%
Viburnum ×burkwoodii 'Conoy'	7/14/1998	0.3	17	8/11/1998	17	100%
Viburnum ×burkwoodii 'Conoy'	5/29/2002	0.5	17	6/21/2002	17	100%
Viburnum ×burkwoodii 'Conoy'	6/25/2003	0.5	16	7/23/2003	15	94%
Viburnum ×burkwoodii 'Mohawk'-02-03	7/19/2005	0.5	4	8/30/2005	3	75%
Viburnum ×burkwoodii 'Mohawk'-11-03	9/22/2005	0.5	9	12/2/2005	2	22%
Viburnum ×burkwoodii 'Mohawk'-12-03	7/19/2005	0.5	9	8/30/2005	9	100%
Viburnum ×burkwoodii 'Mohawk'-15-03	7/19/2005	0.5	9	8/30/2005	9	100%

TAXA	DATE COLLECTED	HORMONE (KIBA) CONCEN-TRATION	NUMBER OF CUT-TINGS TREATED	DATE SAMPLED FOR ROOTING	NUMBER ROOTED	PERCENTAGE ROOTED
Viburnum ×burkwoodii 'Mohawk'-20-03	9/22/2005	0.5	8	12/2/2005	4	50%
Viburnum ×burkwoodii 'Mohawk'-29-03	7/19/2005	0.5	11	8/16/2005	11	100%
Viburnum ×burkwoodii 'Park Farm Hybrid'	6/8/2000	0.5	16	7/12/2000	15	94%
Viburnum ×burkwoodii 'Park Farm Hybrid'	5/1/2002	0.5	16	6/5/2002	15	94%
Viburnum ×burkwoodii 'Park Farm Hybrid'	6/13/2002	0.5	8	7/10/2002	7	87%
Viburnum ×burkwoodii 'Park Farm Hybrid'	6/13/2002	0.5	8	7/10/2002	8	100%
Viburnum ×burkwoodii 'Park Farm Hybrid'	7/9/2003	0.5	8	8/28/2003	3	37%
Viburnum ×burkwoodii 'Park Farm Hybrid'	7/9/2003	0.5	8	8/28/2003	4	50%
Viburnum ×burkwoodii 'Park Farm Hybrid'	7/19/2005	0.5	16	8/30/2005	9	56%
Viburnum ×burkwoodii 'Park Farm Hybrid'	7/19/2005	0.5	16	8/30/2005	13	81%
Viburnum ×carlcephalum 'Eskimo'-02-03	7/19/2005	0.5	8	8/16/2005	8	100%
Viburnum carlesii DJH 288	6/13/2002	0.5	8	7/26/2002	8	100%
Viburnum carlesii DJH 288	7/9/2003	0.5	8	8/28/2003	6	75%
Viburnum cassinoides	6/13/2002	0.5	8	7/26/2002	8	100%
Viburnum cassinoides	7/9/2003	0.5	8	8/6/2003	8	100%
Viburnum cassinoides	7/19/2005	0.5	16	9/21/2005	8	50%
Viburnum cassinoides Hillier Form	6/13/2002	0.5	8	7/26/2002	5	62%
Viburnum cassinoides Hillier Form	7/9/2003	0.5	8	8/28/2003	2	25%
Viburnum cassinoides 'Nanum'	6/13/2002	0.5	8	7/10/2002	7	87%
Viburnum cassinoides 'Nanum'	7/9/2003	0.5	8	8/28/2003	8	100%
Viburnum chingii	6/8/2000	0.5	8	7/12/2000	6	75%
Viburnum chingii	6/21/2002	0.5	8	8/9/2002	3	37%
Viburnum chingii	7/9/2003	0.5	8	8/6/2003	7	87%
Viburnum 'Chippewa'	6/8/2000	0.5	16	7/12/2000	16	100%
Viburnum 'Chippewa'	6/13/2002	0.5	8	7/10/2002	7	87%

TABLE 5, continued

TAXA	DATE COLLECTED	HORMONE (KIBA) CONCEN-TRATION	NUMBER OF CUT-TINGS TREATED	DATE SAMPLED FOR ROOTING	NUMBER ROOTED	PERCENTAGE ROOTED
Viburnum 'Chippewa'	7/9/2003	0.5	8	8/6/2003	8	100%
Viburnum cinnamomifolium	10/17/2001	0.5	16	12/4/2001	10	62%
Viburnum cinnamomifolium	6/21/2002	0.5	8	7/23/2002	5	62%
Viburnum cinnamomifolium	7/9/2003	0.5	8	8/28/2003	7	87%
Viburnum cotinifolium	6/8/2000	0.5	10	7/12/2000	9	90%
Viburnum dentatum	7/5/2002	0.5	9	7/31/2002	7	79%
Viburnum dentatum Autumn Jazz® ('Ralph Senior')	6/8/2000	0.5	16	7/12/2000	16	100%
Viburnum dentatum Autumn Jazz® ('Ralph Senior')	6/13/2002	0.5	8	7/10/2002	7	87%
Viburnum dentatum Autumn Jazz® ('Ralph Senior')	7/9/2003	0.5	8	8/28/2003	6	75%
Viburnum dentatum Cardinal™ ('KLMthree')	6/8/2000	0.5	16	7/12/2000	9	56%
Viburnum dentatum Cardinal™ ('KLMthree')	6/13/2002	0.5	8	7/26/2002	7	87%
Viburnum dentatum Cardinal™ ('KLMthree')	7/9/2003	0.5	8	8/6/2003	8	100%
Viburnum dentatum Chicago Lustre® ('Synnestvedt')	6/8/2000	0.5	16	7/12/2000	16	100%
Viburnum dentatum Chicago Lustre® ('Synnestvedt')	6/13/2002	0.5	8	7/10/2002	8	100%
Viburnum dentatum Chicago Lustre® ('Synnestvedt')	7/9/2003	0.5	8	8/6/2003	6	75%
Viburnum dentatum Northern Burgundy® ('Morton')	6/8/2000	0.5	16	7/12/2000	10	62%
Viburnum dentatum Northern Burgundy® ('Morton')	6/13/2002	0.5	8	7/26/2002	5	62%
Viburnum dentatum Northern Burgundy® ('Morton')	7/9/2003	0.5	8	8/6/2003	5	62%
Viburnum dentatum 'Perle Bleu'	6/8/2000	0.5	16	7/12/2000	16	100%

TAXA	DATE COLLECTED	HORMONE (KIBA) CONCEN- TRATION	NUMBER OF CUT- TINGS TREATED	DATE SAMPLED FOR ROOTING	NUMBER ROOTED	PERCENTAGE ROOTED
Viburnum dentatum 'Perle Bleu'	6/8/2000	0.5	16	7/12/2000	14	87%
Viburnum dentatum 'Perle Bleu'	6/13/2002	0.5	8	7/10/2002	8	100%
Viburnum dentatum 'Perle Bleu'	7/9/2003	0.5	8	8/6/2003	8	100%
Viburnum dentatum var. *scabrellum* (*V. ashei*)	6/21/2002	0.5	8	7/23/2002	8	100%
Viburnum dentatum var. *scabrellum* (*V. ashei*)	5/14/2003	0.5	16	6/26/2003	16	100%
Viburnum dentatum var. *scabrellum* (*V. ashei*)	7/9/2003	0.5	8	8/6/2003	6	75%
Viburnum dentatum var. *scabrellum* (*V. ashei*)	6/26/2004	0.5	32	7/29/2004	32	100%
Viburnum dilatatum 'Michael Dodge'	6/8/2000	0.5	4	7/12/2000	2	50%
Viburnum dilatatum 'Michael Dodge'	6/13/2002	0.5	8	7/10/2002	7	87%
Viburnum dilatatum 'Michael Dodge'	7/9/2003	0.5	8	8/28/2003	4	50%
Viburnum dilatatum 'Ogon'	7/16/2004	0.5	16	8/5/2004	16	100%
Viburnum dilatatum seedling	7/5/2002	0.5	8	8/9/2002	5	62%
Viburnum dilatatum seedling	7/9/2003	0.5	8	8/28/2003	8	100%
Viburnum erubescens	7/9/2003	0.5	8	8/6/2003	8	100%
Viburnum foetidum var. *rectangulatum*	6/8/2000	0.5	16	7/12/2000	13	81%
Viburnum foetidum var. *rectangulatum*	6/21/2002	0.5	8	7/23/2002	8	100%
Viburnum foetidum var. *rectangulatum*	10/24/2002	0.5	16	12/13/2002	15	94%
Viburnum foetidum var. *rectangulatum*	7/9/2003	0.5	8	8/6/2003	8	100%
Viburnum henryi	3/7/1995	0.3	22	1995	5	23%
Viburnum ×hillieri 'Winton'	6/8/2000	0.5	16	7/12/2000	8	50%
Viburnum ×hillieri 'Winton'	7/9/2003	0.5	8	8/6/2003	7	87%
Viburnum 'Huron'	6/8/2000	0.5	16	7/12/2000	14	87%
Viburnum 'Huron'	6/13/2002	0.5	8	7/10/2002	8	100%

TAXA	DATE COLLECTED	HORMONE (KIBA) CONCENTRATION	NUMBER OF CUTTINGS TREATED	DATE SAMPLED FOR ROOTING	NUMBER ROOTED	PERCENTAGE ROOTED
Viburnum 'Huron'	7/9/2003	0.5	8	8/6/2003	7	87%
Viburnum luzonicum	6/8/2000	0.5	16	7/12/2000	12	75%
Viburnum luzonicum	6/8/2000	0.5	4	7/12/2000	3	75%
Viburnum luzonicum	6/13/2002	0.5	8	7/10/2002	8	100%
Viburnum luzonicum	7/9/2003	0.5	8	8/6/2003	8	100%
Viburnum luzonicum	8/26/2004	0.5	8	10/13/2004	8	100%
Viburnum luzonicum	7/19/2005	0.5	16	8/30/2005	13	81%
Viburnum macrocephalum f. *keteleeri*	6/8/2000	0.5	16	8/7/2000	4	25%
Viburnum macrocephalum f. *keteleeri*	5/1/2002	0.5	8	7/10/2002	4	50%
Viburnum macrocephalum f. *keteleeri*	6/13/2002	0.5	8	7/26/2002	7	87%
Viburnum macrocephalum f. *keteleeri*	7/9/2003	0.5	8	8/28/2003	2	25%
Viburnum mullaha	6/8/2000	0.5	16	7/12/2000	12	75%
Viburnum mullaha	6/21/2002	0.5	8	7/23/2002	4	50%
Viburnum mullaha	7/9/2003	0.5	8	8/28/2003	8	100%
Viburnum National Arboretum 69852	6/8/2000	0.5	16	8/7/2000	8	50%
Viburnum National Arboretum 69852	9/27/2000	0.5	16	11/1/2000	11	69%
Viburnum National Arboretum 69852	7/24/2001	0.5	8	9/7/2001	6	75%
Viburnum National Arboretum 69852	6/13/2002	0.5	16	7/26/2002	16	100%
Viburnum National Arboretum 69852	7/9/2003	0.5	8	8/28/2003	7	87%
Viburnum National Arboretum 69852	7/19/2005	0.5	16	9/21/2005	10	62%
Viburnum nudum	6/8/2000	0.5	16	7/12/2000	11	69%
Viburnum nudum	6/21/2002	0.5	8	7/23/2002	8	100%
Viburnum nudum	6/21/2002	0.5	8	7/23/2002	8	100%
Viburnum nudum	7/9/2003	0.5	8	8/6/2003	8	100%
Viburnum nudum	7/9/2003	0.5	8	8/6/2003	8	100%
Viburnum nudum var. *angustifolium*	6/8/2000	0.5	16	7/12/2000	9	56%

TAXA	DATE COLLECTED	HORMONE (KIBA) CONCEN-TRATION	NUMBER OF CUT-TINGS TREATED	DATE SAMPLED FOR ROOTING	NUMBER ROOTED	PERCENTAGE ROOTED
Viburnum nudum var. *angustifolium*	6/13/2002	0.5	8	7/10/2002	8	100%
Viburnum nudum var. *angustifolium*	7/9/2003	0.5	8	8/6/2003	8	100%
Viburnum nudum 'Earth Shade'	6/8/1995	0.3	23	1995	23	100%
Viburnum nudum 'Earth Shade'	5/15/1996	0.3	16	6/11/1996	16	100%
Viburnum nudum 'Earth Shade'	7/14/1998	0.3	17	8/11/1998	16	94%
Viburnum nudum 'Pink Beauty'	7/9/2003	0.5	8	8/6/2003	8	100%
Viburnum nudum 'Pink Beauty'	6/26/2004	0.5	32	7/29/2004	31	97%
Viburnum obovatum	5/10/1991	0.8	8	7/11/1991	0	0%
Viburnum obovatum	6/8/2000	0.5	16	7/12/2000	8	50%
Viburnum obovatum	10/24/2002	0.5	8	1/6/2003	2	25%
Viburnum obovatum	10/24/2002	0.5	8	1/6/2003	2	25%
Viburnum obovatum	7/9/2003	0.5	8	8/28/2003	7	87%
Viburnum obovatum	7/19/2005	0.5	16	8/30/2005	16	100%
Viburnum obovatum 'Best Densa'	6/21/2002	0.5	8	7/23/2002	6	75%
Viburnum obovatum 'Best Densa'	10/24/2002	0.5	8	1/6/2003	1	12%
Viburnum obovatum 'Best Densa'	7/9/2003	0.5	8	8/6/2003	7	87%
Viburnum obovatum 'Best Densa'	7/19/2005	0.5	16	8/30/2005	16	100%
Viburnum obovatum 'Christmas Snow'	6/21/2002	0.5	8	8/9/2002	5	62%
Viburnum obovatum 'Christmas Snow'	10/24/2002	0.5	8	1/6/2003	4	50%
Viburnum obovatum 'Christmas Snow'	7/9/2003	0.5	8	8/6/2003	5	62%
Viburnum obovatum 'Christmas Snow'	7/19/2005	0.5	16	8/30/2005	15	94%
Viburnum obovatum 'Mrs. Schiller's Delight'	6/21/2002	0.5	8	8/9/2002	5	62%

TAXA	DATE COLLECTED	HORMONE (KIBA) CONCEN-TRATION	NUMBER OF CUT-TINGS TREATED	DATE SAMPLED FOR ROOTING	NUMBER ROOTED	PERCENTAGE ROOTED
Viburnum obovatum 'Mrs. Schiller's Delight'	10/24/2002	0.5	8	1/6/2003	0	0%
Viburnum obovatum 'Mrs. Schiller's Delight'	7/9/2003	0.5	4	8/28/2003	3	75%
Viburnum obovatum 'Mrs. Schiller's Delight'	7/19/2005	0.5	16	8/30/2005	16	100%
Viburnum obovatum 'Reifler's Dwarf'	8/23/2001	0.5	16	10/15/2001	10	62%
Viburnum obovatum 'Reifler's Dwarf'	8/28/2001	0.5	16	10/30/2001	14	87%
Viburnum obovatum 'Reifler's Dwarf'	5/1/2002	0.5	16	6/21/2002	16	100%
Viburnum obovatum 'Reifler's Dwarf'	6/13/2002	0.5	8	7/26/2002	8	100%
Viburnum obovatum 'Reifler's Dwarf'	7/9/2003	0.5	8	8/28/2003	2	25%
Viburnum obovatum 'Reifler's Dwarf'	7/19/2005	0.5	16	8/30/2005	16	100%
Viburnum obovatum 'St. Paul'	6/13/2002	0.5	8	7/26/2002	5	62%
Viburnum obovatum 'St. Paul'	7/9/2003	0.5	8	9/17/2003	3	37%
Viburnum obovatum 'Whorled Class'	6/21/2002	0.5	8	8/9/2002	7	87%
Viburnum obovatum 'Whorled Class'	10/24/2002	0.5	6	1/6/2003	0	0%
Viburnum obovatum 'Whorled Class'	7/9/2003	0.5	8	8/6/2003	8	100%
Viburnum obovatum 'Whorled Class'	7/19/2005	0.5	16	8/30/2005	16	100%
Viburnum plicatum f. *plicatum* 'Mary Milton'	7/9/1996	0.5	8	9/3/1996	4	50%
Viburnum plicatum f. *plicatum* 'Mary Milton'	7/9/1996	0.3	8	9/3/1996	8	100%
Viburnum plicatum f. *plicatum* 'Mary Milton'	5/4/1998	0.3	13	6/1/1998	12	92%
Viburnum plicatum f. *plicatum* 'Mary Milton'	4/25/2003	0.5	8	5/30/2003	7	87%

TAXA	DATE COLLECTED	HORMONE (KIBA) CONCEN- TRATION	NUMBER OF CUT- TINGS TREATED	DATE SAMPLED FOR ROOTING	NUMBER ROOTED	PERCENTAGE ROOTED
Viburnum plicatum f. *plicatum* Newport® ('Newzam')	7/20/1992	0.1	~40	8/?/1992	23	57%
Viburnum plicatum f. *plicatum* Newport® ('Newzam')	6/8/2000	0.5	16	7/12/2000	15	94%
Viburnum plicatum f. *plicatum* Newport® ('Newzam')	6/13/2002	0.5	8	7/10/2002	8	100%
Viburnum plicatum f. *plicatum* Newport® ('Newzam')	5/14/2003	0.5	16	6/26/2003	14	87%
Viburnum plicatum f. *plicatum* Newport® ('Newzam')	7/9/2003	0.5	8	8/6/2003	8	100%
Viburnum plicatum f. *plicatum* Newport® ('Newzam')	7/19/2005	0.5	16	8/16/2005	16	100%
Viburnum plicatum f. *plicatum* 'Popcorn'	5/14/1999	0.3	10	6/22/1999	10	100%
Viburnum plicatum f. *plicatum* 'Popcorn'	6/23/1999	0.5	10	7/15/1999	8	80%
Viburnum plicatum f. *plicatum* 'Popcorn'	6/8/2000	0.5	16	7/12/2000	16	100%
Viburnum plicatum f. *plicatum* 'Popcorn'	5/1/2002	0.5	8	5/17/2002	8	100%
Viburnum plicatum f. *plicatum* 'Popcorn'	6/13/2002	0.5	8	7/10/2002	8	100%
Viburnum plicatum f. *plicatum* 'Popcorn'	5/14/2003	0.5	32	6/26/2003	31	97%
Viburnum plicatum f. *plicatum* 'Popcorn'	7/9/2003	0.5	8	8/6/2003	8	100%
Viburnum plicatum f. *plicatum* 'Popcorn'	7/19/2005	0.5	16	8/16/2005	16	100%
Viburnum plicatum f. *plicatum* 'Sawtooth'	6/8/2000	0.5	8	7/12/2000	8	100%
Viburnum plicatum f. *plicatum* 'Sawtooth'	6/13/2002	0.5	8	7/10/2002	8	100%
Viburnum plicatum f. *plicatum* 'Sawtooth'	7/9/2003	0.5	8	8/6/2003	8	100%

TAXA	DATE COLLECTED	HORMONE (KIBA) CONCEN-TRATION	NUMBER OF CUT-TINGS TREATED	DATE SAMPLED FOR ROOTING	NUMBER ROOTED	PERCENTAGE ROOTED
Viburnum plicatum f. *tomentosum*	2/26/1992	0.1	28	4/21/1992	0	0%
Viburnum plicatum f. *tomentosum* 'Shasta'	7/24/1992	0.1	7	8/7/1992	7	100%
Viburnum plicatum f. *tomentosum* 'Shasta'	7/5/2002	0.5	8	7/31/2002	5	62%
Viburnum plicatum f. *tomentosum* 'Shasta'	7/9/2003	0.5	8	8/6/2003	8	100%
Viburnum plicatum f. *tomentosum* 'Shoshoni'	6/8/2000	0.5	8	7/12/2000	8	100%
Viburnum plicatum f. *tomentosum* 'Shoshoni'	6/13/2002	0.5	8	7/10/2002	8	100%
Viburnum plicatum f. *tomentosum* 'Shoshoni'	5/14/2003	0.5	16	6/26/2003	16	100%
Viburnum plicatum f. *tomentosum* 'Shoshoni'	7/9/2003	0.5	8	8/6/2003	8	100%
Viburnum plicatum f. *tomentosum* 'Shoshoni'	7/19/2005	0.5	16	8/16/2005	16	100%
Viburnum plicatum f. *tomentosum* 'Summer Snowflake'	6/8/2000	0.5	16	7/12/2000	16	100%
Viburnum plicatum f. *tomentosum* 'Summer Snowflake'	6/13/2002	0.5	8	7/10/2002	8	100%
Viburnum plicatum f. *tomentosum* 'Summer Snowflake'	7/9/2003	0.5	8	8/6/2003	8	100%
Viburnum prunifolium	6/13/2002	0.5	8	7/10/2002	6	75%
Viburnum prunifolium	7/9/2003	0.5	8	8/28/2003	8	100%
Viburnum rafinesquianum 'Louise's Sunbeam'	5/5/2005	0.1	16	6/10/2005	12	75%
Viburnum ×*rhytidophylloides* 'Willowwood'	3/26/1997	0.5	19	5/27/1997	11	58%
Viburnum ×*rhytidophylloides* 'Willowwood'	6/8/2000	0.5	16	8/7/2000	8	50%
Viburnum ×*rhytidophylloides* 'Willowwood'	6/21/2002	0.5	8	8/9/2002	4	50%

TAXA	DATE COLLECTED	HORMONE (KIBA) CONCEN-TRATION	NUMBER OF CUT-TINGS TREATED	DATE SAMPLED FOR ROOTING	NUMBER ROOTED	PERCENTAGE ROOTED
Viburnum ×rhytidophylloides 'Willowwood'	7/9/2003	0.5	8	8/28/2003	7	87%
Viburnum rhytidophyllum 'Variegatum'	7/15/1998	0.1	2	8/31/1998	0	0%
Viburnum rufidulum	5/12/1994	0.5	11	6/28/1994	7	64%
Viburnum rufidulum	5/12/1994	0.1	11	6/28/1994	10	90%
Viburnum rufidulum	5/29/1997	0.3	16	8/1/1997	11	69%
Viburnum rufidulum	6/8/2000	0.5	8	8/7/2000	8	100%
Viburnum rufidulum	5/1/2002	0.5	16	7/10/2002	7	44%
Viburnum rufidulum	6/13/2002	0.5	8	7/26/2002	6	75%
Viburnum rufidulum	6/21/2002	0.5	8	8/9/2002	7	87%
Viburnum rufidulum 'Royal Guard'	6/21/2002	0.5	8	8/9/2002	3	37%
Viburnum schensianum	6/8/2000	0.5	8	7/12/2000	8	100%
Viburnum tinus	3/18/1993	0.5	32	6/21/1993	10	31%
Viburnum tinus 'Variegatum'	1/31/2002	0.5	2	4/12/2002	1	50%
Viburnum utile	7/9/2003	0.5	8	8/6/2003	3	37%
Viburnum utile	8/29/2003	0.5	18	10/1/2003	13	72%
Viburnum utile Big Leaf Form	6/13/2002	0.5	8	7/10/2002	7	87%
Viburnum utile Big Leaf Form	7/9/2003	0.5	8	8/6/2003	8	100%
Viburnum utile Wavy Leaf Form	6/13/2002	0.5	8	7/10/2002	4	50%
Viburnum utile Wavy Leaf Form	10/24/2002	0.5	8	11/19/2002	8	100%
Viburnum utile Wavy Leaf Form	7/9/2003	0.5	8	8/6/2003	8	100%

Viburnum setigerum, fruits

APPENDIX

Seed, Cutting, and Grafting Propagation Techniques

From *Reference Manual of Woody Plant Propagation*
(Dirr and Heuser 2006)

VIBURNUM FRUITS SHOULD be collected as mature color change occurs, soaked, macerated, and the cleaned seeds dried and stored under refrigeration or planted. Viburnum seeds are often doubly dormant and require extended warm stratification of three- to nine-month duration followed by three months of cold. A classic paper by L. V. Barton [*Contrib. Boyce Thompson Instit.* 9:79 (1937)] describes seed propagation of viburnums.

Viburnum acerifolium
MAPLELEAF VIBURNUM

Seed. A pound of cleaned seed contains 13,000 seeds. Mapleleaf viburnum requires a warm stratification of six to 17 months followed by two to four months of cold stratification at 34 to 41°F. Some growers collect the seed early in the fall and plant immediately; this circumvents the warm period.

Cuttings. Late June, 8000 ppm IBA-talc + thiram, sand:perlite, mist, rooted 100 percent. Control cuttings rooted about 50 percent [*The Plant Propagator* 18(1): 7 (1972)]. Probably best to leave rooted cuttings in place and transplant after new growth occurs in spring.

Viburnum betulifolium

BIRCHLEAF VIBURNUM

Seed. Five months cold/three months warm.

Viburnum bitchiuense

BITCHIU VIBURNUM

Seed. Should be handled as described for *V. carlesii*.

Cuttings. Late May, 8000 ppm IBA-talc + thiram, perlite:sand, mist, rooted 63 percent. June cuttings are easily rooted.

Viburnum ×bodnantense

BODNANT VIBURNUM

Seed. A hybrid between *V. farreri* and *V. grandiflorum*, represented in the trade by the cultivars 'Charles Lamont', 'Dawn', and 'Deben', which are vegetatively propagated.

Cuttings. Softwoods produced from the first flush of growth (late May and June) are the best. Treat with 8000 ppm IBA-talc and place under mist in a peat moss and perlite medium. Late July cuttings treated with 3000 ppm IBA-talc rooted 100 percent in seven weeks, while cuttings in polytents rooted 100 percent with 4000 ppm IBA-talc + thiram. In Denmark, low white polyethylene tunnels are used. The cuttings are inserted in August, potted up in March, and placed under heated glass. Hardwood cuttings are an economical method of producing this species, according to the Proceedings of the International Plant Propagators Society [*PIPPS* 20:378 (1970)]. Refer to *V. dentatum* for hardwood propagation details.

Small quantities can be produced by French layering. Plants are stooled back to produce a low crown and many vigorous shoots. Ten to 12 of the most vigorous shoots are selected and pegged down, horizontal to the ground, early in the new year so that the lateral buds on the stems break into growth and grow upward. The timing is important to allow sufficient time for apical dominance to be dissipated before bud break. In the spring, when the new shoots have grown out 4 to 6 inches, the layer leads are dropped 4 inches into the soil and then covered with earth to their tips; they are covered again in early summer. Further attention is not required until after leaf fall in autumn, when the layers are harvested.

Viburnum bracteatum

BRACTED VIBURNUM

Seed. Should respond like *V. dentatum*. Five months warm/three months cold produced poor germination.

Cuttings. Refer to *V. dentatum* for cutting propagation details. Easily rooted from May–June softwoods.

Viburnum buddleifolium
WOOLLY VIBURNUM

Cuttings. Early July, 4000 ppm IBA-talc + thiram, sand:perlite, mist, rooted 75 percent with heavy root systems in 11 weeks.

Viburnum burejaeticum
MANCHURIAN VIBURNUM

Cuttings. Easy to root, late July, 4000 ppm IBA-talc + thiram, rooted 90 percent with excellent root systems.

Viburnum ×burkwoodii
BURKWOOD VIBURNUM

Seed. This hybrid between *V. carlesii* and *V. utile* is asexually propagated to maintain its unique characteristics. Handle as described under *V. carlesii*.

Cuttings. The rooting of stem cuttings is not a problem, especially under mist. Established plants that are flowering produce cuttings with a lower capacity to regenerate, whereas stock plants that are pruned regularly produce shoots with high rooting capacity. Timing extends into July–August for this species; however, softwood cuttings in June are better. The earlier the cuttings are taken, the better, because a subsequent growth flush often occurs. The cuttings are inserted into a well-drained medium under mist after treating with a hormone such as a 1000 ppm IBA-quick dip. Mid August cuttings treated with 8000 ppm IBA-talc + thiram rooted 100 percent. Late August cuttings treated with 8000 ppm IBA-quick dip also rooted 100 percent in eight weeks. If possible, do not disturb the cuttings after they have rooted. 'Mohawk' can be easily propagated only when growth is very soft. In Denmark, low white polyethylene tunnels are used in the propagation of *V. ×burkwoodii*. The cuttings are inserted in August and potted in March under heated glass. Any *Viburnum* species or cultivar containing *V. carlesii* as a parent is most logically rooted early and left in place. Some nurserymen actually leave the cuttings in the rooting beds (outside) for two seasons. I root *V. ×burkwoodii*, 'Chesapeake', 'Eskimo', etc., in individual containers in early summer. Root systems are not disturbed, and the rooted cuttings are overwintered in a double-layer inflated polyhouse. Survival is excellent.

Grafting. Burkwood viburnum can be readily propagated by budding on *V. lantana* or *V. opulus* rootstocks. Well-established field-lined rootstocks are budded in August using a T-bud method. The rootstocks are headed back in

February, after which continued attention to removal of suckers is necessary. This technique is not desirable because of suckering and incompatibility problems and has largely been superseded by cuttings [*PIPPS* 20:378 (1970)].

The traditional grafting system is bench grafting during August and September. Seedling rootstocks of *V. lantana* are potted the previous autumn into 3-inch pots. The grafting operation is conducted on understocks headed back to within ⅓ inch of the soil and grafted with a two-bud scion using a whip graft. A good union should form in four to five weeks. The use of rootstocks produced from cuttings that have had the lower buds removed will eliminate the suckering problem.

Viburnum ×*burkwoodii* 'Chenaultii'
CHENAULT VIBURNUM

Cuttings. Easily rooted from June and July cuttings; late July cuttings, treated with 3000 ppm IBA-talc, mist, rooted 90 percent. Overwinter as described under *V.* ×*burkwoodii*. Chenault viburnum can be propagated by layering.

Viburnum ×*carlcephalum*
CARLCEPHALUM VIBURNUM, FRAGRANT VIBURNUM

Seed. This hybrid between *V. carlesii* and *V. macrocephalum* f. *keteleeri* is asexually propagated.

Cuttings. Relatively easy to root from softwood cuttings. Refer to *V.* ×*burkwoodii* for details. 'Cayuga' can be propagated only when growth is very soft and before the terminal flower buds have been initiated. Late June (Boston) cuttings treated with 8000 ppm IBA-talc + thiram under mist rooted 84 percent in four weeks. Late August (Boston) treated similarly rooted 80 percent in eight weeks. This hybrid species can prove difficult to overwinter and might be handled like *V.* ×*burkwoodii*.

Viburnum carlesii
KOREANSPICE VIBURNUM, MAYFLOWER VIBURNUM

Seed. One of the easiest viburnums to grow from seed. Some nurseries propagate Koreanspice viburnum from seed because seedlings grow faster than cuttings. Collect fruits from large-flowered, -fruited and -leaved forms before coats are soft and black; clean and sow at this time. Many seeds germinate the following spring. Two months warm (68 to 86°F) stratification followed by two months cold (41°F) stratification induces good germination.

Cuttings. Softwoods up to mid July, 8000 ppm IBA-talc, peat:perlite, mist, rooted about 80 percent. Root in flats in the fall and move to a cold frame, poly-

or pithouse maintained at 35°F. A large Tennessee grower roots cuttings from summer softwoods using 1 percent IBA-quick dip, a sandy soil, and mist in a shaded poly tunnel outside. Rooted cuttings are kept in the beds two years before lifting. The grower noted that all cultivars or hybrids with *V. carlesii* parentage should not be lifted until the second growing season. 'Compactum' rooting conditions include softwoods, 2000 ppm IBA + 5000 ppm NAA, and mist [*J. Amer. Soc. Hort. Sci.* 93:699 (1968)]. June (Rhode Island) cuttings are best, and the cuttings are overwintered in a cold frame without disturbing. Fall cuttings are dormant and fail to root. Propagation by layering is also possible.

Grafting. Koreanspice viburnum can be grafted onto *V. lantana* or *V. dentatum*. This is not a preferred method because both understocks sucker. When *V. dentatum* is used as an understock, one-year seedlings are used because they have fewer sucker buds. Pot the seedlings in the winter and graft by the end of August. Any sucker buds left will be forced out by the grafting operation and can be cut out. Overwinter the grafts in a cold frame and plant out the following spring [*PIPPS* 21:384 (1971)]. Refer to *V. ×burkwoodii* for details when using *V. lantana*.

Viburnum cassinoides

WITHEROD VIBURNUM, SWAMP VIBURNUM, APPALACHIAN TEA VIBURNUM, SWAMP BLACKHAW, FALSE PARAGUAY TEA, WILD RAISIN

Seed. A pound of cleaned seed contains 27,600 seeds. Seeds of witherod viburnum are doubly dormant and require warm stratification at 68 to 86°F for two months followed by three months cold stratification at 34 to 41°F.

Cuttings. Easy to root from June and July cuttings. Treat with 3000 to 5000 ppm IBA-quick dip and place under mist. Overwintering can be a problem. Follow the procedures described under *V. ×burkwoodii*. 'Nanum' rooted 100 percent in six weeks from late June cuttings when treated with 8000 ppm IBA-talc and placed in sand under mist.

Viburnum cylindricum

TUBEFLOWER VIBURNUM

Seed. Three months cold stratification produced good germination.

Viburnum davidii

DAVID VIBURNUM

Seed. Seven months of warm stratification followed by three months of cold stratification induces germination.

Cuttings. Very soft shoot tips taken early in the season and placed under mist root well. Later cuttings root with 8000 ppm IBA + 500 ppm NAA solution. A liquid formulation hastens rooting and induces a heavier root system. Hardwoods with flower buds removed, 8000 ppm IBA-talc, a suitable medium, and mist will root [*PIPPS* 22:123 (1972) and 31:109 (1981)]. Overwintering may be a problem; procedures described under *V.* ×*burkwoodii* should be followed.

Viburnum dentatum
ARROWWOOD VIBURNUM

Seed. A pound of cleaned seed contains 20,400 seeds. Germination requirements for this species are as varied as its distribution. With seeds from the southern part of the range, temperature is not critical. Northern seed sources may require 12 to 17 months of warm stratification at 68 to 86°F followed by 15 to 30 days of cold stratification at 41°F. If the fruit is picked just prior to ripening and sown directly, germination will occur the following spring for northern sources [*American Nurseryman* 86(5): 58 (1947); *PIPPS* 8:126 (1958)]. Refer to *V. acerifolium* for additional details on seed germination.

Cuttings. Arrowwood can be propagated from softwood, hardwood, or root cuttings. Softwoods are preferred because the cuttings root easily and establish quickly. A wide range of hormone treatments, varying from 1000 ppm IBA + 500 ppm NAA solution to 8000 ppm IBA-talc, have been used successfully. Place in a suitable medium such as peat moss:perlite or sand, and mist. Rooting percentages of 94 to 100 percent are reported. Hardwoods selected from flowering plants are not suitable. Plants cut back hard produce suitable cuttings. At leaf fall the canes are cut into 5- to 6-inch-long nodal cuttings, treated with 8000 ppm IBA-talc, and placed in a cold frame protected from frost. Basal sections of the shoots should be used, as there is a demonstrable positional effect on regeneration. Peat moss:sand (2:1, v/v) is used, and the cuttings are inserted so that only the top ½ inch is exposed. As the cutting will remain and develop in place until the following autumn, sufficient space must be allowed (3 by 4 inches). In the spring, harden off gradually as the cuttings leaf out.

Viburnum dentatum var. *pubescens*
DOWNY VIBURNUM
Seed. Four months warm/three months cold induces good germination.

Viburnum dilatatum
LINDEN VIBURNUM
Seed. Seeds have a complex dormancy and are difficult to germinate. Five

to seven months of warm stratification followed by three to four months of cold stratification is recommended, but germination response is variable: five months warm with three months cold produced only 8 percent germination. The same treatment produced heavy germination of 'Xanthocarpum' (yellow-fruited form).

Cuttings. Softwoods under mist in early summer with 8000 ppm IBA-talc or solution, peat moss:perlite, sand, or suitable medium, mist. Rooting will average 80 to 100 percent [*The Plant Propagator* 17(4): 3 (1971)]. Early August (Boston) cuttings, treated with 4000 ppm IBA-quick dip, rooted 60 percent. If the cuttings are rooted early and kept under long days (18 hours) to induce a flush of growth, they will overwinter in a cold frame. Later-rooted cuttings that do not make a new growth flush must be overwintered in a cool greenhouse. In general, this species is not as difficult to overwinter as *V. carlesii* but should not be disturbed after rooting.

Viburnum erosum
BEECH VIBURNUM

Seed. Three to five months warm/three months cold.
Cuttings. Early August, 3000 ppm IBA-talc, rooted 80 percent.

Viburnum erubescens

Cuttings. Roots readily from softwoods; follow procedure described under *V. farreri*.

Viburnum farreri
FRAGRANT VIBURNUM

Seed. Seed is sparsely produced because the very early flowering habit results in frost damage. Also, the absence of different clones or seedlings for cross-pollination probably affects fruit set.

Cuttings. Softwoods root easily. The earlier the cuttings are selected, the better, for ultimate survival the first winter. Author has rooted the species in June using 1000 ppm IBA-solution, peat:perlite, and mist. 'Nanum' rooted 80 percent in early August when treated with 4000 ppm IBA-quick dip. Hardwoods from stock hedges are an economical means of producing this species. Cut into 5- to 6-inch lengths, 8000 ppm IBA-talc, insert in a cold frame, and protect from frost. Small quantities can be produced by French layering [*PIPPS* 20:378 (1970)]. This technique is described under *V. ×bodnantense*.

Viburnum furcatum
FORKED VIBURNUM

Cuttings. Late June, 8000 ppm IBA-talc, rooted 21 percent.

Viburnum hupehense
HUBEI VIBURNUM

Seed. Seeds are doubly dormant and require five months at 60 to 85°F followed by three months at 41°F [*Arnoldia* 14(5): 25 (1954)].

Cuttings. July cuttings root readily.

Viburnum japonicum
JAPANESE VIBURNUM

Cuttings. Readily rooted from June, July, and August cuttings. Treat with 3000 to 8000 ppm IBA-talc or solution and place in a well-drained medium under mist. Leave in place and transplant in spring. Can also be rooted in October through March from hardwood cuttings. Bottom heat coupled with the above treatments would be beneficial.

Viburnum ×juddii
JUDD VIBURNUM

Seed. A hybrid between *V. carlesii* and *V. bitchiuense*. Occasionally fruits are produced, and the resultant seedling populations might prove interesting. Treat as described for *V. carlesii*.

Cuttings. This hybrid species roots more easily than *V. carlesii*. Cuttings taken in late June, treated with 3000 ppm IBA, placed in sand:peat moss medium with mist, rooted about 90 percent in 12 weeks. Overwintering the rooted cuttings can be a problem. For additional details on rooting and overwintering, refer to *V. ×burkwoodii*. Can also be propagated by layering.

Grafting. Judd viburnum can be grafted on *V. lantana* and *V. opulus*. Refer to *V. ×burkwoodii* for details. This is not a preferred method because of the suckering problem.

Viburnum lantana
WAYFARINGTREE VIBURNUM

Seed. This species is commercially propagated from seed. A pound of cleaned seed averages 8,700 seeds. Two months cold stratification at 40°F is adequate to stimulate germination. Embryos extracted from dormant seeds germinate readily, which indicates that the dormancy problem does not reside in the embryo itself [*PIPPS* 12:150 (1962)]. Collect seed before it turns black, clean, and sow; many seedlings will germinate the following spring.

Cuttings. Softwoods root easily [*PIPPS* 30:398 (1980)]. Treat with 3000 to 5000 ppm IBA-talc or -quick dip, peat:perlite (1:1, v/v) or suitable medium, and mist. Refer to *V.* ×*burkwoodii* for additional information on rooting from softwood cuttings. In one study, 'Mohican' rooted 89 percent from semi-hardwoods, 5000 ppm IBA, peat:perlite, mist [*The Plant Propagator* 26(3): 5 (1980)].

Viburnum lantanoides

HOBBLEBUSH

Seed. A pound of cleaned seed contains 11,500 seeds. The seed requires a warm stratification of five months at 68 to 86°F followed by two-and-a-half months cold stratification at 34 to 41°F.

Viburnum lentago

NANNYBERRY VIBURNUM, SHEEPBERRY VIBURNUM

Seed. This species is primarily grown from seed. A pound of cleaned seed averages 5,900 seeds. The seed requires five to nine months of warm stratification at 68 to 86°F fluctuating temperatures followed by two to four months cold stratification at 41°F.

Cuttings. Roots easily from softwood cuttings. Treat with 2000 to 8000 ppm IBA-talc or solution and place under mist or in a plastic tent. Overwintering may be a problem.

Viburnum lobophyllum

Seed. Seeds are doubly dormant and require five months at 60 to 85°F followed by three months at 41°F [*Arnoldia* 14(5): 25 (1954)].

Viburnum macrocephalum

CHINESE SNOWBALL VIBURNUM

Seed. Sterile form and sets no fruit.

Cuttings. Can be rooted from summer softwood cuttings when the wood has firmed at the base. Soft succulent cuttings should be avoided, and this applies to most viburnums. If tips are soft they should be removed. Treat with 5000 to 10,000 ppm IBA-talc or solution, and place under mist in a well-drained medium. A rooting percentage of 90 to 100 percent can be expected. Treat rooted cuttings as described for *V. carlesii*. This species resists moving after rooting. A Tennessee nurseryman related that this is a difficult species to root. I collected mid August cuttings, 1.0 percent KIBA solution, rooting plugs, mist, with 30 percent rooting in nine to ten weeks.

Viburnum nudum

SMOOTH WITHEROD

Seed. Requires no pretreatment for germination.

Cuttings. Easily rooted as described under *V. carlesii*. No problem overwintering this species. Can also be propagated by layering.

Viburnum opulus

EUROPEAN CRANBERRYBUSH VIBURNUM

Seed. A pound of cleaned seed contains 13,600 seeds. The seed requires warm and cold stratification to germinate. A two- to three-month warm stratification at 68 to 86°F followed by one-and-a-half months cold stratification at 41°F is most effective [*PIPPS* 8:126 (1958)]. One reference noted five months warm and three months cold was satisfactory.

Cuttings. *Viburnum opulus* and its cultivars are easy to propagate. Soft summer cuttings root well. Treat with 1000 ppm IBA and place under mist in peat moss and perlite or suitable medium. If the cuttings are taken from the first flush of growth, the long growing season promotes the development of a well-established plant by autumn. Overwintering is the main concern as with many other viburnums. Supplemental light has been used to induce new growth on *V. opulus* 'Nanum' rooted cuttings and improve survival. I have observed "after-rooting" decline and overwinter survival problems. Unless cuttings are rooted early and induced to grow, they should be handled like *V. ×burkwoodii* [*PIPPS* 20:378 (1970)].

It is probable that this plant would propagate satisfactorily from hardwood cuttings if stooling was practiced. Make sure the cuttings are nodal, as this plant has a large pith. Refer to *V. dentatum* for hardwood cutting methods.

For small quantities, simple layering or French layering (refer to *V. ×bodnantense* for method) is possible.

Viburnum plicatum f. *plicatum*

JAPANESE SNOWBALL VIBURNUM

Viburnum plicatum f. *tomentosum*

DOUBLEFILE VIBURNUM

Seed. Forma *tomentosum* is fertile and sets viable seed. Ripened seed should be cleaned and sown immediately, with germination taking place the following spring.

Cuttings. Overwintering rooted cuttings is a problem, although it is not as serious as with *V. carlesii*. Softwoods, mist, 1000 ppm IBA solution, peat:perlite, root easily [*The Plant Propagator* 18(1): 7 (1972)]. It is important to encourage new vegetative growth after rooting and not transplant until new growth starts. The best cuttings are produced from pruned stock plants that develop vigorous young growth. Cuttings rooted early are more easily overwintered than those rooted in August. The rooted cuttings can be left in place after rooting for two years.

Hardwood cuttings root provided they are in a vigorous vegetative condition. The technique is the same as that described for *V. farreri* and *V. dentatum*.

A reliable method for the propagation of small numbers is layering, such as French layering (refer to *V. ×bodnantense* for method).

Viburnum 'Pragense'
PRAGUE VIBURNUM

Cuttings. Firm wood cuttings in June, July, August, and later are rooted 90 to 100 percent with 1000 to 3000 ppm IBA-quick dip. Place in peat moss:perlite or suitable medium under mist. Rooted cuttings transplant easily and continue to grow if fertilized. Probably can be rooted year-round except from extremely soft growth.

Viburnum prunifolium
BLACKHAW VIBURNUM

Seed. A warm stratification period of five to nine months followed by one to two months of cold stratification is required.

Cuttings. June cuttings should root if treated with 3000 to 8000 ppm IBA in talc or solution and placed in peat moss:perlite or suitable medium. Overwintering may be a problem.

Viburnum ×rhytidophylloides
LANTANAPHYLLUM VIBURNUM

Seed. A hybrid of *V. lantana* and *V. rhytidophyllum* and must be asexually propagated, although prodigious quantities of fruits are often set if another seedling or related species is in the vicinity.

Cuttings. Cultivars of this hybrid are easy to root from softwoods using 1000 ppm IBA, peat moss:perlite, and mist. Rooted cuttings present no overwintering problems. 'Alleghany' in one study rooted above 90 percent with semi-hardwoods in June, 5000 ppm IBA, peat:perlite, and mist [*The Plant Propagator* 26(3): 5 (1980)]. Small quantities can be produced by layering.

Viburnum rhytidophyllum
LEATHERLEAF VIBURNUM

Seed. Possibly similar to *V. lantana* in germination requirements.

Cuttings. This evergreen species is easily propagated throughout summer into fall and winter. Ideally, 1000 to 3000 ppm IBA-solution, well-drained medium, mist, produce excellent results. Hardwoods taken in March and April, 8000 ppm IBA, peat:perlite, 65°F bottom heat, mist, root readily. Wounding is helpful with hard cuttings [*PIPPS* 24:207 (1974)].

Summer (June, July, August) cuttings, fairly small in size, can be rooted very easily with no apparent seasonal decline in rooting capacity. Rooting has been reported under thermoblankets.

Viburnum rufidulum
RUSTY BLACKHAW VIBURNUM, SOUTHERN BLACKHAW VIBURNUM

Seed. A pound of cleaned seed contains 5,500 seeds. Southern blackhaw requires a warm stratification of six to 17 months followed by three to four months of cold stratification.

Cuttings. Cuttings root easily when taken as soft or maturing wood from late May through August and treated with 3000 to 8000 ppm IBA-talc or -quick dip and placed under mist. Cuttings taken in late May, 4000 ppm IBA-talc + thiram, mist, rooted 71 percent. Growth ceases after the cutting is taken, and overwintering may be a problem. Refer to *V. ×burkwoodii* or *V. carlesii* for additional information on overwintering rooted cuttings.

Viburnum sargentii
SARGENT VIBURNUM, SARGENT CRANBERRYBUSH

Seed. Seeds possess a double dormancy, similar to *V. opulus*. A warm stratification of two to three months followed by cold stratification for one to two months promotes germination. In one test, five months warm/three months cold produced excellent germination. 'Flavum' shows radical emergence after three months of warm stratification.

Cuttings. It is important to induce a flush of growth for successful overwintering. Cuttings rooted early and kept under long days until a flush of growth has occurred will overwinter. Treat with 8000 ppm IBA, peat moss:perlite or perlite:vermiculite, and mist. Cuttings can be rooted in place and left for two years before digging. 'Onondaga' rooted 78 percent from semi-hardwoods in June using 5000 ppm IBA, peat:perlite, and mist [*The Plant Propagator* 26(3): 5 (1980)].

Hardwood cuttings can be rooted from shoots produced in stool beds. Cuttings have a large pith and should be nodal.

For small quantities layering is a useful method, either simple layering of individual stems or French layering. In either case it is necessary to stool the plants.

Viburnum setigerum
TEA VIBURNUM

Seed. A three- to five-month warm period followed by three months of cold produces the best results.

Cuttings. Very easy to root. Although the species can be rooted into September, the earlier the cuttings are taken the better. Treat with 8000 ppm IBA-talc or solution and place in a peat:perlite medium under mist. The major problem is the overwintering of the rooted cuttings. Stimulating a flush of growth is important. Refer to *V. ×burkwoodii* and *V. carlesii* for details. Propagation from hardwood cuttings and layering are additional possibilities, although neither is reported.

Viburnum sieboldii
SIEBOLD VIBURNUM

Seed. Cold stratification for three months produced 36 percent germination. Perhaps a brief warm period (one to two months) prior to cold stratification would improve germination.

Cuttings. Summer cuttings from early June to August are the best: the earlier the better to overcome the overwintering problem. Treat with 8000 ppm IBA-talc and place in a peat moss:perlite medium under mist. Early August (Boston), 4000 ppm IBA-quick dip, rooted 100 percent with a profuse root system.

Viburnum suspensum
SANDANKWA VIBURNUM

Cuttings. Treat like *V. tinus*.

Viburnum tinus
LAURUSTINUS

Cuttings. This species and its cultivars are very easy to root from stem cuttings and it is merely a question of when to fit it into the propagation schedule. Softwoods, mid summer, 8000 ppm IBA-talc, peat moss:perlite, mist, are the best. Cuttings will be well rooted in three to four weeks. June cuttings in low plastic tunnels rooted satisfactorily when treated with 8000 ppm IBA-talc. Autumn and winter hardwoods with a wound under mist root in high percentages.

Viburnum trilobum

Seed. Four months warm/three months cold has produced good germination.

Cuttings. Handle as described under *V. opulus*.

Viburnum wrightii

Seed. Treat as described under *V. dilatatum*.

Cuttings. Softwoods, 2000 ppm IBA + 500 ppm NAA solution, mist, root. See *V. dilatatum* for additional information.

Useful Conversions

INCHES	CENTIMETERS		FEET	METERS		TEMPERATURES
⅛	0.3		¼	0.08		$°C = 5/9 \times (°F\text{-}32)$
⅙	0.4		⅓	0.1		$°F = (9/5 \times °C) + 32$
⅕	0.5		½	0.15		
¼	0.6		1	0.3		
⅓	0.8		1½	0.5		
⅜	0.9		2	0.6		
⅖	1.0		2½	0.8		
½	1.25		3	0.9		
⅗	1.5		4	1.2		
⅝	1.6		5	1.5		
⅔	1.7		6	1.8		
¾	1.9		7	2.1		
⅞	2.2		8	2.4		
1	2.5		9	2.7		
1¼	3.1		10	3.0		
1⅓	3.3		12	3.6		
1½	3.8		15	4.5		
1¾	4.4		18	5.4		
2	5.0		20	6.0		
3	7.5		25	7.5		
4	10		30	9.0		
5	12.5		35	10.5		
6	15		40	12		
7	18		45	13.5		
8	20		50	15		
9	23		60	18		
10	25		70	21		
12	30		75	22.5		
15	38		80	24		
18	45		90	27		
20	50		100	30		
24	60		125	37.5		
30	75		150	45		
32	80		175	52.5		
36	90		200	60		

References

Author(s) unknown. *Illustrated Important Forest Trees of Japan*. Vols. 2–5.
 Citation incomplete. (Excellent descriptions of native viburnums along with
 superb illustrations and distribution maps.)

Barton, L. V. 1958. Germination and seedling production of species of
 Viburnum. Plant Propagator 8:126–136.

Bartram, Douglas. 1958. *Hydrangeas and Viburnums*. John Gifford, Ltd.,
 London. (Good guide to species, culture, and uses.)

Bean, W. J. 1981. *Trees and Shrubs Hardy in the British Isles*. Vol. 4. St.
 Martin's Press, New York.

Brenzel, Kathleen N. 2001. *Western Garden Book*. Sunset Publishing, Menlo
 Park, Calif.

Cappiello, Paul. 2002. Koreanspice viburnum is an all-star performer. *Nursery
 Management and Production* 18(8): 12, 87–89.

Coombes, Allen J. 1980. *Viburnum ×globosum. Plantsman* 2(1): 63–64.

Dirr, Michael A. 1975. Effect of nitrogen form and pH on growth, NO_3-N,
 NH_4-N and total N content of container-grown doublefile viburnum. *J.
 Amer. Soc. Hort. Sci.* 100:216–218.

———. 1979. Snowball viburnums offer rare beauty in many varieties.
 American Nurseryman 150(9): 14–15, 73–78, 96–97.

———. 1981. Viburnums old and new. *Brooklyn Botanic Gardens Handbook*
 37(1): 32–35, 94.

———. 1983. *Viburnum plicatum* f. *tomentosum*. Cover illustration. *American
 Nurseryman* 157(8): 22.

———. 1992. *Viburnum plicatum*, Japanese snowball: it's a magnificent shrub best suited for zones 5–7. *Nursery Manager* 8(8): 22.

———. 1998a. *Manual of Woody Landscape Plants*. Stipes Publishing, Champaign, Ill.

———. 1998b. Two worthy viburnums primed for selection. *Nursery Management and Production* 14(1): 14–15, 72.

———. 1999. Viburnums are early-flowering and, often, fragrant. *Nursery Management and Production* 15(10): 14–15, 78–80, 82–88.

———. 2002. Which viburnums resist deer browsing? *Nursery Management and Production* 18(10): 12–13, 81.

Dirr, Michael A., and C. A. Heuser, Jr. 2006. *The Reference Manual of Woody Plant Propagation*. Varsity Press, Cary, N.C.

Donoghue, M. J., B. G. Baldwin, J. Li, and R. C. Winkworth. 2004. Viburnum phylogeny based on the chloroplast trnK intron and nuclear ribosomal ITS DNA sequences. *Syst. Bot.* 29:188–198.

Egolf, Donald R. 1956. Cytological and interspecific hybridization studies in the genus *Viburnum*. Ph.D. dissertation. Cornell University, Ithaca, N.Y.

———. 1962. A cytological study of the genus *Viburnum*. *J. Arnold Arboretum* 43:132–172.

———. 1966a. Two new cultivars of *Viburnum*, 'Cayuga' and 'Mohawk' (Caprifoliaceae). *Baileya* 14:24–28.

———. 1966b. Eight new *Viburnum* cultivars (Caprifoliaceae). *Baileya* 14:106–122.

———. 1971. *Viburnum dilatatum* Thunb. cv. 'Erie' (Caprifoliaceae) N.A. 32226, P.I. 347259. *Baileya* 18:23–25.

———. 1979. 'Shasta' viburnum. *HortScience* 14:78–79.

———. 1981a. 'Chesapeake' viburnum. *HortScience* 16:350.

———. 1981b. 'Eskimo' viburnum. *HortScience* 16:691.

———. 1986. 'Shoshoni' viburnum. *HortScience* 21:1077–1078.

———. 1987. 'Chippewa' and 'Huron' viburnum. *HortScience* 22:174–176.

———. 1988. 'Conoy' viburnum. *HortScience* 23:419–421.

Fisher, Kathleen. 1989. Donald Egolf's viburnums. *American Horticulturist* 68(10): 30–35.

Hara, H. 1983. *A Revision of Caprifoliaceae of Japan with Reference to Allied Plants in Other Districts and the Adoxaceae*. Academia Scientific Books, Inc., Tokyo.

Hartman, P., and David Parsons. 2006. Viburnum borer research: 2002–2005. *Landscape Plant News* 17(2): 4–5.

Hickman, James C., ed. 1993. *The Jepson Manual: Higher Plants of California*. University of California Press, Berkeley.

Hillier, John, and Allen Coombes. 2002. *The Hillier Manual of Trees and Shrubs*. David & Charles, Newton Abbot, England.

Houtman, Ronald. 1998. Viburnum. *Dendroflora* 35:96–148.

Hulton, Eric. 1968. *Flora of Alaska and Neighboring Territories*. Stanford University Press, Stanford, Calif.

Kenyon, Lloyd. 2001. *Viburnum*. NCCPG, Stable Courtyard, Wisley, Woking, Surrey, England. (Excellent reference.)

Krüssmann, Gerd. 1985. *Manual of Cultivated Broad-leaved Trees and Shrubs*. Vol. 3. Timber Press, Portland, Ore.

Ladman, Gary, and Susan Ladman. 2007. Classic Nurseries (1385 Q Rd., Upland, NE 68981) reference catalog, Upland, Neb.

Lancaster, Roy. 1989. *Travels in China*. Antique's Collector's Club, Ltd., Woodbridge, England.

———. 1998. *Viburnum furcatum*. *The Garden* 123(10): 702–703.

———. 2000. *Viburnum conundrum*. *The Garden* 125(11): 822–823.

———. 2003. Winter-flowering viburnums. *Gardens Illustrated* (February): 57–59.

Li, Hui-Lin. 1963. *Woody Flora of Taiwan*. Livingston Publ. Co., Narberth, Pa.

Lord, Tony. 2006. *RHS Plant Finder*. Dorling Kindersley, London.

Meyer, Frederick G., Peter M. Mazzeo, and Donald H. Voss. 1994. *A Catalog of Cultivated Woody Plants of the Southeastern United States*. USDA-ARS. USNA Contribution No. 7.

Morton, C. V. 1933. The Mexican and Central American species of *Viburnum*. *Contributions from the U.S. National Herbarium*, vol. 26, part 7: 339–366.

Ohwi, Jisaburo. 1965. *Flora of Japan*. Smithsonian Institution, Washington, D.C.

Rose, Nancy, and Harold Pellett. 1994. *Viburnum* 'Emerald Triumph'. *J. Environmental Horticulture* 12:59–60.

Rehder, Alfred. 1951. *Manual of Cultivated Trees and Shrubs*. Macmillan, New York.

Rodda, Kelli. 2003. *Viburnum* 'Emerald Triumph'. *Nursery Management and Production* 19(2): 10.

Steward, Albert N. 1958. *Manual of Vascular Plants of the Lower Yangtze Valley*. International Academic Printing Co. Ltd., Tokyo.

Taylor, Nigel, and Daniela Zappi. 1997. *Viburnum grandiflorum* forma *foetens* 'Desmond Clarke'. *Curtis's Botanical Magazine* 14(3): 120–124.

Vines, Robert A. 1960. *Trees, Shrubs and Woody Vines of the Southwest*. University of Texas Press, Austin.

Weston, Paul A. 2004. Viburnum leaf beetle, a formidable new pest in the landscape. *Landscape Plant News* 15(3): 1–4.

Weston, Paul A., Brian Eshenaur, Joel M. Baird, and Jana S. Lamboy. 2002. Evaluation of insecticides for control of larvae of *Pyrrhalta viburni*, a new pest of viburnums. *J. Environmental Horticulture* 20:82–85.

Wiegrefe, Susan J. 2002. Quest for superior native viburnums. *Landscape Plant News* 10(4): 9–10.

Winkworth, Richard C., and Michael J. Donoghue. 2005. Viburnum phylogeny based on combined molecular data: implications for taxonomy and biogeography. *Amer. J. Bot.* 92:653–666.

Wyman, Donald. 1933. Untitled article. *Arnold Arboretum Bulletin of Popular Information*, ser. 4, vol. 1, no. 4.

———. 1937. Viburnums. *Arnold Arboretum Bulletin of Popular Information*, ser. 4, vol. 5, nos. 14–15: 73–79.

Zucker, Isabel. 1966. *Flowering Shrubs*. D. Van Nostrand Co., Inc., New York.

Index